AS RIVETING AS
THE HUNT FOR RED OCTOBER.
ONLY, THIS STORY IS TRUE.

RED STAR ROGUE

The Untold Story of a Soviet Submarine's Nuclear Strike Attempt on the U.S.

"Full of dramatic circumstances, tales of impending world danger, and the possibility of a nuclear war. . . . A TRUE STORY THAT WILL HORRIFY READERS AS THEY REALIZE THAT A NUCLEAR ATTACK ON THE UNITED STATES WAS SECONDS AWAY."

—The Associated Press

"CHILLING . . . WITH TWISTS AND TURNS THAT ARE POSITIVELY BREATHTAKING. . . . As fascinating as it is frightening. . . . Sewell takes us inside the once top-secret Soviet nuclear navy. . . . His scholarship is impeccable."

—*The Flint Journal* (MI)

"READS LIKE A SPY THRILLER. . . . Many interesting twists . . . g   le (OH)

"Beyond chill   son, WI)

This title is also available as an eBook

RED STAR ROGUE

THE UNTOLD STORY OF A SOVIET SUBMARINE'S NUCLEAR STRIKE ATTEMPT ON THE U.S.

★

KENNETH SEWELL

WITH CLINT RICHMOND

POCKET STAR BOOKS
New York London Toronto Sydney

A Pocket Star book published by
POCKET BOOKS, a division of Simon & Schuster, Inc.
1230 Avenue of the Americas, New York, NY 10020

Copyright © 2005 by Kenneth Sewell and Clint Richmond

Maps on pp. 14, 123 and 162 copyright © Jeffrey L. Ward

All rights reserved, including the right to reproduce
this book or portions thereof in any form whatsoever.
For information address Simon & Schuster, Inc.,
1230 Avenue of the Americas, New York, NY 10020

ISBN-13: 978-0-7432-6112-8
ISBN-10:   0-7432-6112-7
ISBN-13: 978-1-4165-2733-6 (Pbk)
ISBN-10:   1-4165-2733-8 (Pbk)

This Pocket Books paperback edition October 2006

10 9 8 7 6 5 4 3 2 1

POCKET STAR BOOKS and colophon are registered trademarks
of Simon & Schuster, Inc.

Cover design by Jon Valk; Cover photograph © Kulik photo

Manufactured in the United States of America

For information about special discounts for bulk purchases,
please contact Simon & Schuster Special Sales at
1-800-456-6798 or business@simonandschuster.com.

For the men and women of the United States military who served our country with little or no recognition, at countless outposts guarding land, sea, and sky during the long years of the Cold War

ACKNOWLEDGMENTS

ABOVE ALL, my appreciation goes to fourteen men and women now living in the United States and the former Soviet Union who must remain unnamed, as exposing their contributions to this book might adversely affect their well-being. Without their willingness to share critical information concerning the events revealed here, the public might never have learned how close the Cold War world came to ending in an incalculable catastrophe rather than a victory for democracy.

Others, who can be named, were also devoted to lifting the veil of secrecy so that these truths could be shared with the public. Among these, my thanks go to David Hughes in America for his translation of Russian documents, Svetlana Stepanova [pseud.] and Eugene Soukharnikov for researching open files and conducting follow-up interviews in Russia, Nam Nguyen for research in Hawaii, D. D. Dacosta for research at the University of Hawaii, and Linda Chatfield for archival and technical research.

A special thanks to Captain Third Rank (Ret.) Igor Kolosov, current caretaker of the Foxtrot submarine B-427 on display at Queen Mary Attractions in Long Beach, California, for descriptions of the day-to-day life experienced by Soviet submariners during the Cold War era. Edward L. Blanton YNC USN (Ret.) and U.S.

Navy Commander (Ret.) Paul Grandinetti provided valuable assistance in authenticating American naval defensive warfare techniques of that period. Andy Frank and Adam VonIns gave their time and expertise to examine and evaluate the book's premises about how the mysterious incidents that occurred during this critical period of history were interrelated.

Thanks to Beth Green for photo restoration, Chris Haggy for technical illustrations, and Frank Parker for photography. The staff of the Operational Archives Branch of the Naval Historical Center, Washington Navy Yard, was especially helpful. And a special thanks to Judith Morison for creative manuscript rewrites that made often complex and technical information accessible to the widest possible reading audience.

Heartfelt appreciation to my literary agent, John Talbot of the John Talbot Agency, Inc., who was enthusiastic about the project from the start, and who shepherded this work from proposal, through drafts, to final manuscript with insightful and sensitive critique and patience. Thanks to Jim Hornfischer of Hornfischer Literary Management, L.P., for bringing Clint Richmond to the project, as well as his own valuable knowledge of the nonfiction military genre. I appreciate both agents for their professionalism and guidance, and for finding the perfect placement for this work.

Last, but not at all least, my sincere appreciation goes to my senior editor at Simon & Schuster, Robert Bender, for making the publication of this information possible. His unflagging dedication to seeing this story told, and the diligent work of his editorial assistant, Johanna Li, brought the project to life as a book. His gentle editing hand and respect for his writers made polishing the final work a pleasant, rather than a painful task. Others at Simon & Schuster who contributed to the project were Al Madocs and Sean Devlin in copyediting, Rachel Nagler in publicity, and Michael Accordino in the art department.

Kenneth Sewell
Columbus, Ohio
September 2005

CONTENTS

FOREWORD

SHORTLY AFTER THE OPENING of trade relations with the People's Republic of China (PRC) in the early 1980s, I was assigned to work with Chinese engineers at the Beijing research facility of the Ministry of Aeronautics Industry. It was, for me, the first of many memorable trips to this once-secluded country. It was likewise memorable for my Chinese hosts, because I was the first American they had ever met.

The scientists and engineers I worked with were well educated in the basic technical skills of their fields. But they were completely ignorant of what the world was like outside China. The leadership had only recently permitted peasant farmers to sell their excess produce in the cities, though many Chinese had not yet learned to cook since leaving their communes. This was years before the Tiananmen Square massacre, and everywhere there was a feeling of optimistic uncertainty.

Like most visitors to China in those days, I had been assigned a "government watcher." One day as we ate lunch, he was called away, leaving me alone with a group of engineers I had come to know fairly well. They were nervously glancing around to see if anyone was watching. A man was placed at the entrance, obviously as a lookout.

With a great show of courtesy and some embarrassment, the young engineer who spoke the best English began by asking me, "Mr. Sewell, may we inquire about an incident that we heard of some time ago?"

The question took me by surprise, and I must admit to feeling a twinge of fear. It had been only a few years since I had served on the crew of an American submarine under the command of a highly classified organization. Maybe I was being paranoid, but I did have information that could compromise intelligence operations critical to American security, and I had no idea how much these people knew about my past.

"Here it comes," I told myself, preparing for the third degree. So I was stunned when my chief inquisitor timidly asked his question.

"We have heard rumors for some time now, that American spacemen have landed on the moon," the young engineer whispered, with a grave look on his face. "Is this correct?" He quickly produced a Western trade magazine and pointed to an article. Over half the magazine had been censored, blacked out; but in one obscure paragraph was a reference to the American Apollo moon missions of the 1960s and 1970s.

I stood dumbfounded for several seconds. These highly trained engineers, the finest of Red China's aeronautical specialists, were surely joshing me. But they all leaned closer to hear my answer. They were not kidding.

During the remainder of our lunch break, the Chinese engineers pressed me for the details of the U.S. astronauts' seven moon landings. When the commissar—my minder—returned, the enlightenment abruptly ended.

Mao had warned his comrades, "When you open windows, you let in the flies." In this case, I was proud to be one of the first flies. The Chinese government was so repressive, their society so closed and secretive, that information about one of the greatest engineering and scientific accomplishments in human history had been withheld from the country's best technical minds.

Years later, in the aftermath of September 11, 2001, this memory came back to me. *What haven't we been told?*

No one knows better than an American submariner the need to protect our military and technological secrets for the security of our nation. But archiving old secrets long after the crisis has passed deprives us of knowledge that free people need to make enlightened choices. Burying our history beneath layers of cover stories, security classifications, and deliberate deceit for the purpose of protecting mistakes or reputations of bygone leaders is a violation of a free people's rights. In the military, the highest restriction placed on a document is called a "need to know" classification. But at some point, after a crisis has passed, there is a higher authorization that we Americans must be granted—and that is the "right to know."

If our democratic way of life and the self-rule of free people everywhere are to survive, then those we elect to lead us are not entitled to keep vital information from us forever.

On September 11, we learned that Islamist fanatics would resort to any and all means to achieve their goal, the destruction of the United States of America and the freedom it represents. It has long been reported that these terrorists have actively sought to obtain nuclear weapons. There is no doubt, now, that they would use them if given the chance.

This is why I have written *Red Star Rogue*. For some time I have known about a horrifying incident, perhaps the darkest secret of the Cold War era. It involved a failed attempt by a lone Soviet submarine, a rogue, to launch a nuclear missile against a sleeping American city. Yet, for no reason of national security, this three-decades-old secret remains buried in mystery, rumor, and purposefully leaked disinformation.

In 1968, in a desperate bid to win the Cold War, a small group of radical Stalinists came within seconds of a sneak attack that would have killed a half-million Americans.

After spending years searching for answers to satisfy my own concerns about this incident, I submitted a detailed outline of my research to one of the few people still living who knew the entire story. Because of this person's impeccable credentials and integrity, I was sure if my conclusions were wrong, this man would tell me.

A few days later he responded, "You have made a great start in developing the credible and probable scenarios that have had that effect on history that we call the end of the Cold War (it is not over yet)."

As I dug deeper, it became increasingly difficult to have *in the clear* contact with my covert mentor, and my inquiries exposed me to those whose job it is to keep these things secret. Because of the classified nature of his former career and his lifetime commitment of confidentiality, my contact was unable to go public.

But I still managed to update him on my findings. Near the conclusion of my research I again asked him to review my work. His last response was, "So go, man, go. They do not yet suspect that you have an important message for the American people."

The public not only has a right to know, but now they have a need to know. In the current climate of perpetual war against terrorism, we can only hope that lessons learned from this Cold War incident will provide insights that can help us make the right choices in this increasingly dangerous, post–9/11 era.

Kenneth Sewell

PROLOGUE

THIS WAS NOT SIMPLY AN ESPIONAGE WAR. IT WAS NOT JUST ONE SIDE AGAINST THE OTHER. IT WAS A DEADLY STRUGGLE OF IRRECONCILABLE IDEOLOGIES, WHERE THE DEFEAT OF THE OTHER SYSTEM WAS THE SOLE GOAL.

—*Former KGB Major General Oleg Kalugin*

IN EARLY 1968, the world nervously watched as the armies, air forces, and navies of the United States and the Soviet Union taunted each other in dangerous face-to-face standoffs around the globe. This tension was at its highest in the oceans of the world, where submarines of both sides played deadly games of hide-and-seek. At no point during the Cold War, including the dramatic confrontation of the Cuban Missile Crisis in September and October 1962, was the stalemate as close to escalating into World War III as in the first six months of 1968. Yet only a handful of military men and espionage agents—and a few key politicians in the inner sanctums of the Kremlin and the White House—knew just how close the world came to the long-feared nuclear Armageddon.

Asia and the Far East were aflame, with the Cold War turning hot in a major conflict fueled by the United States and the Soviet Union. American boys were dying by the scores each week in the steaming jungles of Indochina. That year, 1968, was the bloodiest of the war, with 16,869 Americans killed in action.

In the People's Republic of China, Mao's Red Guards

were well along in the murderous Great Proletarian Revolution, better known as the Cultural Revolution. Mao's criticism of the post-Stalin Soviet leadership had resulted in a split between these two Red giants. The followers of a radical Maoist policy turned on Red China's longtime patron, the Soviet Union, in the early 1960s, which led to open clashes at several spots along their twenty-four-hundred-mile border. Having originally supplied the Chinese with Russian nuclear missile and submarine technology, the Soviets withdrew their military assistance. Relations had deteriorated to the point that Soviet diplomats and military advisors and their families were forced to flee their posts in China, some barely getting out of the country with their lives.

On January 23, 1968, North Korean gunboats, in a brazen act of piracy on the high seas, fired on and captured the American surveillance ship USS *Pueblo*.

On January 30, 1968, war-weary Americans were shocked by the news that the Vietnam War, far from nearing the end that politicians had promised, had blazed into a new inferno. The North Vietnamese regular army and battalions of Viet Cong guerrillas launched a surprise attack on thirty provincial capitals in South Vietnam. Within days of the Tet Offensive, America suffered its highest casualty counts of the war: 543 GIs killed and 2,547 wounded in a single week.

Exhausted by the war, on March 31, President Lyndon Baines Johnson announced he would not seek re-election. Just four days later, Martin Luther King was assassinated in Memphis.

On May 24, 1968, an American attack submarine, the USS *Scorpion*, went missing off the Azores while conducting a clandestine mission to investigate an unusual assembly of Soviet warships in the eastern Atlantic. Immediately, U.S. officials suspected a possible Soviet navy connection with the disappearance. Ninety-nine American officers and sailors were lost.

After successfully winning the California presidential primary, Senator Robert F. Kennedy was assassinated in Los Angeles on June 5. Two hundred thousand antiwar protesters marched in New York City, a major event in the long national war protest that would divide the nation for years to come.

Across the globe, Communist-inspired, Soviet-supported insurgencies raged in Southeast Asia, the Middle East, Africa, and Latin America. Overtly, the Soviets began supplying client states such as Syria and Egypt with the latest missile technology, while behind the scenes they were supplying arms to revolutionaries throughout the Third World.

In Moscow, resentment over the Cuban Missile Crisis still simmered in some elements of the military, the KGB, and the Kremlin, despite the replacement of the bellicose Nikita Khrushchev by Leonid Brezhnev three years earlier. Seldom during the long years of the Cold War did the Soviets more aggressively rattle their sabers. In Europe, the Cold War heated up with the Prague Spring. Western intelligence learned that the Warsaw Pact was about to put down the unrest in Czechoslovakia with a brutal invasion.

In short, America and the world were seething in violence and bitter turmoil during the first months of 1968, when the events described in this book took place.

It was into this volatile mix of intrigue and open hostilities that an obscure incident involving an older-model, diesel-electric Soviet submarine operating off the coast of Hawaii edged the world to the brink of nuclear war. The people of the United States and the Russian Federation have never been told the truth of this near-catastrophe.

The last mission of the Soviet ballistic missile submarine K-129 was to become one of the greatest enigmas of the Cold War. None of the crew members survived to offer historic testimony about that clandestine trip. The author uses physical evidence found at the wreck site, interviews with former Soviet submarine officers, post–Cold War writings of retired Soviet admirals from the Pacific Fleet, recently released Soviet naval equipment journals and procedural manuals, and his own experience as a Cold War submariner to answer many of the most important remaining questions. Based on these sources, early chapters of this book offer a vivid re-creation of living conditions and actions that likely took place aboard K-129 on its final voyage. For example, since the operating procedures and launch sequence of a Soviet ballistic missile submarine never varied, the background of what occurred on this boat can be reasonably reenacted.

PART ONE

THE INCIDENT

1

IN THE DARK HOURS OF March 7, 1968, a lone submarine slowly prowled the surface in open waters of the North Pacific. The slender sub rolled easily in swells raised by a twenty-knot wind. Occasionally, the whitecaps racing ahead of wave crests broke over the low forward deck, sending foaming rivulets of seawater to hide the rust streaks weeping from the boat's aging welds.

A coast watcher might have mistaken the submarine for some naval relic with an oddly long fin emerging from the depths to fight a sea battle of the Second World War. Such identification would have been only partly right. This sub, despite its angular U-boat appearance, carried three atomic-age ballistic missiles snugly housed in tubes in its extended sail.

On the bridge, in the brisk wind, an officer quickly scanned the horizon through powerful naval binoculars, and then raised them to search all quadrants of the night sky.

A seaman in an ill-fitting sheepskin coat focused his attention closer to home, climbing to the highest point in the aft section of the bridge. The coat was much too large for his slight frame, and he was much too young to have attained the rank entitling him to wear the storm raglan coat, quilted pants, and expensive lined boots of a fleet officer.

From his new perch he examined the long, flat area of the conning tower behind the bridge. The faintest glow of starlight provided just enough illumination for the sailor to discern the outline of the three launch-tube doors. The doors appeared to be clear of any flot-sam that might have been picked up during surfacing. Beneath the steel doors, like giant elongated eggs, were forty-two-foot-long ballistic missiles. Each carried a one-megaton thermonuclear warhead.

The massive doors were tightly sealed, to keep salt water out of the missile tubes. The powerful hydraulic arms that opened them could be activated only from the missile control panel inside the submarine.

The officer gazing through his binoculars at the front of the bridge had seen no threat to their position—no running lights of surface ships, no antisubmarine warfare planes patrolling the sky. He acknowledged the other man's report that the missile doors were clear, then ducked back down the ladder and into the submarine.

As the boat broke through the swells at an almost leisurely two knots, the crewmen below eagerly breathed the fresh air rushing in through hatches opened to the conning tower. It was the first time the boat had been on the surface long enough to flush out the foul air that had accumulated in the living chambers during two weeks of submerged sailing. The cool sea air replacing oily diesel fumes created a slight draft in the control center as it flowed from compartments fore and aft.

The usual elation of the crew at finally being back in

man's normal realm on the surface was suddenly cut short when they heard an order barked over the intercom. The order was for battle stations, missile launch. All compartments were to report ready when sealed. The order was followed by: "This is not a drill."

That harsh command, which may have startled even the few crewmen in the operating compartments who knew what to expect next, was more shocking for five dozen officers and sailors confined against their will in the forward two compartments of the submarine.

With an efficiency born of a thousand drills, all the steps to fulfill a missile submarine's ultimate purpose were methodically taken.

The officer who had just returned from lookout duty on the bridge entered the control room to assume the post of deputy commander. He reported that all was clear from his visual observations, and that the doors over the missile tubes were free of flotsam. Only the sailor in the bulky, foul-weather coat remained on the bridge in the open night air.

Another officer pronounced the stations manned and ready for live fire of the main missile batteries.

Before surfacing, several skilled seamen trained as missile technicians had worked feverishly for nearly an hour preparing for the next order. An inspection of the missile tubes through small hatches in compartment four revealed no fuel leaks or seepage of seawater that might hamper a launch. Now all preparations were complete. A small knot of anxious men in the control center waited for the commander to issue the final instructions to activate the emergency firing procedure for nuclear weapon release.

A missile officer standing at the launch console watched a warning light blink on. The door of number-one missile tube was open.

Atop the submarine, the sailor in the raglan coat visually confirmed that the missile door had opened properly. He closed the outer hatch in the floor of the bridge and knelt behind a steel protective shield. His job was to remain in this somewhat precarious spot—the only person outside the hull—to be available in the event of any last-minute problems.

Below the bridge in the action center, an officer peering through the periscope confirmed number-one missile hatch open and clear.

The commander provided a large cassette containing the computerized codes required to arm the missile warhead. Normally, the codes would have been locked inside the captain's safe, to be retrieved by the captain and the submarine's political officer only after orders were received from fleet headquarters. This time, the officer in charge simply handed the cassette to a young man, who turned and plugged the packet into the launch console.

Some of the crewmen waited to hear the procedure they had followed in dozens of simulated and live drills. The political officer should have announced that headquarters had confirmed launch authority. But this critical procedure was ignored. There had been no communication with headquarters in more than a week.

The officer in the action center directly above the control room made one last sweep of the horizon with the attack periscope. He checked again to make sure the missile door was completely deployed and shouted down to the control room that the missile was clear for launch.

At the launch control panel, an officer confirmed he had powered the number-one console.

An assistant navigation officer, a lieutenant, told the commander they were three minutes to launch position at latitude 24° north, longitude 163° west. Their course was east-southeast, at a speed of two knots.

The missile technician at the launch panel confirmed the target coordinates on a southeast heading from the boat: 21°18' north, 157° west.

With that information, the commander, his deputy, and a third sailor stepped up to the launch panel. Each man inserted a key in the panel face. They turned the keys and stepped back to allow the missile officer to complete his task at the console.

The commander gave the order to proceed to activation of the warhead on number-one missile. He hurried up the ladder to the periscope in the action center, shouting to his deputy as he climbed to prepare for emergency dive after launch.

A small spotlight in the ceiling above the chart table in the control room threw a bright beam onto a naval chart. A penciled X, crudely drawn in the center of the chart, partially covered the name printed on the map. Just below the mark was another name: HONOLULU. The target was Pearl Harbor. But the explosive power of a one-megaton yield from the thermonuclear warhead would extend far beyond the military base to the civilian metropolitan area that adjoined it.

The sailor at the launch control panel announced the system ready for firing sequence.

The commander looked toward the man standing at the navigator's station. The man held a stopwatch in one hand and dividers in the other. "Two minutes to launch point on my mark . . . mark!"

Instantly, the commander activated his own stopwatch. The second hand swept one full turn around the face. He ordered missile one to be fired.

The man at the control panel complied, setting in motion the last step to launch missile one. Time to launch was sixty seconds.

Officers and seamen in the control room instinctively braced themselves for the jolt that would come when compressed air ejected the eighteen-ton missile out of the launch tube, just feet away from the command center.

At the control panel, a sailor pressed a black button, removing the last manual override of the system. It was fifteen seconds to launch.

The men locked in the forward compartments could hear each order in the launch sequence over the intercom. Any outcry they made was muffled by the watertight hatch separating them from the men giving the orders in the control center.

A young assistant missile officer, who by training would have known more than most crewmen about what was to happen next, curled up helpless in his bunk in one of the officers' cabins in compartment two. A small journal lay by his side.

It was ten seconds to launch.

Standing in front of the control panel, the officer commanding the submarine began the staccato countdown:

"*Dyesyat, dyevyat, vosyem, syem . . .*"

2

THE COLD WAR SAGA of the Soviet submarine known as K-129 began two months earlier, on the fog-shrouded Kamchatka Peninsula of the Soviet Union's Pacific Far East. In the first week of January 1968, the diesel-electric, ballistic missile submarine returned to its base from one of its autonomous missions, a seventy-day patrol somewhere in the North Pacific.

These lengthy assignments were called "autonomous" because the submarines were sent out alone, with sealed instructions meant for only two people, the captain and the political officer. After sailing, a boat would limit communications with headquarters to coded microburst transmissions when it reached specific, predetermined locations along its course.

K-129 had departed on such a mission in late October 1967, and returned to home port after the successful conclusion of the assignment, on approximately the sixth of January 1968.

The submarine sailed in from the open Pacific and entered Avachinskaya Bay on the southeastern coast of the Kamchatka Peninsula. The huge deepwater bay had provided safe harbor for Russian sailors since the

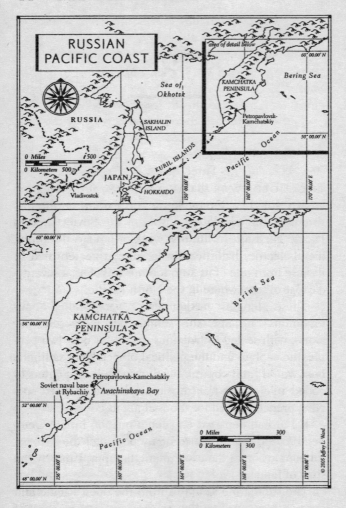

RUSSIAN
PACIFIC COAST

Sea of
Okhotsk

area of detail below

60° 00.00' N

KAMCHATKA
PENINSULA

Bering Sea

RUSSIA

SAKHALIN
ISLAND

50° 00.00' N

Petropavlovsk-
Kamchatskiy

0 Miles   500

0 Kilometers   500

KURIL ISLANDS

Pacific

JAPAN

150° 00.00' E

160° 00.00' E

170° 00.00' E

Vladivostok

HOKKAIDO

60° 00.00' N

Bering Sea

KAMCHATKA
PENINSULA

56° 00.00' N

Petropavlovsk-Kamchatskiy

Soviet naval base
at Rybachiy   Avachinskaya Bay

52° 00.00' N

Pacific Ocean

0 Miles   300

0 Kilometers   300

48° 00.00' N

156° 00.00' E

160° 00.00' E

164° 00.00' E

168° 00.00' E

170° 00.00' E

© 2005 Jeffrey L. Ward

1600s, serving as an unconquered Pacific outpost for czars and commissars alike, in wars against the British and French in 1854, the Japanese in 1903 and 1945, and finally, against the United States Navy in the protracted Cold War. At the time of this incident, that global stalemate had already lasted two decades.

K-129 returned to the windswept bay not far from where it had submerged to begin its clandestine mission two months and ten days earlier. The submarine surfaced near the Three Brothers Sea Stacks, the natural rock formation that stood sentinel at the bay's entrance. In the morning light, the base of one of the volcanic peaks, 3,456-foot Mount Koryakskaya, could be seen looming behind the port city of Petropavlovsk-Kamchatskiy. The mountain's peak was covered by clouds and fog during most of the winter months.

The captain, wearing a sheepskin coat and an expensive fur *ushanka* covering his head, appeared at the bridge atop the submarine's high sail. A seaman, also dressed in a heavy woolen coat and headgear, but not of the distinctive fur and sheepskin worn by senior officers, hurriedly took the ship's Soviet navy ensign from a locker in the action center of the conning tower and followed the captain to the bridge. The young seaman attached the flag to the ship's mast.

A strong north wind snatched the flag from the sailor's arms and unfurled it in a flapping streamer over the conning tower. He rendered a smart salute and proceeded to his lookout post. The flag's bright colors—a large red star leading the red hammer and sickle on a white field above a sea-blue stripe—were in stark contrast to the wintry gray waters of the bay, eroded brown shoreline, and snow-covered hills and mountains. The wind snapped the flag briskly above the submarine as it plowed at fourteen knots through small whitecaps on the surface.

The temperature hovered between a seasonal norm of 10° to 12°F, but the biting cold was welcomed by most of the crewmen gathered on the bridge. For them, it was a physical release to take the first deep swigs of open air, no matter how numbing the chill. It was an even greater pleasure to see the familiar landmarks along the bay shore for the first time in more than two months.

The man in the distinctive fur hat was Captain First Rank Vladimir Ivanovich Kobzar, one of the most competent and respected officers in the Soviet Pacific Fleet. At age thirty-eight, he was already a seasoned submarine commander and had captained the K-129 for three and a half years.

Before the waters brought up from the deep were fully drained from the deck, sailors had opened the hatch above the aft torpedo room. Even on this overcast morning, the men's first glimpse of sky caused them to squint sharply against the light.

Almost as soon as K-129 surfaced, a small tugboat that did double duty as an icebreaker signaled, "Follow me." The auxiliary boat, sent out when K-129 radioed flotilla headquarters that it was entering the bay, had been waiting to escort the sub. It would lead K-129 through the thin ice shelf that formed along the shore all winter, and into Rybachiy Naval Base. While the open waters of the huge bay were largely clear of ice, the shorelines remained ice-bound from late autumn until the middle of spring. The tug led the submarine into Krashennini Cove at the southeastern end of the bay and crunched a path through the ice shelf to a center berth that had been reserved for the arriving sub.

The docking area consisted of twelve long, concrete piers that made up Rybachiy's main submarine pens. Other submarines, some much longer and wider than K-129, were secured in the shelter on either side of the piers. The facility could easily hold four dozen submarines tied up at one time. Just inland, adjoining the piers, were concrete warehouses and industrial buildings where supplies were stored and machinery hummed with constant demands for spot repairs on the fleet. The concrete docks, buildings, and treeless muddy yards all blended into a muted gray that echoed the drab hues of the idled submarines.

While the tug gently nudged the K-129 into the assigned berth, a small knot of grim-looking officers in black greatcoats watched from the pier—the only reception party. Unlike its American counterpart, the Soviet submarine service did not encourage families and friends to greet their returning submariners.

The crew was required to remain on board while the captain, first officer, and political officer reported to the division commander. Only after a brief report on the mission had been satisfactorily delivered could the captain return to the boat to allow the first of the crew—those officers and senior petty officers with family members billeted nearby—to depart the boat. If anything at all had gone wrong on the long mission, no one would be allowed to leave the submarine until the chain of command was fully satisfied that all questions had been answered. Even the wives of the most senior officers were not informed of K-129's return until this debriefing had been completed to the satisfaction of headquarters.

There had been many cases, particularly during the unsuccessful ventures of Soviet submarines to Cuba during the 1962 crisis, when submariners were confined aboard their boats for weeks after returning from months at sea. Often this cruel, extended confinement had been imposed for minor infractions that were no fault of the seamen and officers, such as being forced to surface for identification by harassing U.S. Navy destroyers. The Americans would stalk the submarines, pounding them with their powerful active sonars. They positioned their warships over the Soviet subs to prevent them from snorkeling to recharge their batteries or replenish their air. Ultimately, the sub commanders had no choice but to surface. The Soviet admiralty blamed the crews and officers all the same.

The ice surrounding the pier had offered little resistance to the K-129, cracking into sheets that rode up on the curved pressure hull as the sub came to rest against the rubber bumpers of the concrete pier. Sailors wearing life jackets over winter coats caught the knotted lines thrown by the men on the pier. These ropes were attached to the heavier mooring lines that would secure the sub.

The seamen kept busy as they waited for their captain to return. The deck of the submarine was a beehive of activity as men set up safety lines and engineers worked at connecting the heavy auxiliary cables that would supply the submarine with electrical power while in port. A gangway had been hoisted from the pier to the deck, but nobody dared cross it. They wouldn't have to wait long, anyway. The crew was certain there would be no extra confinement this time—the mission had gone without incident.

The eighty-three crew members had every reason to expect a well-deserved six months in port, with only brief coastal drills and routine maintenance and repair work until midsummer, when they would sail again.

Concrete submarine pens lined the entire south shore of Krashennini Cove, a bristling arm of naval activity off the larger bay. The cove provided slight relief from the strong winds that occasionally lifted the low clouds for brief views of the snowy peaks. In midwinter, at this latitude, there were just four hours of gloomy daylight, made even grayer by the incessant fogs and scudding low clouds off the Bering Sea. Rybachiy was less than 750 miles south of the Arctic Circle.

When the north winds were strong, waves lapped over the decks of the boats tied up at the concrete piers built low to the water to accommodate submarines. Wet and icy in patches, the decks appeared a darker gray than the looming conning towers and launch tubes encapsulated behind them.

The submarine base was located across the bay from the city of Petropavlovsk-Kamchatskiy, the capital of the Kamchatka *oblast*. With a civilian population of three hundred thousand, it was the largest city on the 470,000-square-mile, mostly wilderness peninsula. Naval yards, military camps, and KGB border-guard stations dotted the bay shores. Because of its secret installations, the region, including the city of

Petropavlovsk-Kamchatskiy, was closed to everyone except Soviet citizens and visiting allies. Commercial fishing was the only nonmilitary economy of the region. Even then, the ostensibly civilian trawlers of the fishing fleets doubled as military intelligence boats.

This fogbound bay sheltered the submarine pens for the deadly Kamchatka Flotilla, to which K-129 was assigned. The facility, exclusively dedicated to the dispatch of Soviet missile and attack submarines, was one of the most guarded installations of the Soviet navy.

By the mid-1960s, Avachinskaya Bay had become the Soviet Pacific Fleet's most important submarine center. It was a major naval asset in the Communist giant's mighty striving to compete with the rapidly modernizing United States Navy.

The Soviets had struggled for the first decade of the Cold War to meet Joseph Stalin's impossibly audacious military goal of building the world's largest submarine force. The Soviet dictator believed that the outcome of World War II would have been far different if Hitler had invested more of Germany's resources in submarines. In the early 1950s, Stalin ordered more than twelve hundred submarines built.

Although that grandiose plan was abandoned at Stalin's death in 1953, his successor, Nikita Khrushchev, saw the submarine service as an essential part of the Soviet military strategy and placed an emphasis on upgrading the Red Navy with fewer, but more modern, submarines.

Construction of nuclear-propelled, ballistic missile submarines was once again given top priority when Leonid Brezhnev assumed power after a Moscow cabal ousted Khrushchev in 1964. Admiral Sergey G. Gorshkov, commander in chief of the Soviet navy, believed that nuclear submarines were best suited to lead the way in the development of the Soviets' new blue-water navy.

However, the naval construction program, along with rapid expansion of land-based intercontinental nuclear weapons, was crippling the economy of the Communist behemoth. The Kremlin was expending as much as 60 percent of the country's gross national product on military and space budgets. The Soviet people knew only that their shoes were ill-fitting and the shelves were usually empty at the cooperative stores.

Despite this huge military outlay, the Americans continued to outpace the Soviets in construction of nuclear weapons and the missiles, ships, and aircraft needed to deliver them. More important than numerical superiority was the quality of the weaponry. The United States was producing more technologically advanced, longer-range, multiwarhead missiles and a new generation of nuclear-powered submarines.

The bellicose rhetoric of Kremlin politicians did not fool everyone. A few Moscow economists already knew the Communist system of centralized control had failed to live up to expectations and stood no chance of competing with modern Western economies. Many generals and admirals in the Soviet Union watched the rapid modernization of the U.S. Air Force and Navy with growing apprehension.

To counter the widening nuclear weapons gap, Kremlin strategists pinned hopes on what they deemed to be America's greatest weakness, the inability of Americans to sacrifice their people for the good of the collective. They knew Americans could never face the terrible prospect of losing even a single city to a nuclear attack. Soviet leaders based their beliefs on observations of American battle tactics during World War II. On the battlefield, U.S. commanders favored maneuver and firepower over frontal assault to achieve victory. The public outcry over casualty figures in Vietnam seemed to verify their assumptions. Some cynical leaders in the Soviet Union believed that as long as they could guarantee the incineration of just one U.S. city, it would be enough to hold the American hawks in check.

The key to the success of this "have-not" strategy was the ballistic missile submarine. While the Americans held vast technological and numerical superiority in airborne nuclear missiles and intercontinental ballistic missiles, the Soviets believed their sea-launched ballistic missiles would be more than enough to deter a first strike. A crash program of naval construction also focused on launching a number of destroyers and cruisers armed with surface-to-surface missiles. But since these ships were vulnerable, too, the primary element in the short-term deterrence plan was the missile submarine.

By 1967, the Soviet navy had launched a powerful and dangerous blue-water armada in the Atlantic Ocean and, for the first time, was a force to be reckoned with in the Mediterranean Sea. Soviet fleets began sailing missile cruisers and submarines into the ports of Third World countries, a strategy that won new converts to Communism. The increasingly powerful Red fleet served to further intimidate vassal Socialist Republics around the Baltic and Black seas, and to keep the always-restive Warsaw Pact countries of Eastern Europe in line.

The Soviets boasted of their new sea power. Marshal Rodion Malinovsky, the Soviet minister of defense, pronounced in a speech shortly before his death in 1967: "First priority is being given to the strategic missile forces and atomic missile-launching submarines—forces which are the principal means of deterring the aggressor and decisively defeating him in war."

In October 1967, Admiral Gorshkov clearly defined the new Soviet ambitions in a speech delivered on the fiftieth anniversary of the Soviet fleet. He warned, "In the past our ships and naval aviation units have operated primarily near our coast, concerned mainly with operations and tactical coordination with ground troops. Now, we must be prepared for broad offensive operations against sea and ground troops of the imperialists on any point of the world's oceans and adjacent territories."

Nowhere was the role of the Soviet navy, and particularly the Soviet submarine force, as essential to the strategic ambitions of the motherland as in the Soviet Pacific Far East. Soviet naval bases were strung the length of the Soviet Pacific coast, from Rybachiy Naval Base on the Kamchatka Peninsula to Vladivostok, fourteen hundred miles to the south. The warships of the Soviet Pacific surface fleet and Pacific Fleet headquarters were located at bases near Vladivostok.

The Soviet navy also had several submarine bases at Vladivostok, around the eastern edges of Peter the Great Bay, in Vladimir Bay off the Sea of Japan, on the Tatar Strait between Sakhalin Island and the mainland,

and in several bays on the Sea of Okhotsk. In addition
to its own permanent submarine facilities, the Soviet
Union had secured a submarine base from its client
state North Korea at the port of Wonsan near the De-
militarized Zone. That facility was about to become the
focus of one of the bitterest confrontations in the already heated Cold War.

Rybachiy Naval Base on the Kamchatka Peninsula
was the home port for the Soviets' increasingly menacing ballistic missile force in the Pacific. In part because
of its isolation, Avachinskaya Bay was one of the most
important strategic assets in the USSR's Pacific battle
plan. Although the huge natural bay was in the far
northern Pacific on the edge of the Bering Sea, a cli-
matic anomaly left its main open waters ice-free the
year round. This all-weather bay provided the home
port for more than half of the Soviet Union's sizable Pacific submarine fleet. The bay was deep enough that
departing submarines could submerge well before leaving the narrow inlet for the open sea.

The U.S. Navy was well aware that Rybachiy Naval
Base was the key to the new Soviet submarine strategy
in the Pacific. It was almost as close to American military bases in the Aleutian Islands of Alaska as it was to
its own headquarters at Vladivostok. This proximity, and
the fact that it was primarily a ballistic missile submarine base, made the entrance to Avachinskaya Bay one
of the most watched waterways on earth.

Elsewhere in the Pacific region, America was mired in
the Vietnam War. The Soviet navy aimed to take advantage of the situation to lay claim to a share of America's
undisputed Pacific realm. The U.S. Navy had ruled this

ocean from the Ross Sea to the Bering Sea, and from the Americas to Southeast Asia, since the end of World War II. In 1968, the Soviets, with their far-flung submarine and naval bases from the Arctic Circle to the Sea of Japan, were poised to challenge the American claim. In the early 1960s, the Soviet naval formations from the Pacific bases had begun making calls throughout Southeast Asia and into the Indian Ocean. The Soviets became the naval patron for the nonaligned nations of Indonesia and India, giving the Red fleet new, friendly ports of call for refueling.

The United States Navy, with its major bases in Japan, Okinawa, the Philippines, and Vietnam, and its midocean headquarters at Hawaii, still ruled the Pacific realm, but the Soviets' new emphasis on a sea-launched ballistic missile navy was intended to challenge that supremacy.

In the mid-1960s, a new problem appeared on the Pacific horizon that boded trouble for both the Soviets and the Americans. The impenetrable naval ring these great powers sought to build around the Pacific Ocean had a sizable gap in its southwestern front. The People's Republic of China (PRC) had joined the fraternity of nuclear nations in 1964, when it successfully tested its first atomic bomb. The Chinese wasted no time in adapting their new nuclear capability to tactical and strategic missiles. In a matter of a few months, there was a major new nuclear-armed threat in the Pacific Ocean.

Although Communist China had been a near-vassal state to the mighty Soviet Union from its creation in 1949, in the early 1960s the sleeping giant turned on its patron. By 1967–68, the relationship had become so hostile, a powerful faction in the Kremlin was urging that Mao Tse-tung's China be designated people's enemy number one, replacing the United States and its NATO allies as the prime target.

The American CIA watched the developing feud between the two Red giants with growing interest.

"[Soviet] relations with China have deteriorated to the point that major hostilities could occur. It is clear that the Soviets now regard China as a major threat to the USSR, and they apparently see this threat as active, growing, and of long duration," revealed a top-secret National Intelligence Estimate (NIE), which was declassified at the end of the Cold War. "The Soviet military buildup in the Sino-Soviet border area has primarily involved the theater forces, but there have been some related developments in the strategic forces. Substantial Soviet forces will almost certainly be stationed on the eastern frontier for the foreseeable future."

The instability was made all the more frightening by the near-anarchy that spread throughout the Chinese mainland with the Great Proletarian Cultural Revolution, which had begun in 1966. The thought of an out-of-control nation with nuclear weapons posed a nightmare scenario for both Washington and Moscow.

The NIE pointed out that the developing hostility between the Soviets and Red Chinese had critically stretched the Soviet military capabilities. It stated that "the Soviets only five years ago faced two major military problems: the strategic capabilities of the West and the security of Eastern Europe. Now there is a third, a hostile China with an emerging nuclear capability."

Thus, the rapid Soviet naval buildup in the Pacific

was designed to confront a new enemy, as well as the old American nemesis. The ballistic missile submarine was the primary weapon in the Soviet arsenal to carry out that new military policy.

The Chinese nuclear threat was equally disturbing to the United States, especially in light of Chairman Mao's repeated harangues that China would welcome an all-out nuclear war. The Chairman boasted that China alone could prevail after the nuclear holocaust because of its vast population and immense land area. He predicted the Soviet Union and the United States would be reduced to postindustrial wastelands.

Even as this new nuclear adversary in the Pacific theater emerged, the United States Navy remained focused on the Soviets' rapidly expanding submarine force. In a 1968 confidential report, the Navy told Congress: "Of all elements of Soviet naval strength, the most alarming is the growth of its submarine force. The chief naval threat comes from the USSR's huge underseas fleet of 250 attack submarines and 100 missilefiring submarines, the largest force of submarines ever created."

The report warned that the Soviet Union was developing an offensive maritime strategy and was seeking supremacy at sea. Admiral Thomas H. Moorer, chief of naval operations, provided this assessment:

"By any measuring stick, they [the Soviets] are today the second largest sea power in the world. In a mere ten years, the Soviet Union with dedication of purpose, large outlays of funds, and with priorities equivalent to or even surpassing their space program, has transferred itself from a maritime nonentity to a major sea power."

The new Soviet naval capabilities for offensive action in the Pacific Ocean temporarily relied on weapons systems such as the Soviet diesel-electric submarine K-129, known as a Golf-class sub to the United States and its NATO allies. (To facilitate identification and communication among its multilingual members, NATO assigned code names to Soviet submarine classes, using the standard military phonetic alphabet, although in no particular order.)

K-129's seventy-day mission at the end of 1967 may well have been one of the first probes under the new strategy that called for sending missile submarines to within close range of the Pacific coast of the United States. Supreme Navy Commander Gorshkov and his political counterparts in the Kremlin would have certainly been fully aware of such a mission before Gorshkov's aggressive anniversary speech in October of that year.

The American Navy, which was only beginning to deploy systems in the Pacific to track Soviet submarines, argued in frustration for more funding to match the new threats, but the Vietnam War was soaking up every penny of increases in the defense budget.

The U.S. Navy's report to Congress concluded that the USSR's "transformation from a land power to also being an aggressive oceanic power" was bound to produce new belligerence.

Other reports not shared with Congress at the time were even more specific about the new submarine-launched missile threat in the Pacific. A National Intelligence Estimate prepared by the CIA warned that, while the Soviets were building and launching large numbers of new nuclear-propelled ballistic missile submarines, the Golf-class diesel submarines with nuclear missiles had already become a major threat in the Pacific. The secret NIE concluded: "We believe that G-class [Golf] submarines operating in the Pacific would probably be used against Alaska, Hawaii, Asia, and other targets in the Pacific Ocean. A few may be committed against targets in the northwest U.S., perhaps as an interim measure until more nuclear-powered types become available."

The Kamchatka Flotilla based at Rybachiy was the largest submarine force structured to carry out that threat in the Pacific. K-129 was one of six boats of the Golf type assigned to the 29th Ballistic Missile Division of the Kamchatka Flotilla. In January 1968, K-129 was part of the 15th Squadron, tactical number 574, which was under the command of *Kontr* (Rear) Admiral Rudolf A. Golosov. The division commander was Admiral Viktor A. Dygalo.

The Kamchatka Flotilla also included three other major divisions. The 45th Nuclear Submarine Division consisted of the Soviets' first nuclear-powered, ballistic missile submarines known to NATO as the Hotel class. The 8th and 25th divisions were deploying the newer Yankee-class, nuclear-powered, ballistic missile submarines as rapidly as they could be turned out at overextended shipyards. In addition to the ballistic missile boats, the Kamchatka Flotilla also included scores of smaller attack submarines, which were sent out to protect the Soviet coasts and to spy on the Americans and their allies in the Pacific and on the fledgling Red Chinese navy.

Although K-129 was a transitional model between the upgraded technology of World War II and the nuclear-age boats, its stealth and long-range capability made it a formidable adversary. It was almost certainly one of the first Soviet ballistic missile submarines to challenge the Americans on their own shores. Before 1967, there was no evidence that Soviet missile submarines were approaching closer than their maximum missile range, about eight hundred miles, to the U.S. Pacific Fleet headquarters at Pearl Harbor, Hawaii. U.S. intelligence knew the Soviets frequently sent smaller attack subs much closer on spy missions. The Soviets had not even sent missile boats near the American coasts during the Cuban Missile Crisis; they had dispatched only the attack boats to Cuban waters. The U.S. Navy's antisubmarine warfare (ASW) capabilities to protect the base at Pearl Harbor were fearsome, and the Soviets knew it.

Soviet missile subs regularly patrolled in midocean within a one-hundred- by two-hundred-mile rectangular mission box northwest of Hawaii. The outer edge of that patrol area was approximately 750 miles northwest of Hawaii. This patrol area brought the Soviets to within striking range of Pearl Harbor, but not close enough to provoke an incident between the two most powerful navies the world had ever known.

K-129 had probably conducted autonomous missions to this patrol box in the mid-Pacific. Whether this submarine had patrolled off Hawaii in 1967, farther north on the coast of Alaska, or along the northwest coast of the United States, is still a secret of the Soviet navy.

A mission did not necessarily have to be spectacular to be shrouded in secrecy. As with all its extended solo missions, information on the exact patrol areas navigated by K-129 in 1967 remains top-secret within the Soviet navy. Sealed orders came from Moscow to fleet headquarters in Vladivostok and were delivered unopened to the Kamchatka base. The mission orders were opened by the captain and political officer only after the submarine sailed.

When K-129 returned to Avachinskaya Bay after its seventy-day patrol in the Pacific on that frigid day in early January 1968, the Soviet Pacific Far East was the front line in the escalating Cold War. Bombs were not falling, but the Kamchatka Flotilla was at the highest level of wartime readiness.

No family members were waiting to greet the returning crew, and civilians along the shore went about their business, inured to the sight of a submarine returning from some deep-sea mission. In America, tourists would line the causeways to gawk at submarines arriving at Pearl Harbor or San Diego, and Navy wives and children thronged the piers for homecomings. In this isolated part of the Soviet Union, the Cold War was waged in grim earnest.

The very isolation of the Kamchatka submarine base, four thousand miles from Moscow, provided the required cloak of obscurity for the most dangerous Soviet-American confrontation of that undeclared war.

3

UNDERSEAS WARFARE WAS FOREVER changed in the summer of 1960, when the Americans achieved a breakthrough in submarine technology. On July 20, off Cape Canaveral, Florida, the USS *George Washington*, a hybridized attack submarine modified as the first nuclear-powered, ballistic missile submarine, fired two Polaris A-1 missiles. The Polaris had a range of twelve hundred miles. It was not only the breathtaking range of the new missile that astounded the world's admirals, but the fact that these missiles were successfully launched while the *George Washington* was completely submerged.

This single event set off an arms race that would ultimately break the bank in the Soviet Union, as Moscow desperately tried to keep up with the West. By the late 1960s, the United States had nearly completed the conversion of its underseas missile fleet to nuclear-powered, multiwarhead carriers. Though Soviet technology lagged behind that of the Americans, a few new nuclear-powered, Yankee-class submarines were beginning to come off the production line.

It was apparent that the Soviet Union's limited industrial capacity, coupled with technological weaknesses, would cause a shortage of modern submarines for many years to come. The urgency to remain competitive forced the Soviet navy to continue its dependency on older diesel submarines such as K-129 to carry sea-launched ballistic missiles during this critical transition period.

K-129 looked rawboned next to the newer and larger Yankee-class, nuclear-powered submarines that had arrived at the Rybachiy base in 1967. While most of the new sixteen-missile subs were assigned to European fleets in the Baltic and Black seas, two had been sent to the Kamchatka Flotilla.

The new boats were slow in coming and plagued with reactor problems. By necessity, the Soviet navy's older missile boats, the diesel-electric Golf class and the nuclear-powered Hotel class, remained the first-line weapons of the Pacific Fleet.

In the second week of January, the sailors of K-129 were performing the routine repair and maintenance required after return from a long mission. The seamen, with one lieutenant still aboard as duty officer, moved unhurriedly about their chores; everyone expected a long stay in port.

The volcanic peaks, visible from time to time when winter winds blew breaks in the overcast skies, gave the Rybachiy Naval Base a false sense of security, as if the submarines tied up at the piers were protected by a natural mountain bastion. But these submariners knew better than most that in this age of nuclear missiles the circle of high peaks would provide no protection from attack. A single intercontinental or sea-launched ballistic missile such as the ones they carried could obliterate the base and the city across the bay in a single thermonuclear flash.

The crew of K-129 was happy to be back in port with its relatively comfortable quarters on dry land. Another autonomous mission was certainly the last thing on their minds as they worked in the frigid air. Now the wind, which had felt so refreshing the day they sailed into the bay after weeks of breathing foul fumes of diesel oil and sweat, was a miserable 12°F at midday. Any pleasure they had initially derived from the fresh air was supplanted by the ache of freezing fingers and toes for those sailors whose tasks required them to work on the deck or make trips to supply rooms for replacement parts. The bay water splashing over K-129's deck and the adjacent pier froze almost immediately, making their chores uncomfortable and footing hazardous.

From the outside, the K-129 appeared ready for retirement to a naval museum. It looked much like the advanced German U-boats the Allies had captured at the end of World War II. Soviet engineers and captured Nazi scientists, who had been brought back from Germany as prisoners, worked from looted blueprints to design a better boat. They kept the best technology of the most advanced German submarine of World War II and added a number of improvements. The result was the development of the attack submarine designated as Foxtrot by NATO naval intelligence. The design for the highly reliable and successful Foxtrot submarine was later modified by adding three launch tubes in the center of the boat to make it the Soviet Union's first production ballistic missile submarine. This missile boat was called the Series 629 by the Soviets and designated the Golf by NATO.

In appearance and operational characteristics the Foxtrot and Golf submarines were close copies of the German U-XXI electro-diesel submarines. The snorkeling system copied from the German model was state-of-the-art technology, which allowed submarines to remain submerged while recharging their main batteries.

The Soviet innovations to this design included greatly extended battery life, quieter electric motors and diesel engines, an acoustically muted five-blade propeller, and other operating features. Some American Navy men, charged with stalking this class of boat, believed it was even stealthier than the first generation of nuclear-powered Soviet subs.

These improvements, along with extended mission range of twenty thousand miles and a top submerged speed of fifteen to sixteen knots, brought the boat into the postwar era.

The Golf submarine was 324 feet in length and 27 feet wide. Fueled and armed, the submarine displaced approximately 2,850 tons submerged.

Because the submarine was basically powered by diesel engines and electric motors that had been improved and tested in years of service, the Golf soon became the most dependable boat in the Soviet submarine fleet. It had a problem-free propulsion system. The Golfs were driven by three 2,000-horsepower diesel engines, two 1,350-horsepower electric motors, and one 2,700-horsepower electric motor. In addition, they employed one 180-horsepower electric motor for slow-speed, ultraquiet operations. A similar system had been in use since the 1940s in the German electro-diesel submarine, which had approximately the same configuration of motors.

Golf submarines served in Soviet fleets from 1960 until the early 1990s. Many are still in service in the navies of former Soviet clients. In all the years this class of boat was in active service with the Soviet navy, there is no record of a Golf being lost due to mechanical failure—a record that sadly would not be duplicated by any of the newer Soviet nuclear-powered submarines. Because of its reliability, the Golf—far from being ready for the mothball fleet—remained in the Soviet naval arsenal through the end of the Cold War, and was one of the weapon systems most surveilled by NATO forces.

During the late 1960s, more Soviet nuclear-propelled submarines were tied up in shipyards for repairs than were on station in the Atlantic or Pacific, or any of the seas adjoining those oceans. As U.S. submarine and sea-launched missile technology was advancing rapidly, the crews on the Soviet nuclear-propelled subs were still suffering crippling or mortal injuries in accidents and equipment failures. For this reason, the workhorse diesel submarines were considered to be among the safest, and therefore choice, assignments for career officers and senior enlisted men in the Soviet navy.

While the Golfs were based on World War II designs, any similarity between the Soviet Golfs and their Nazi predecessors ended when it came to weaponry. The mission of the Nazi U-boat was to sink ships with torpedoes, as was that of the Soviet attack boat, the Foxtrot. But the Golf was developed as a strategic weapons platform with a mission to obliterate cities and sink whole armadas with nuclear missiles. In addition to its three ballistic missiles, the Golf submarine had six torpedo tubes and could carry as many as sixteen torpedoes. The Soviet mission planners designated two of the torpedoes on each Golf to be armed with nuclear warheads. These nuclear torpedoes were meant to destroy U.S. carrier groups or seashore installations.

But the main threat of this submarine was its ballistic missiles. As the Golfs steadily came off the assembly lines, they provided the Red Navy with a sea-launched ballistic missile capability that nearly tripled the range and destructive yield of earlier Soviet subs.

The Golf-class subs' vertically mounted missiles were enclosed in tubes built into the sail and located immediately behind the conning tower bridge. The first generation of Golf-type submarines to be deployed could stand off more than 375 miles from an enemy's coast and hurl three one-megaton missiles at cities or military targets. Before the Golfs were introduced, the combat role of Soviet missile submarines was limited to close-in missions near coasts, in support of ground forces. These earlier missile submarines carried one or two missiles, each with a yield of only ten kilotons, and a limited range of approximately one hundred miles.

The first of the twenty-two Golf submarines to enter service were assigned to operational squadrons beginning in 1960. Boats for the Atlantic and Baltic fleets were built in Europe at the closed city of Severodvinsk on the White Sea. These first European boats may well have been built by slave labor, since Severodvinsk itself was entirely built by Stalin-era political prisoners. A huge gulag in the city provided most of the labor at that shipbuilding plant.

The Golfs for the Pacific Fleet were built at Plant 199 in eastern Siberia, at Komsomolsk-on-Amur. This closed city was created exclusively as a military-industrial supply and manufacturing center to service the Soviets' Far East armies. Because of the great distances from the industrialized western Soviet Union to the Far East, all fleet submarine maintenance and repair facilities were duplicated in shipyards in Soviet Asia, a continent away from Moscow. This military-industrial center was located far inland, to provide maximum cover from the prying American submarines that might lurk off a port city. The planned secrecy did not work for long. By the time the Soviets were launching the Golf submarines, the United States had penetrated the veil with spy satellites.

Every submarine built at Plant 199 and at the other shipyards of the Soviet Union was photographed by U.S. satellite cameras from the time it left the plant to its arrival at an assigned naval base. The Americans went a step beyond simply watching the progress of shipbuilding. Each Soviet submarine that sailed was catalogued. U.S. Navy intelligence also made acoustical sound tracks of engine, motor, and propeller noises recorded by tracking spy submarines. Information on Soviet submarines in the active-duty fleets was entered into a database in the U.S. Navy's Cray computers. When a submarine left port the Americans knew exactly the type, capabilities, and weaponry the Soviets were sending against them.

Even though they proved to be operationally reliable, the Golfs were not without defects. Whether slave labor was used in the shipbuilding plant at Komsomolsk-on-Amur is not known, but the United States Navy would later learn that some of the workmanship on the K-129 was quite shoddy. The welds and steel used in hull plates were inferior. Wooden timbers were used in parts of the frame. Such built-in structural weaknesses would have been considered criminal in U.S. and Western submarines, which used the highest quality steel and advanced alloys to ensure that underseas boats could withstand the pressure of the depths and stressful maneuvers required of this type of war machine.

One of the major design flaws in the Golf submarine resulted from adapting the boat as a missile carrier. A long, reinforced, keel-like structure was added to strengthen the frame in the center of the submarine to support the weight of the missiles. But the boat still could not make sharp-angle turns or withstand steep dives without putting dangerous stress on its structural integrity.

The Golf was built with double hulls that gave the submarine the ability to operate at a maximum depth of 853 feet. The submarine could withstand a maximum depth of 984 feet. The space between the hulls provided storage for diesel fuel, fresh water, and compressed air. Some of the space was used for ballast, allowing the boat to take on seawater for extra weight in diving. The double walls and the liquids stored between them also provided insulation from the cold waters of the deep ocean.

At about the time the Soviets began introducing the Golf submarines into service, the People's Republic of China was clamoring for assistance in upgrading its own navy. To placate their Chinese ally the Soviets agreed to provide one of the prototype missile submarines. The submarine they gave to the Chinese was one of the original test Golf boats, which had a much less advanced weapons system and had never been produced in any quantity by the Soviets. It was armed with a missile designated R-11FM, which was little more than an upgraded SCUD surface-to-surface missile of the type used on the earliest Soviet missile submarines. That missile system was limited in range, accuracy, and maximum throw weight. These limitations restricted the operational range to less than one hundred miles and the nuclear warhead yield to ten kilotons. Prelaunch preparations had to be performed on the surface and took more than an hour, making the boat an easy target for any antisubmarine aircraft or ships guarding an enemy's waters.

Along with this prototype Golf, seven of the R-11 missiles were transferred to the Chinese in late 1959 or early 1960. The Soviets would rapidly come to regret supplying the Chinese with a ballistic missile submarine, because relations soured soon after this transfer of technology.

The first Golf submarines deployed by the Soviets had been vastly improved over the prototype model they gave to the Chinese. Soviet engineers had adapted a new weapons system to provide for greater flexibility of missions before their boats were assigned to the Atlantic and Pacific fleets. This system was designated SS-N-4, and featured an improved launcher called the D-2. It was designed to launch a new R-13 missile, with a maximum range of 372 miles and a warhead yield of one megaton. The system also provided for more rapid deployment and launch of the missile. The new R-13 missile was called the Sark. Though preparation for launch could be accomplished while the boat was still submerged, the submarine still had to surface to fire the missile. Thus, it remained vulnerable in the face of the Allies' rapid deployment of antisubmarine aircraft, ships, and submarines.

The Americans' underseas launch of missiles by the USS *George Washington* created a major new challenge to the Soviets. Even though the Soviets began rapidly increasing submarine production, they continued to fall behind Western underseas warfare technology.

After completion in 1960 at the inland shipyard at Komsomolsk-on-Amur, the submarine designated K-129 sailed down the Amur River to the Tatar Strait and into the open ocean. K-129, which was built on the original Golf blueprint, was assigned to a Soviet submarine pack operating from the Pavlovsk Naval Base on Strelok Bay, forty miles east of Vladivostok. In 1964,

K-129 was transferred to Rakushka Naval Base, 185 miles northeast of Vladivostok on the northern edge of the Sea of Japan.

It was at Rakushka on Vladimir Bay that the young Captain Second Rank Kobzar took command of K-129. Along with command of the boat came the promotion to captain first rank. Kobzar was thirty-four years old.

An event in Asia in 1964 had a dramatic impact on the strategists in the Kremlin and the mission of the Soviet Pacific Fleet. On October 16, the People's Republic of China—the increasingly hostile former client state— successfully tested an atomic bomb. In less than a year the Chinese would up the ante with a successful test of their first hydrogen bomb. The Soviets knew the Chinese could rapidly weaponize their nuclear technology since they had transferred submarine and missile technology to China before the Sino-Soviet rift. Between 1950 and 1960, the Soviets had also provided the then-friendly Asian neighbor with blueprints for more advanced weapons systems, probably including the plans for the upgraded R-13 Sark missile and the D-2 launcher for the Golf submarine.

China's sudden entry into the exclusive club of nuclear-armed nations was a greater threat to the Soviets than to the Americans, because of the immense size of the PRC army and its proximity to the Soviet border. KGB intelligence studies warned Soviet leaders that the large Asian population of eastern Russia was increasingly being drawn to Mao Tse-tung and the Chinese style of Communism. From the early 1960s, Chairman

Mao had viciously lashed out at Soviet premier Nikita Khrushchev for deviating from the true path of Marxism. Beijing was challenging Moscow for hegemony over world Communism. The dispute quickly turned to direct confrontation along the twenty-four-hundred-mile-long common border in the Soviet Far East.

In 1963, the Kremlin made a final desperate effort to patch up the rift with China. A delegation led by its top China hand, Mikhail Andreyevich Suslov, met with Chinese officials and offered to restore good relations between Moscow and Beijing. Suslov was the Soviet Communist Party's chief ideologue and an unrepentant Stalinist. Rudely rebuffed by the Chinese, the delegation was convinced that the PRC—and Mao in particular—had suddenly replaced the United States as the Soviet Union's primary adversary.

Thus, by 1964, the Soviets in the Far East found themselves between the devil and the deep blue sea, with a nuclear-armed and hostile China next door and an even more powerful U.S. Navy in the Pacific Ocean. The Soviet navy had to be modernized quickly. The Soviet Union desperately needed a submarine that could launch ballistic missiles while submerged. To improve the balance of terror, the Soviets wanted submarines that could carry a nuclear strike to the enemies' cities and missile sites farther inland.

The Soviets had a more advanced missile system on the drawing boards, a system they determined could be adapted and retrofitted on the diesel-electric Golf submarines while improved nuclear submarines were being designed, built, and deployed.

The new sea-launched ballistic missile system designated the R-21 (Serb), with an effective range of more than 840 miles and a one-megaton warhead, was ready for installation by the mid-1960s. More important, the engineers had designed a new launch system, the D-4, which provided a capability for submarines to launch while surfaced or submerged. The combined system, known as the SS-N-5, would give the Soviet fleets their first truly atomic-age, sea-launch missile capability.

The Golf submarines in the retrofit program were designated Series 629A by the Soviets. NATO would identify them as Golf IIs, at which point the boats not retrofitted were designated Golf Is. When the retrofit was completed, the Soviets had a major new sea-launched missile system that could temporarily compete with the Americans' superior SLBM technology, and an ability to put sea-launched, one-megaton nuclear warheads on practically every major city in China, as well.

Of the twenty-two Golf-type submarines in service in 1965, fourteen were selected to be retrofitted with the new Serb missile and underwater launch system. Captain Kobzar's K-129 was one of these boats.

The K-129 was ordered to the Dalzavod shipyards for the missile retrofit and a complete overhaul. As was customary, the captain and senior crew members stayed with their ship for this work. The Dalzavod facility had been the premier Russian shipyard in the Far East since the late 1880s. It was located in a suburb of the bristling Soviet naval facilities at Vladivostok. This huge shipyard was as well equipped as any in the Soviet Union, with a giant quay wall, three dry docks, two side-launching ways, and two floating docks. The six Golf submarines in the Pacific Fleet were to be retrofitted with the improved missile systems and returned to duty as soon as the conversion was completed.

While the extensive missile launch retrofit was taking place, K-129's captain arranged to have another, customized modification made to his boat. Kobzar wanted more space in compartment two where the officers' cabins were located, along with the cipher room, the sonar room, and one of the sub's three communal toilets. One way to achieve this was to move the cipher room out of that area. During the overhaul at the Dalzavod shipyards, the captain bribed an engineer with a case of vodka to make the additional, unauthorized alterations to his boat.

The cipher room was a closetlike enclosure where the encryption codebooks and decoding machines were kept in a locked safe. One of the few underused spaces on the submarine was in compartment four, which housed the three huge missile tubes. There was space between the tubes and in walkways between the tubes and hull. The cipher room was replicated there, and the equipment moved from compartment two to compartment four.

Moving the cipher gear to compartment four not only freed some space in the officers' quarters but placed the critical cipher equipment and codebooks much closer to the communications room and the control center. Thus, the unauthorized innovation was both a convenience for the officers and a practical improvement to the boat's overall utility.

Captain Kobzar's uncharacteristic independent streak did not go unnoticed by his superiors. The captain's action was so unusual that it sparked an investigation by Soviet naval intelligence. The chief engineer from the Dalzavod shipyards was questioned about having accepted the case of vodka as a bribe and ultimately forced to sign an affidavit admitting complicity.

While the K-129 and other Golfs were being retrofitted with the modern missile and launch system in the shipyard at Vladivostok, China was wasting no time modernizing its own navy. Coincidentally, in September 1966, a submarine almost identical in appearance and operations to the Series 629 Golf (Golf I) originally deployed by the Soviets was completed at the Dalian shipyards on the north shore of the Yellow Sea in China, approximately 750 miles southwest of Vladivostok.

The Americans soon became aware that the Chinese had launched this improved Golf with enhanced ballistic missile range. The intelligence agencies of both the Soviets and the Americans watched with growing concern as missiles with ever greater range and capacity were tested in the deserts of western China. China had been testing its own missile delivery systems since at least 1958.

In addition, a dozen Chinese attack submarines began to appear around the fringes of the Asian continent. China had been rapidly turning out Soviet-style, diesel-electric attack submarines at shipyards at Jiangnan, Wuchang, and Fulin. With typical Western bias, the Free World had hardly noticed Mao's ambition to build an offensive naval force until the Chinese tested the first Asian atom bomb.

The KGB knew the Chinese had also married their newfound nuclear warhead and missile technology to at least one submarine and they assumed that U.S. military intelligence knew it, too.

When the conversion of K-129 to a Golf II–type submarine was completed in 1966, the Soviets had a greatly improved weapon to send back into the Pacific. With its extended missile range, the Golf II submarine could hide and launch its missiles from an area of ocean six times larger than before. That meant it was a much more elusive weapon, and posed a greater threat to American cities, ports, and military installations located anywhere within eight hundred miles of a coastline. The new Serb missile was not as good as the American Polaris system, but the Golf II submarines such as K-129 now had the ability to fire while running submerged at four or five knots.

After the retrofit, K-129 was reassigned to a new unit as part of the Kamchatka Flotilla. There was no visible difference to the sub's external features, since the improvements were all internal. However, the wet launch system did add considerable weight to the submarine and additional stress to the hull.

In early January 1966, Captain Kobzar sailed his newly refurbished submarine fourteen hundred miles from Vladivostok to the submarine base near Petropavlovsk-Kamchatskiy on the Kamchatka Peninsula. K-129 was one of six of the remodeled boats assigned to the Soviet 29th Ballistic Missile Squadron.

The retrofitted subs operating out of the Rybachiy

Navy Base on the Kamchatka Peninsula became a menace to America and the object of intense surveillance by the U.S. attack submarines operating near the Soviet Asian coasts. Assignments from that deep-water port took K-129 to the edges of the territorial waters of the United States for the first time. It is known that K-129 completed at least two of these long-range missions in 1967.

While the Americans and Soviets were rushing into production a new generation of nuclear-powered submarines, it was this aging diesel-electric boat that would soon become, for both sides, the most hunted submarine of the Cold War.

4

THE SUBMARINE OFFICER of the Cold War Red Navy was as close as the Marxist system ever came to producing the idealized "new Soviet man."

These naval officers, along with the few cosmonauts and a smattering of top aviators, were the first generation of men born and reared entirely under the control of a Communist state. By selection, training, and discipline they were sterling examples of what the proletariat could accomplish under the best that the Soviet system had to offer.

While these men were not state-controlled robots, their intensive indoctrination made them both technically well educated and extremely patriotic. The submarine commanders never hesitated to risk their lives and boats for the cause and, if given a verifiable order, they would have launched nuclear missiles on an enemy city without qualms. This devotion to state, however, came with a major caveat. These officers strictly adhered to a regimen of procedures and a chain of command that absolutely prevented them from exercising even the slightest degree of personal initiative. Just as the submarine officers would not hesitate to obey orders to the letter, their intensive indoctrination prevented any deviation from their assignments. There were no cowboys in the Soviet submarine service.

The commander of K-129, Captain First Rank Vladimir Ivanovich Kobzar, was recognized by his peers and superiors alike as the embodiment of this first generation of new Soviet men. His loyal service was rewarded in January 1968.

Kobzar was told he was slated for appointment to a command position with the Pacific Fleet headquarters in Vladivostok. This increase in responsibility would almost certainly bring with it the rank of rear admiral. Another unexpected honor was bestowed on him. The veteran submarine captain received the Soviet Union's second-highest military honor, the Order of the Red Star. This prestigious medal was awarded for outstanding achievement in the defense of the USSR by acts or conduct that ensured state security. Captain Kobzar was cited for personal courage and valor. The specific act that merited this recognition was then, and remains today, a state secret. His crew was told only that the medal was awarded for a submarine mission Captain Kobzar headed during 1967. It is reasonable to speculate that he received the honor for commanding the first Pacific Ocean mission to bring a Soviet submarine within ballistic missile range of the American mainland. This was a major step toward establishing nuclear parity with the United States.

The significance of the Red Star to the Soviet submariners went far beyond the name of this medal. The Soviet navy—from the lowest seaman to the top admiral—literally sailed and served under the symbol of the

Red Star. Their ships flew the Red Star on the naval banner when they left and returned to port, and every officer and enlisted man wore a Red Star on the crown of his cap.

Captain Kobzar was one of the most experienced veterans of the post–World War II Red submarine service. Upon graduation from the naval academy at Sevastopol, he received command training at Leningrad before being posted to the Far East in 1952. A "sailor's sailor," Kobzar worked his way up through the ranks, serving on submarines in the Pacific Fleet at Vladivostok and Nakhodka before assuming command of the K-129 at Rakushka in 1964.

He was born in the small Ukrainian village of Ternavshchino. A tall, good-looking man with brown curly hair and a somber demeanor, Kobzar was by all accounts a dedicated and respected officer. He was highly regarded by his superiors and fellow officers and, though a stern commander, was considered fair and protective by those who served under him.

Submarine officers enjoyed the greatest prestige and privileges of any members of the Soviet armed forces, which could have placed them in an elitist class in the minds of other crew members. Still, there was a warm camaraderie between most officers and the men in the enlisted ranks on their subs. The close living accommodations and shared risks of the service fostered a level of cohesion unheard of in other branches of the Soviet military.

Admiral Rudolf A. Golosov, commander of the missile squadron to which the K-129 was attached, summed up the relationship this way:

"Submariners are a special brotherhood, either all come to the surface or no one does. On a submarine, the phrase all for one and one for all is not just a slogan, but reality."

If Captain Kobzar was a respected father figure to the K-129 crew, his first officer, Alexander M. Zhuravin, filled the role of big brother. Captain Second Rank Zhuravin, also exceptionally tall for a submariner at six feet two inches, was popular with the men of the submarine from the moment he assumed the first-officer position. He was known for his good-natured joking and quickly became a favorite officer among the ordinary seamen. On routine trips around the bay when the boat was between missions, Zhuravin often fished with the enlisted men off the submarine's stern.

Captain Zhuravin became K-129's first officer in mid-1967, and had served with this crew on its most recent extended mission. A submariner for more than twelve years, with extensive experience aboard Golf I and Golf II subs, Zhuravin had been selected to replace Captain Kobzar as commander of the K-129 when Kobzar assumed his new duties at Pacific Fleet headquarters. Zhuravin's first major assignment as submarine commander would be the regularly scheduled mission in early summer 1968, at which time he could expect a promotion to captain first rank.

A commander of a smaller attack submarine could hold that position as a captain second rank, but all missile boat skippers had to be at least captain first rank. The higher rank required for missile boat commanders indicated the Kremlin's appreciation for the responsibility these officers assumed. The missile boat commander, despite all the checks and balances of the system, had the ultimate potential to launch nuclear missiles that could start a world war.

Zhuravin came from a family of Leningrad industrial workers. His parents and older brother all worked in the Yegorov Train Car Factory. But during the Russian Revolution his father, Mikhail Grigoriavich Zhuravin, had been a sailor on the famous cruiser *Aurora*. The crew of that ship mutinied against the czarist navy on behalf of the Bolsheviks in February 1917 and fired the first shot that signaled the start of the Communist revolution.

After graduating from the naval academy at Riga, Zhuravin worked through the ranks from lieutenant, senior lieutenant, captain lieutenant, and captain third rank, to his position as first officer of the K-129 with the grade of captain second rank. He served on submarines at Odessa and Feodosiya on the Black Sea.

In 1960, Zhuravin's submarine was transferred from the Black Sea Fleet to the Pacific Fleet. This transfer of men and boat took him on an extraordinary voyage by submarine across the elaborate Russian inland waterway system. Czar Peter the Great had begun construction of the waterway in the early 1700s. Zhuravin's submarine traveled from the Black Sea in southern Russia, through the Volga-Don Canal to the Volga-Baltic Waterway into the White Sea in northern Russia. The submarine then sailed along the top of the world through the Kara Sea, the Laptev Sea, the East Siberian Sea, the Chukchi Sea, and through the Bering Strait into the Bering Sea, and finally, across the northern Pacific Ocean to Vladivostok.

Before being assigned to K-129, Zhuravin served on a Golf I submarine at Vladivostok and later on a retrofitted Golf II, identical to the K-129 he was soon to command. When he was transferred to the Kamchatka Flotilla, he joined the K-129 crew.

The rapid career advancement of both Kobzar and Zhuravin was based solely on merit. In the Soviet submarine officers corps in the late 1960s, political connections and party affiliations did not result in promotion. While submarine officers were required to be members of the Communist Party, and the party vetted candidates for command positions, first and foremost the typical submarine officer had to be technically proficient in the operations of the complicated, and often mechanically flawed, boats.

Captains Kobzar and Zhuravin, like all other Soviet navy officers assigned to high-level command positions aboard submarines, dutifully complied with the party membership requirements, but their careers were dedicated to the navy, not the party. Unlike many of the politicized postings in the Red Army, the submarine commanders were not political hacks. The submarine forces of the Soviet Union were too vital to the security of the Communist state, and the jobs too important to be filled by sycophants. Submarine commanders were handpicked by top admirals in the Soviet Supreme Naval Headquarters from the best officers in the Red Navy.

The candidate officers were selected in their teens from the cream of the Soviet youth. They were chosen strictly on the basis of their tested abilities and largely from the working classes, not from the families of Kremlin elite.

The cadets at the naval academies were educated and trained in specialties related to submarine operations, including weaponry, communications, engineering, and electronics. The submarine commanders, as well as the ships' other officers and petty officers, also had to be jacks-of-all-trades, with a flair for improvising with "bailing wire and Band-Aids," to compensate for the constant shortages of spare parts and technical problems.

The post–World War II submarines of the Soviet Union were constructed under much the same political pressure as Stalin had imposed on slave laborers to churn out vast armies of tanks for the Great Patriotic War. Sheer numbers counted for everything, while mechanical quality was often ignored. There was one obvious major difference. Mechanical failure of a tank engine or transmission was not likely to kill the crew. A leaking pressure hull or faulty hatch on a submarine was quite another matter.

Soviet submarine officers had to contend with dangerous risks to boats and crews created by the Communist bureaucracy, as well as head-to-head competition against superior American submarines and ASW aircraft. Party hacks in charge of shipyards and other production facilities frequently forced the navy to accept unsafe ships and other equipment into service before being properly tested. Submarine commanders bore the brunt of the mistakes made by the submarine builders, who were turning out boats of substandard quality, made by poorly trained workers. These boats often placed the lives of the officers and their men at risk. Between 1946 and 1991, hundreds of Soviet submarine sailors would pay for these mistakes with their lives.

But orders were orders and the Soviet submarine officers were obedient to a fault. Popular American movie plots to the contrary, there was not a single defection of a submarine crew during the entire Cold War. This loyalty to motherland seems even more surprising, in light of the fact that submarine commanders had ample opportunity to sail their boats independently into any harbor in the West.

Men such as Kobzar were indoctrinated from the crib to believe that the hardship of long years of service, isolated from home and family, was essential to protect their country from the imperialistic Western aggressors, particularly the Americans.

To compensate for the inadequacies of the Soviet military-industrial system, extraordinary men had to be raised to operate and fight these dangerous boats. Until the 1960s, most of the world did not consider the Soviet navy to be a competitive blue-water force. Against great odds, that reputation was gradually improving with the expansion of the submarine service.

The Communist system failed repeatedly on the economic front, with disaster after disaster in industrial and agricultural Five-Year Plans. But the Soviet submarine officer corps was honed at its excellent naval academies, and upon graduation these officers became the elite of Soviet society.

In 1968, Captain Kobzar, age thirty-eight, and Captain Zhuravin, four years his junior, were typical of the products of the postwar Soviet navy submarine schools. K-129's captain and first officer had been selected to become submarine officers while in their teens. Each had entered a submarine academy at the age of eighteen: Kobzar, the Admiral Makarov Naval Academy at Sevastopol on the Black Sea in 1948; and Zhuravin, the Riszhskoe Academy for Submariners at Riga, Latvia, on the Baltic Sea in 1952.

Both officers began their naval careers while Joseph Stalin was still dictator of the Soviet Union.

The Soviet navy, which had been decimated by Stalin's liquidation of all officers with the rank of rear admiral and above during the bloody military purges of the late 1930s, had been completely reorganized during and after the Great Patriotic War. As a result of the lingering memory of the purges, line officers in the military, particularly the navy, maintained a distrustful distance from the politics of the Kremlin. Even as they were forced to join and pledge loyalty to the Communist Party in order to attain higher rank, the typical submarine officer was strictly loyal to his fleet and military chain of command. The party was involved in every aspect of life in the Soviet Union, but operational naval command lines of authority were clear.

Like most of the veteran submarine commanders, Captain Kobzar held no position in the Communist Party. The younger Zhuravin held a minor post as secretary in a local party unit in Vladivostok.

Submarine commanders left the party's ideological duties and indoctrination to the *zampolit*, or political officer, stationed aboard every submarine. The *zampolits* were the postwar equivalent of the infamous commissars of World War II. In the modern Soviet military, they did not stand in the rear with machine guns waiting to mow down retreating soldiers, but their presence in every major unit was nonetheless a powerful influence. Every Soviet submarine had a regular *zampolit* assigned. On K-129, that man was Captain Third Rank Fedor E. Lobas.

Before modernization of the Soviet navy in the 1960s, the *zampolit* was sometimes called the second commander of Soviet submarines. But even with the shortage of trained submarine officers created by the rapid expansion of the submarine fleet, the political officer played almost no role in routine operations of the submarine. Theoretically, the political officer was put aboard every submarine to educate and make sure the crew maintained proper attitudes toward the state. In reality, it was also the political officer's job to guarantee that submarine commanders did not take any unauthorized action, particularly with the nuclear weapons.

All aspects of an assignment were preapproved by fleet headquarters or higher up the chain of command. Detailed, sealed orders were delivered simultaneously to the submarine captain and the political officer before each sailing. These orders were not opened until the boat was at sea. Every major decision made by a submarine commander had to conform to either written orders delivered before sailing or coded orders communicated by radio. In either case, it was the *zampolit*'s job to confirm the authenticity of the orders. There were no exceptions. Any disobedience or deviation could be grounds for harsh punishment to include imprisonment, exile to a gulag, or worse.

While political officer Lobas could never aspire to become commander of a submarine, there were other avenues for promotion. Stalin, Khrushchev, and Brezhnev had all been political officers or commissars in the Soviet army during their early careers. The political officer's career path was through the Communist Party structure. The *zampolit* did not answer to the captain or the chain of command, but to the Main Political Directorate, a bureau within the Ministry of Defense and an organ of the Communist Party. He was selected, trained, assigned, promoted, or demoted by the party.

Although the political officer could be expected to spy on the activities of officers and crew, most became well integrated into the crews after being assigned to their boats for long periods of time. One former Soviet submarine captain described his *zampolit* as "the party's official cheerleader." As a veteran member of the K-129 crew, Captain Third Rank Lobas was accepted by the other men and liked by many, despite his primary assignment as a party disciplinarian and sometimes spy.

The submarine was ably staffed with officers who had all served on the boat for at least one of the long autonomous patrols. Most had been with the boat on several of these extended missions. In 1967, the K-129 had spent almost six of the twelve months at sea.

At the end of January 1968, there was a full complement of fourteen officers assigned to K-129, all of them regular officers with personal service aboard that boat.

K-129's doctor, Sergey Cherepanov, was not a navy man but a major in the Soviet medical service. He had a medical assignment onshore, but had asked for, and was granted, special permission from Pacific Fleet headquarters to remain as part of the crew. The doctor routinely monitored the health of the whole crew, which was challenged by the environment of the sub itself. Stale air saturated with diesel and battery fumes and close physical contact created chronic problems. In an emergency, such as an appendicitis attack, Doctor Major Cherepanov performed surgery on a galley table. A submarine committed to an autonomous mission could not turn back for the sudden illness or death of one, or even a few, sailors. To keep the men as healthy as possible, the doctor and a seaman medic passed among the crew each day, dispensing vitamins and damp towels for washing.

A special security officer was assigned to Soviet missile submarines, under the cover of an operational position as deputy to the commander. It was common practice to put an officer from a separate naval branch in charge of the security and control of the nuclear missiles. On K-129 this officer was Captain Third Rank Vladimir Motovolov. Although Motovolov was called the commander's deputy, Captain Zhuravin actually held the number-two spot on the sub.

Since it was well known that Zhuravin was next in line among young submarine officers in the Pacific Fleet for command of his own boat, on K-129's last mission of 1967, he served as de facto commander. As first officer, Zhuravin was in day-to-day control of the submarine. He would have immediately returned the boat to Kobzar's command during difficult operations such as maneuvers to evade a stalking enemy submarine, or entry and departure from home port.

Two of the most important positions on a submarine crew were held by technical officers. The engineer and engineering assistant played vital roles in keeping the boat operating. These highly trained officers were responsible for the diesel engines and battery-powered electric motors, as well as maintenance and repair of all mechanical equipment. They were also responsible for monitoring fuel levels to conserve the diesel oil necessary to complete a mission and return. There were no refueling facilities in the North Pacific.

The men in the engineering section checked the battery charges hourly, to ensure the boat maintained power for running the electric motors used for submerged sailing. The commander was notified well in advance when a snorkeling operation would be required for recharging. Because of these important and multiple tasks, these officers supervised the largest number of regular crewmen on the submarine. The K-129's chief engineer was Captain Third Rank Nikolai Orechov. The assistant engineering officer was Captain-Lieutenant Alexander Egorov.

The submarine commander had to know his location in the vastness of the ocean at all times, a navigational challenge made all the more difficult since the boat usually traveled for days without surfacing. It was the job of the senior navigator and his assistant to keep precise charts.

To successfully launch a ballistic missile, the commander had to know the exact location of his submarine and the exact location of the target, calculations that were difficult to achieve, since the boat was constantly moving. K-129 had probably not been equipped with a new satellite-based navigational system, which was just coming online at that time. However, the latest radio-navigational system had been installed during the retrofit.

When running on the surface or snorkeling, the navigator would extend an antenna from the conning tower to obtain a radio-navigational signal transmitted from a known geographic location. Under ideal conditions, the submarine's position could be established within a hundred-foot radius. A sextant was built into the navigational periscope, giving the navigator a secondary method of calculating his position, using celestial bodies. Positions were periodically confirmed to headquarters through coded, microburst radio transmissions. The senior navigator was Captain-Lieutenant Nikolai Pikulik, and the assistant navigator was Lieutenant Anatoly Dykin.

The submarine's radio room was one of the most secure posts in the boat—only specifically cleared personnel could enter the room. It was the submarine's lifeline to headquarters and the critical nerve center for receiving changes in orders, war alerts, and actual clearances from fleet headquarters to activate and fire missiles. The Soviets knew the Americans were listening to every radio transmission, even though they were sent out over the airways in undecipherable microbursts. The job of radio man was one of the submarine's most important, and Senior Lieutenant Alexander Zarnakov held the post of radio electronic officer.

The K-129 had another assigned officer whose job went beyond the functions of the boat itself. A radio intelligence officer was stationed on the submarine to collect information on enemy shipping, antisubmarine warfare activities, and land-based military facilities. This officer eavesdropped on maritime, aviation, and shore radio traffic wherever the boat sailed. Senior Lieutenant Vladimir Mosyachkin was the radio intelligence officer. He assisted the radio operator in transmitting and receiving signals involved in the boat's regular operations.

When the Soviets and Americans began deploying strategic nuclear missiles, a new type of high-tech submarine officer had to be trained. These specialists—submarine missile officers—were required to become expert in nuclear weaponry, ballistics, and the emerging new launch technology. K-129's weapons officer was Captain Third Rank Gennady Panarin. The assistant weapons officer was Captain-Lieutenant Victor Zuev.

In addition to its three Serb ballistic missiles, K-129 carried two other strategic weapons. Two of the submarine's sixteen torpedoes were equipped with nuclear warheads, to be used in an attack on a U.S. carrier task force or fired into an enemy's harbor, shoreline city, or military installation for maximum strategic damage. The remaining, regular torpedoes were intended for use against Allied submarines or surface warships. The torpedo/mine officer was Captain Third Rank Eugeny Kovalev.

While these operational officers had to display a high degree of technical initiative to keep their substandard boats working, there was no room for innovation when it came to carrying out the mission. The strict controls of missile submarine operations extended all the way up the chain of command to Moscow.

No other arm of the Soviet military establishment was more rigidly controlled than the ballistic missile submarine force. Even fleet commanders, such as Admiral Ivan Amelko of the Pacific Fleet, had little discretion in assigning missions to the missile boats. The

K-129's division commander, Admiral Dygalo, and squadron commander, Admiral Rudolf A. Golosov, had no authority to dispatch or alter a mission for any of the missile submarines under their commands. These frontline admirals were primarily conveyors of the orders to the boat captains.

Authority for the strategic deployment of K-129 and other missile submarines in the fleets was vested in supreme naval headquarters in Moscow. Admiral of the Soviet navy Sergey Gorshkov was the real commander of the Soviet missile submarine fleets. He took his orders exclusively from General Secretary Leonid Brezhnev and that dictator's small circle of top Politburo defense officials. There were others in the Kremlin who were envious of this tight structure, and who endlessly tried to circumvent the system to gain more power in the Communist empire. Most of these schemers were in some way or another in a camp that believed the control of the system should be exercised through the parallel hierarchy of the KGB.

The Soviet naval system had built-in checks and balances throughout the officer structure, to ensure that official orders involving missile submarines originated at the top, and that these orders were strictly followed down the chain. Admiral Gorshkov, an ironfisted commander with direct lines to the politicians in the Kremlin, was a ruthless disciplinarian. A respected naval hero of the Great Patriotic War, Gorshkov became an admiral at the age of thirty-two, the youngest any Soviet officer had attained that respected rank.

Some deployment of missile submarines—such as the assignment of boats to squadrons, divisions, and flotillas—was invested in superiors at fleet headquarters in Vladivostok. But when it came to the strategic missions for these boats, the authority was executed by Supreme Soviet navy command headquarters in Moscow.

The fourteen command and operations officers of K-129, all regulars, were the final link in the chain of command. Their job was to obediently carry out the orders, and they had practically no authority otherwise.

The next tier of K-129 crewmen was even more rigidly indoctrinated to follow orders without question. These were the senior enlisted men, including three with the rank of *michman* (warrant officer) and six chief petty officers. Most warrant officers and senior petty officers in the Soviet navy were also career professionals. They were highly trained in the technical skills required to operate the submarine and specialized in their fields of expertise, such as electronics, engine mechanics, communications, and weaponry. Unlike enlisted submariners in the American Navy, their Soviet counterparts were not cross-trained, and stayed in their specific jobs for the duration of their service.

The regular K-129 crew also included two dozen petty officers. All the men in these senior enlisted ranks were better trained than the common seamen, and all were volunteers. The typical tour of service of these ranking crewmen was six years. However, since the privileges of housing, clothing, and food for the trained submariner so exceeded what was available to civilians or enlisted personnel in other service branches, many of these petty officers chose to remain in service.

It had been years since many of the K-129 senior enlisted personnel had been granted leave to take the long trips home to western Russia. A handful of eager young Soviet submariners, returning in January from the latest extended mission, were lucky enough to be granted furloughs. These men quickly vanished into the vast Russian winter, hitching rides on whatever military transport they could find, or cramming onto the cheap Aeroflot commercial flights that shuttled between the military outposts of Asia and western Russia.

Normally, Soviet regulations required any active submarine to retain a sufficient number of officers and men needed to sail and fight the ship at a moment's notice. Captain Kobzar had been allowed to bend rules and permitted eight senior enlisted men to take leave. In addition, the duty tours of seven first-class and regular seamen had expired and they were permitted to leave the service. Furloughing so many crew members was a risk the captain thought worth taking. He did not expect to be ordered back to sea for an extended patrol until early summer.

The majority of the K-129 crew members, approximately four dozen, were lower-ranking enlisted men. These seamen received no leave for the duration of their conscription. They were drafted for three- to four-year stints and remained on duty until their service obligation was fulfilled.

When the K-129 returned from an extended mission these sailors, who lived in barracks, worked around the submarine performing repairs, cleaning, and routine maintenance. While the navy skimmed the best of the conscripts, these men received little specialized training. They were placed on the job and given specific duties.

Most of the lower-ranking members of the normal, eighty-three-man complement serving aboard Golf-type subs were from villages and towns scattered across the Union of Soviet Socialist Republics. Many of them were from the Soviet *Stans,* predominantly Moslem republics. Others were conscripted from Tatar ethnic groups of the steppes and Siberia. The conscripts in the lower ranks were treated as younger members of the K-129 family. These sailors from the collective farms and herder villages obeyed whatever orders they received from any authority figure they encountered. In general, their greatest ambition in the Soviet submarine service was to finish their hitch and return home as soon as possible.

5

THE SOVIET SUBMARINE OFFICER was effectively indoctrinated throughout his training to dedicate life and career to the state, and yet, paradoxically, a strong devotion to wife and children humanized this "new Soviet man."

The senior staff officers of K-129 had been carefully selected, highly trained at the best naval schools, and drilled in the Marxist tenet of "State above all." At the same time, there is ample evidence that these men's families strongly influenced how they carried out their duties to the motherland.

Homecoming after a long patrol was an occasion of real celebration for the officers and crew. Naturally, the men were glad to be back on land where their accommodations, though Spartan by Western standards, were luxurious compared to the cramped bunks and stagnant air on the boat. The return to port was even more significant for those who would be reuniting with their families. Many of the senior crew members had wives and children living in government-provided apartments on or near the base, or in housing in nearby military villages. Some lived across the bay in the city of

Petropavlovsk-Kamchatskiy. A few families of officers recently transferred to Rybachiy still lived at large naval complexes near Vladivostok, waiting for housing assignments closer to the base.

Despite the strictness of the Soviet military system, the navy actually encouraged cadets to marry at the end of their academy training. The navy provided transportation for their brides to follow them to the far-flung naval bases where they were assigned.

The submariner families lived insular lives, far removed from most population centers and still more distant from the realities of the failing Soviet economy. The pay of junior officers was low, but the navy compensated in other ways, offering families a privileged lifestyle compared with that of average Soviet citizens. Free housing, often with a television set and sometimes a private bath, was furnished whenever available. The families enjoyed better food, a wide selection of otherwise scarce clothing, and a few luxury items. Almost everything needed for a relatively comfortable lifestyle was provided more generously to the families of submarine officers than to any other military or workers group in Soviet society.

An especially popular perk for the submariners in the Pacific Fleet was a health resort holiday provided at the end of each extended mission. The Soviet bureaucrats justified the expense of the recreational junkets by calling the resorts "sanitariums" and including rehabilitation sessions on the agenda. But the accommodations and programs at the sanitariums were more like the vacation spas offered as rewards to European workers and their families. If the submariner's wife lived near the base, she was included in the holiday.

When the K-129 returned in January, the crew members were offered twenty-day respites at such a spa. Shortly after being cleared from the mission, approximately half the crew left for the spa, while the other half did light duty around the Rybachiy submarine base. When the first group returned, the other half went.

The hot springs spa, which included family cottages as well as recreational, medical, and therapy facilities, was located at Paratunka Village, about twenty miles from Petropavlovsk.

Captain Kobzar enjoyed the privileges of a submarine commander, and his family had been awarded comparatively comfortable quarters in the officers' housing section at Rybachiy Naval Base. He and his wife, Irina Ivanova, had two children, sixteen-year-old daughter Tatiana and son Andre, who was eight. As a submarine commander, Kobzar was already among the elite of the Soviet navy, and his family was accorded the privileges of that rank.

The circumstances of his younger first officer, Captain Third Rank Zhuravin, were more representative of the lifestyle of the average Soviet submarine officer in the Pacific Fleet.

Captain Zhuravin's wife, also named Irina, still lived in an apartment in Vladivostok, waiting for housing at the base. Zhuravin telephoned her as soon as he could get permission to use a secure phone line. The telephone link between the Kamchatka base and Vladivostok was made through an undersea cable. Coincidentally, the U.S. Navy was already designing bugging equipment to tap this underwater cable. A U.S. spy submarine would later plant the bugging equipment.

Irina Zhuravina, age thirty-three, had married the dashing young submariner immediately after graduating from Moscow State University of Foreign Relations with a degree in international economics. Her new husband had graduated from the Riga naval academy the year before, with honors.

About a year after joining him for his first assignment to a submarine stationed on the Black Sea, Irina delivered a baby boy, Mikhail. The child was twelve years old and in the sixth grade at school when his father assumed the first-officer position aboard K-129. The family grew close because of Zhuravin's frequent transfers, and when the father was in port, he and his son were inseparable. Irina affectionately called her husband Sasha and her son Misha.

Irina had reluctantly remained in their apartment near the Pacific Fleet headquarters in Vladivostok because Captain Zhuravin had sailed on a long patrol almost immediately after being transferred to Kamchatka in the summer of 1967. Her mother flew out from Moscow to help her with Misha while Zhuravin was at sea, and to assist them later when they moved closer to the base. They would have more choices in housing with his promotion, and they planned to look for a new place before he assumed command of the K-129.

It was years since Zhuravin had been on furlough. In addition to finding a house, the couple hoped to take an extended trip back to Moscow and western Russia to visit family and friends before the submarine's next extended mission. That mission was scheduled for June. The captain had spent an aggregate five years at sea during the last eleven years of their marriage.

This latest homecoming from an extended sea tour should have been an especially happy occasion for the family, but as it turned out, it was less than joyous. Zhuravin returned from the mission suffering from a chronic respiratory illness. He told Irina the ailment was only a side-effect from inhaling diesel fumes and stagnant air during seventy days at sea. But the symptoms were serious enough that Zhuravin was given medical treatment at a base facility. Irina flew in from Vladivostok to be with him.

Captain Zhuravin's illness seemed to worry his wife more than it did him or the doctors. Irina was concerned that the long days submerged in the foul air of diesel fumes and chemicals from the sub's lead acid batteries had done permanent damage to her husband's lungs. After she arrived, he continued to experience bouts of profuse nasal bleeding and other symptoms of respiratory infection.

Following his treatment, Irina and Sasha joined one of the groups of K-129 officers who were taking the coveted recreation trip to the health spa. It was near the end of January when they arrived at the Paratunka Village sanitarium. After several days of relaxation with other officers and their families, Sasha's ailments seemed to improve.

At the spa, couples were billeted in private cabins and had unlimited use of a modern gymnasium and other recreational facilities on the grounds. The Zhuravins spent much of the holiday mixing with other

K-129 officers and their wives. With them at the spa were the weapons officer, Captain Third Rank Gennady Panarin, and his wife, Zoya, and the chief engineer, Captain Third Rank Nikolai Orechov, and his wife, Tamara. During the vacation, Irina also got to know the ship's doctor, Major Sergey Cherepanov, and the *zampolit*, Captain Third Rank Fedor Lobas. Her husband jokingly told her that the party spy Lobas had been ordered to keep an eye on her.

The greatest reward of being stationed in this isolated part of the Soviet Far East was the beauty of its wilderness. Kamchatka Peninsula was not connected by highway or railroad to the more settled Russian mainland. The vacationers occasionally spotted the area's giant Russian bears, cousins of their Alaskan counterparts, the Kodiak grizzlies.

After Zhuravin's recovery, their days at the sanitarium-spa were filled with sledding excursions and day trips to explore the snow-covered slopes of the nearby volcanic mountains: Koryaksky, Avachinskaya, and Kozelsky. There are more than three hundred volcanic peaks and thirty active volcanoes in the region.

It was during this convalescence that the K-129 officers learned of an ominous incident in the Pacific.

On January 23, 1968, patrol boats of the Democratic People's Republic of Korea (DPRK) attacked and seized the U.S. Navy electronic surveillance boat USS *Pueblo*. The American ship was sailing about fifteen miles off the North Korean coast in the Sea of Japan. Most nations recognized a twelve-mile territorial limit. One American sailor was killed in the attack and eighty-two seamen and officers were taken prisoner.

Tensions were already running high in the Pacific. The Vietnam War was also heating up, with the January Tet Offensive escalating that conflict to its most deadly level since the Americans had joined the war. The North Korean attack on the American intelligence-gathering ship became even more of a crisis when U.S. surveillance planes discovered the ship had been hauled to Wonsan harbor. The Soviet navy had recently opened a submarine base at the northern end of that harbor. The Americans learned that Soviet technicians had been given complete access to the pirated boat, with all its sophisticated spy gear. Suddenly, American Pacific forces were placed on high alert. President Johnson ordered the mobilization of six Air Force reserve and National Guard fighter-bomber units. An American naval armada began patrolling the North Korean coastline, dangerously close to the huge Soviet naval facilities at Vladivostok.

The growing tensions caused by the Korean provocation seemed a lifetime removed from the vacationing K-129 submariners and their wives. The Zhuravins and the other K-129 couples were, for all the world, a carefree assembly of sailors on leave. At least for this short time they were shielded by the mysterious vastness of the Kamchatka Peninsula from the machinations of war and the troubled Soviet economy.

The group frolicking in the Paratunka spa hot springs was typical of the young, educated Soviet submarine families sent from their homes in western Russia to the empire's Far East outpost. None was more representative of this new privileged class of submarine families than the Zhuravins.

Irina and Sasha had been introduced when both were in their late teens. Her brother, Stanislav Grigorievich, who was destined to become an admiral of his own fleet in the post–Cold War Russian Federation Navy, was serving as a fellow cadet with Zhuravin at the naval academy in Riga. When Grigorievich gave Zhuravin a photograph of Irina and her address, a three-year correspondence began.

Her brother, whom she called Stas, brought Sasha home on vacation to Moscow. She was eighteen, Sasha a year older. Her classmates were jealous of her handsome naval cadet pen pal.

"When he visited, I was so proud to show him off to my girlfriends and the boys who had been flirting with me," Irina recalls. "Of course, much of the charm was his uniform—he looked wonderful in it."

Although they kept up a steady correspondence during her early years at university, she was not ready to marry. Irina was devoted to her education, and actively involved in Moscow life as an amateur artist and dancer. She was a member of the university's folk dance ensemble, which toured the Soviet Union offering performances at workers' co-ops. Every time the troupe performed near Riga she visited her brother and Sasha. After they graduated from the naval academy, Irina visited Sasha at his first assignment at Sevastopol. It was then that he placed a ring on her finger and said it was his intention to marry her.

"For me it wasn't a surprise," she said. "I had known for a long time that Sasha would be mine. Many girls were after him, but I knew he wasn't going anywhere. I, too, had suitors, but I felt sure Sasha was the man for me. I showed my eleven-year-old cousin a photo of a class of forty cadets and asked her to pick the one I should marry. Without hesitation, she pointed to Sasha and said, 'You should marry *him.*'"

They were married soon after she graduated, and the newlyweds accepted the nomadic life of the Soviet submariner family. Irina went with her husband "from base to base, everywhere he served" during the early years of their marriage.

"I followed him like thread follows a needle," she said.

Although submariners enjoyed perks that were not available to average Soviet families, life was not easy compared to Western standards. But to a young couple in love, who had been raised in the devastated remains of Russia after the Great Patriotic War witnessing purges and famines, their living conditions seemed good and navy life was exciting.

During Sasha's rise through the junior ranks, the Zhuravins often shared an apartment with the families of two or three other submarine officers. They cooked meals over charcoal stoves and made do with whatever groceries were available at food co-ops on the bases.

Then orders came transferring Zhuravin to the Far East. His first assignment there was at a base near the Pacific Fleet headquarters in Vladivostok. He sent for his wife and son immediately after finding an apartment close to the military complex in the big port city.

Their living conditions improved as Zhuravin moved up through the ranks. When Zhuravin was promoted to captain third rank in 1965, they had their own apartment in a modern building with other officers' families.

Irina described it as "one room with all the comforts, even a television set."

After Captain Zhuravin was transferred to the Kamchatka Peninsula to join the K-129, Irina frequently traveled from Vladivostok to the submarine base at Rybachiy. While waiting for a place of their own, they stayed with other submarine officer friends who already had apartments near the base. During her visits in the summer of 1967, the submarine was going out for a day or two at a time. The crews returned home after each short exercise.

She and other navy wives busied themselves tending to the children and exchanging stories about their lives and families back in European Russia. Occasionally, a new film would arrive to be shown at the officers' club and that, for a time, became the center of conversation. But opportunities for entertainment were sparse at this isolated base.

Since the huge bay was home to a year-round Soviet fishing fleet, fresh seafood was always in abundance. Occasionally, a civilian steamer docked at Petropavlovsk-Kamchatskiy and the wives took large bags across the bay to go shopping.

"We would run to the icebreaker for the trip to the city across the bay to buy fresh vegetables and fruit," said Irina. "My friends and I would cook together and take turns minding each other's children."

When Captain Zhuravin sailed with the K-129 on an extended mission in October 1967, Irina returned to their apartment in Vladivostok, and to her job. She was a senior economist at the Primorskiy Kraiispolkom, the regional authority for Primorskiy Krai (province). She

conducted research into programs for developing international trade for Soviet fisheries and forestry products.

In February 1968, Sasha and Irina had been at the spa
for two weeks of their three-week allotted vacation
when unexpected orders arrived. Captain Second Rank
Zhuravin and the other officers were ordered to report
back to K-129 immediately. The submarine was to return to sea as soon as possible on another autonomous
mission of not less than two months.

Zhuravin's promotion to captain first rank and commander of the submarine was put on hold, as was Captain Kobzar's promotion and transfer to Pacific Fleet
headquarters in Vladivostok.

Captain Kobzar, who had every reason to expect a
leisurely refitting of the K-129, was also surprised by the
abruptness of the orders. The order to embark on a new
mission six months before schedule was completely out
of keeping with the Soviet navy's deployment routine
for the missile boats. The sub had been in port only six
weeks. What new mission could be so urgent that the
normal home port call had to be drastically curtailed?
Could replacements be found for the key crew members spread throughout Mother Russia on leave—most
of them thousands of miles and many days' travel away?
Even if the furloughed crewmen could be contacted,
most would never have time to arrange travel and return for sailing on such short notice.

The news of the sailing was more than a disappoint-
ing surprise. It struck the seamen as strange. But orders
were orders. The officers and men of the K-129 would

obey without question, and with a minimum of open complaint.

Captain Kobzar was told only that K-129 was needed to replace another boat for immediate patrol in the northern Pacific. Headquarters gave a vague explanation that another scheduled missile submarine had broken down and could not fill its regular patrol slot. They would provide replacement crew members in time for sailing.

For this mission, like all the others, the details were withheld. K-129 was to sail on February 24, 1968, with an expected return date of May 5. That was all the information the submariners were allowed to tell their wives, and probably all the information they were given.

The hardship was obvious. Captain Kobzar and his crew had settled in for a long period of limited coastal exercises that allowed them to return to their families almost every night. Believing he had six months to spare, the captain had granted extended leaves to eleven senior enlisted crewmen. Most of them were chief and first-class petty officers and warrant officers with key technical responsibilities for operating the boat.

Captain Kobzar was able to round up all his officers, since most of them were either at the spa or with their families on or near the base. He expected to have a difficult time replacing the key enlisted technicians needed for an autonomous mission of this length. Active Soviet submarines were required to keep a crew available for emergency sailing, but as a rule, the crews could be sent on no more than two seventy-day missions in a year. This new mission would be their third in less than a year, meaning that most of the regular K-129 crew would have spent almost eight months of service submerged in their submarine in a little more than a twelve-month period.

Such a rigorous schedule was highly unusual, except in an emergency or time of war. In peacetime, Soviet ballistic missile submarines, because their entire extended missions were spent underwater, were never turned around so suddenly for another arduous assignment. K-129's crew was long overdue for a rest and the boat needed refurbishing and repairs from the most recent mission.

Inexplicably, this time the rules were ignored. The Kamchatka Flotilla was ordered to fill the vacancies in the roster immediately. With manpower shortages always plaguing the navy, K-129's commander and first officer were undoubtedly pleased that a replacement crew was found so quickly. Fourteen replacements were ordered aboard the K-129 to fill the jobs of the regular crewmen on furlough. This brought the roster to eighty-seven, which was four more than the normal complement.

For the most part, the replacements were a ragtag assortment of ordinary seamen and a few senior ranking enlisted men. One warrant officer, seven petty officers, and six ordinary seamen were scrounged from other idled submarines undergoing repairs at the base.

Why K-129 was selected for this particular mission remains a mystery. Although there was a general shortage of missile submarines and trained crews throughout the Soviet navy in 1968, the Soviet Pacific Fleet was able to maintain an aggressive schedule of deployments. There were at least seventeen nuclear-powered ballistic missile submarines stationed at bases scattered up and down the Asian coasts, plus five other Golf II submarines identical to the K-129 and a number of other older-type ballistic missile submarines stationed at Kamchatka. At any given time, some were at sea and on station, others were preparing for deployment or in transit to their assigned patrol areas, and the rest were on their way back or had recently returned to base. It seems logical that one of the boats preparing to depart would have been a better substitute for the submarine that had failed to make its scheduled deployment. K-129 was not the only option headquarters had for a replacement submarine to send on a routine, autonomous patrol.

The sudden order for K-129 to undertake this new mission was apparently as much a surprise to the commanders at headquarters in Vladivostok as it was to the submarine's officers. Later, no one seemed to know why the K-129 had been dispatched on such short notice.

Like the purpose of the mission, the originating command authority has never been revealed. No higher Soviet command ever publicly took credit for issuing the order. One thing is clear, however. In the tightly controlled hierarchy of Soviet ballistic submarine forces, no deviation from standard procedures happened in a vacuum. A missile submarine would never have been assigned an extended mission except by very high authority. The orders that arrived at Rybachiy Naval Base to dispatch the submarine under such unusual circumstances could only have originated in Moscow.

The inexplicable order to rush K-129 back to sea was

only one of several mysterious events that occurred before the boat's departure.

The order to sail early was so odious that some of the sub's officers and sailors risked stern disciplinary action to make their opinions known. In the Soviet navy, with political officers throughout the ranks, there was usually far less open complaining than in most of the world's military establishments. But the peculiarity of the order seemed to overcome the normal reluctance to complain.

In this case, there was more of an air of despondency than bitterness. After they returned to the flotilla headquarters to learn more about the circumstances of being recalled to sea, Captain Zhuravin and some of the other boat officers' behavior became uncharacteristically odd.

Captain Zhuravin, without telling Irina the reasons, visited a banking facility where he kept his business papers and savings account. He asked an official for a form to write a will. The official, a woman who handled his personal papers, told him, "Don't be silly, you do not need to write a will."

In the days before sailing, the submarine's first officer went around the base to all his friends—many of whom had served with him on previous assignments—and asked them to dinner, so he could properly tell them goodbye. He also wrote a letter to his son, Misha, and left it with someone at the base to mail at a future date. In the last line of the letter, Captain Zhuravin wrote, "Son, don't forget your dad."

Irina's husband seemed deeply depressed. It was the first time she had ever seen him react so negatively to any assignment, no matter how difficult. During the years he had served on submarines in the Black Sea and the Pacific, he had been on scores of missions, including some that seemed more unpleasant than this latest assignment. Captain Zhuravin had never openly objected or complained.

He was not the only officer who reacted strangely when they were recalled to sea duty so early. Tamara Orechov, wife of chief engineer Nikolai Orechov, told Irina Zhuravina that her husband was also very distressed by the orders. Tamara said Kolya was understandably exhausted from the last mission, but it was more than that. He became unusually depressed by this sudden assignment. She, too, thought her husband's reaction was unusual. Orechov had always enthusiastically prepared for previous departures.

The slow pace of routine refurbishing, which would normally have taken three to six months, was accelerated as the sailors of K-129, joined by the replacement crew, skipped over routine maintenance and went about performing emergency repairs that would be absolutely necessary to safely sail the submarine.

The boat was fueled with a light-grade diesel called D-37 oil. This fuel was preferred by Soviet submarine commanders because it burned clean, with almost no trace of smoke. The sub's huge electric batteries were serviced, and food and medical stocks quickly stowed to accommodate the early departure. Three tarp-covered trucks from the tightly guarded nuclear armory delivered freshly fueled ballistic missiles. Interior Ministry soldiers, under the watchful eye of a KGB officer, stood rigidly at guard on the windy pier as the missiles were hoisted by crane and carefully lowered into the launch tubes. All nuclear weaponry was under the direct physical control of the KGB and not the Soviet navy. The nuclear-armed missiles were stored in KGB-secured facilities and distributed to the various naval commands as needed for missions.

The senior crewmen and officers, who remained near the Kamchatka base because their dependents were there, worked feverishly to prepare the boat for sea duty, even as they grumbled at having to sail again so quickly. They were naturally reluctant to leave the comfort of their warm barracks or apartments, and the arms of wives and girlfriends on base and in the nearby military towns of Paratunka and Nikolayevka. Their displeasure over the new orders did not prevent them, however, from keeping an especially close eye on the quality of foodstuffs being loaded. As members of the navy's elite Soviet submarine service, they were accustomed to the best of rations, and were even allotted generous supplies of caviar.

The supplies were stowed in every nook and cranny throughout the tight quarters of the submarine. Fresh meats and vegetables were placed within easiest reach, to be consumed early in the mission; dried buckwheat bread and canned foods would be the fare as the mission lapsed into weeks. Since K-129 would make no port calls on these extended missions, everything the crew needed to subsist, including fresh water, had to be brought aboard before sailing.

A day before the scheduled departure, Captains Kobzar and Zhuravin received another jolt. It was an even more drastic deviation from operational protocol than being rushed back into service ahead of schedule.

The submarine's crew roster had already been filled with replacements, and they had been introduced to the section officers they would serve. Since these replacements were from other submarines stationed at the base, they were quickly integrated into the regular crew. The new men were assigned to their duty sections, shifts, and bunk schedules. With the replacements, all work assignments were covered for the upcoming mission.

Then, without explanation, eleven strangers, all in the uniforms of Soviet sailors, showed up at the pier where K-129 was berthed. They carried written orders to join the crew. The latecomers, including nine in the uniform of common seamen and one wearing the insignia of a seaman first class, were led by a chief petty officer. The chief produced orders assigning this squad to duty aboard Kobzar's submarine as temporary replacements for his furloughed key senior enlisted men. These last-minute assignments were especially unusual, because their numbers raised the crew total to ninety-eight, fifteen over the normal complement of eighty-three men.

There is no record of how Captain Kobzar reacted to the sudden appearance of strangers with orders to join his crew. But the appearance of these mystery men may have triggered Captain Zhuravin's unusual behavior. It is certain that the captain or first officer would have brought the overage of personnel to the attention of base authorities. With more than a dozen extra men aboard, the tightly packed submarine would be even more uncomfortable, if not operationally hampered, on a long sea voyage.

The Golf and other diesel-electric submarines had limited space in which to store food for an extended mission. The normal stockpile was barely adequate for the regular crew. Just as supplies were limited, space to accommodate an acceptable level of living and working conditions was at a premium on a submarine of this type. Sanitation, not to mention health and adequate rest, would be jeopardized on a seventy-day mission with ninety-eight men aboard a submarine designed to accommodate eighty-three. During the mission, each man was allocated one liter of fresh water per day for drinking, bathing, and laundry. The submarine had only three toilets.

Sleeping arrangements were likewise carefully designed. Officers had small cabins forward of the control center, but regular crewmen were assigned sleeping space that was barely adequate to get the rest needed for the long mission. Some petty officers fashioned beds in their workstations, and others strung hammocks in whatever space they could find that would not interfere with operations.

There were twenty-seven fixed bunks in the aft torpedo room for approximately seventy sailors. This arrangement required what is known in the submarine service as "hot bunking." The sailors slept in shifts, three each day, with most bunks shared by two or three sailors. The ordinary seaman had to take his turn in one of the bunks, stacked three-high in the uncomfortable rear of the submarine.

Witnesses to the preparations for sailing recalled that the regular K-129 crewmen had another complaint about these extra sailors—beyond the fact that they would consume precious resources. From the time they boarded, the unneeded newcomers kept to themselves and were oddly uncommunicative with the rest of the crew. Their aloofness was considered strange for submariners, normally known for their open embrace of other crew members who would be sharing their rations, cramped space, and often perilous life aboard a Soviet sub. On the other hand, their interaction with each other suggested there was a bond among them, an established order of command that transcended their official rank and duties.

Whatever the response Kobzar received in answer to his concerns about the additional crewmen, the orders came from an authority high enough to keep them on the mission. K-129 was completely fitted for sea and the anxious hour of sailing approached. Select crewmen and officers were allowed a few last hours of shore leave to say their goodbyes.

Captain Zhuravin had secured an Aeroflot ticket for his wife to fly home from the Petropavlovsk-Kamchatskiy civilian airport to Vladivostok, where their son was being cared for by Irina's mother. Though there had been many such farewells, this one could have been a scene from an epic Russian novel.

The parting of the Soviet couple—he a dashing military officer and she a beautiful former dancer—took place against a backdrop of swirling snow on a Siberian winter night. Captain Zhuravin had been denied permission to board the Soviet airliner, but managed to find his wife seated by a window. He approached as close as he could to the side of the airplane to bid her farewell.

"Under the light from the plane I saw Sasha's face, streaked with tears. I had never seen him cry before," Irina recalled. "I thought to myself, *he must be afraid for me*—that I am flying in this snowstorm, that the plane might crash. He didn't wave, he just stood there like a pillar under the light, crying. It was our last good-bye—a picture of him I have carried my whole life. Standing under the plane, snow falling on his dark uniform, his face wet with tears."

But this was not a novel or a movie. Their parting, like the unusual circumstances of the sailing itself, was real.

The officers and sailors of K-129 reported back to the submarine and readied for departure. They would leave in the dark, as it maximized their chances of eluding detection by orbiting American spy satellites.

The sailing date fell during one of the most significant holiday periods for the Soviet military. The Bolsheviks celebrated the founding of the Red Army and Navy from February 23 through 25. Soviet Army and Fleet Day was a time for military parades and celebratory dinners at bases across the vast Eurasian empire.

There was no celebrating aboard K-129. Sometime during the night, Vice Admiral Rudolf Golosov, commander of the 15th Squadron, received permission from Captain First Rank Vladimir Kobzar to board the submarine. Kobzar, dressed in his great raglan sheepskin coat and fur hat, saluted the admiral. The admiral's arrival was greeted by the traditional ringing of the ship's bell, located behind the bridge in the conning tower. The bell was used only to announce that a high-ranking officer was coming aboard, or for tolling warnings when the submarine sailed on the surface in dense fog.

A bitter cold Siberian wind was blowing across Avachinskaya Bay in the early hours of February 24, 1968. The wind whipped the Soviet naval banner as a sailor lowered and carefully folded it. Another sailor removed the clapper from the submarine's bell, an important last precaution to make sure it did not bang with the current and give away the boat's location. The young sailors stowed the bell clapper and the folded flag in a locker in the action center where the periscopes were housed.

Admiral Golosov handed sealed orders to Captain Kobzar and *zampolit* Lobas. After reminding them that the orders were not to be opened until the submarine had cleared the bay and was in open sea, he wished them a safe and successful mission. The admiral saluted and returned alone to the icy pier and his waiting staff car.

6

SOVIET SUBMARINE K-129 sailed on the surface toward the mouth of Avachinskaya Bay under full diesel power, hidden by the darkness of the predawn hours of February 24, 1968. The boat used no running lights, to avoid visual detection of its departure by any American submarine that might be patrolling off the coast.

As the submarine approached the outlet from the bay into the open ocean, the first huge waves pounding through the narrows rocked the boat violently. The Golf's rounded narrow hull, with a beam width of only twenty-seven feet, was not designed to sail comfortably on the surface, even in calm seas. And the seas of the wintry North Pacific were never calm.

The northerly winds off the ocean roared through the land gap, causing the eastbound submarine to shudder from their ferocity. Captain First Rank Vladimir Kobzar, commanding the submarine from the exposed bridge for the duration of the departure from Rybachiy Naval Base, was bundled against the subfreezing wind. The broad flap of his fur *ushanka* was turned down, covering much of his face, ears, and neck. Only the captain and two lookouts, also bundled in heavy storm gear, stood watch for the departure, while the officers and crewmen below busily prepared the boat for the open sea and the beginning of their extended mission.

The submarine bucked through the watery turmoil. From the bridge, Captain Kobzar and the enlisted men strained their eyes in the dark, searching for any sign of icebergs, a common threat to submarines and small ships along the coast of the Kamchatka Peninsula that time of year. The ice menace from bergs and growlers that calved from glaciers in the far northern reaches of the Bering Sea extended out as far as 160 miles from shore. Careful watch while operating on the surface was an important part of the departure of all submarines before reaching deeper water to submerge.

The veteran submarine captain assumed this cold duty of bridge watch himself, even though he could have assigned the unpleasant task to another officer. It was customary in the Soviet navy for the commander to take his boat to sea before turning over control to his first assistant for routine operations.

K-129 left the entrance narrows and plunged into the Pacific Ocean well before daylight. The boat entered the northwestern Pacific near where it merged with the even stormier Bering Sea. The winter winds in this part of the ocean blew straight out of Arctic Siberia, without any intervening landmass to temper them. Seaforce winds in gusts of more than thirty-five knots produced giant swells and crashing waves, leaving the men aboard in no doubt they were about to enter the domain of the open ocean.

Only a short distance out of the sheltering bay of the

peninsula, waves pounded spume against the K-129 conning tower. In heavy seas even veteran submariners working to secure loose gear in the boat's compartments had difficulty keeping their footing. Some among the crew were embarrassed by how quickly seasickness, caused by the violent rolling and the lingering stench of diesel engine fumes, sent them dashing for the closest head, sink, or receptacle. The old hands knew they would be living for the rest of the mission with whatever smells their sickness produced, mingled with the acrid mixture of diesel and body odors.

With fully charged batteries at his disposal, the captain would waste no time in switching from diesel to electric engines and diving beneath the storm-roiled ocean surface. Captain Kobzar sent the lookouts below, and then dropped into the manhole leading into the action center. The final duty of the commander before entering the open sea was to close the heavy steel hatch and give the locking wheel an extra hard twist, to assure the safety of the boat and crew. Back in the command center, the captain routinely turned the submarine over to his first assistant, Captain Second Rank Alexander Zhuravin, and ordered him to take the submarine down for commencement of the assigned mission.

On Zhuravin's order to prepare to dive, sailors discharged sewage and dumped what little refuse had collected since departing the base. Diesel engines were stopped, and the snorkel and diesel exhaust valves were closed. Each compartment warden reported that his section was prepared to dive, and the dive alarm was sounded.

Captain Zhuravin gave orders to dive and instructed

the helmsman to set the initial depth and course. He ordered the periscope up. Port and starboard electric motors were engaged for slow speed. With Captain Kobzar observing in the control room, his assistant climbed the ladder into the action center and went to the periscope. Exiting the narrow passage from the busy ports in the bay to the Pacific required extreme caution, to avoid colliding with other warships and commercial vessels.

Port and starboard motors slowly propelled the submarine, as the order was given to open bow and stern valves to flood the sub's ballast tanks. Seawater rushed into the tanks. The submarine immediately plunged into the giant waves. When the bow and stern tanks flooded, the middle ballast tanks were opened and the submarine began to submerge. As the waters closed over the decks, the boat seemed to sigh, like the great whales it so resembled. Hissing sprays of air-blasted water spewed from ballast tanks, and the ship simply vanished beneath the angry sea.

The retractable bow diving planes were extended. Crew members in each compartment checked the interior hull, valves, flanges, and pipes to make sure there were no water leaks. Captain Zhuravin lowered the periscope and returned to the control room. He ordered all masts lowered.

The submarine continued its dive to 150 feet. All ventilation valves were closed and all ballast tanks sealed.

The crewmen, even those who had grumbled the loudest about having their shore time cut short, welcomed the news when an officer's voice boomed over the internal address system that the dive had been completed. At last the boat had taken the crew into smooth underseas waters. K-129 had entered the natural realm of cold, silent darkness for which it was designed. They were now gliding quietly through a realm completely alien to human beings, and more hostile than outer space.

As a test of the fitness of the submarine, first officer Zhuravin put K-129 into a steep dive to its maximum operational depth, so the men could examine the seams and fittings for leaks. The submarine had been in continuous service for almost eight years, except for a period in 1966, when it was retrofitted with the Serb missile system and had a general overhaul. Over the years, the salty sea waters had eaten away at the welds that held the enormous steel plates in place, and corroded the plates, as well.

Despite creaks and groans, K-129 easily withstood the stress of the test dive. As the sub sank deeper, the sailors were aware that their already cramped quarters were compressing ever so slightly around them. This phenomenon, caused by the extreme pressure, was experienced by all submariners.

When the test dive was completed, Captain Zhuravin ordered the boat back up to a comfortable operating depth of two hundred feet. Though far below the turbulence of the ocean surface, the wild motion of the sea above still caused a gentle roll. The first officer conferred with the navigator, then ordered the helmsman to set a course bearing due east to clear the shoreline shallows. That course would take K-129 into the great void in the middle of the North Pacific, before heading for an assigned patrol area close enough to launch an attack on a coastal city or military base on the North American continent, Hawaii, or other American asset in the Pacific Ocean.

The officers were satisfied that the boat had been safely submerged and that the huge electric motors were operating efficiently. The commanders then cere-moniously prepared for one of the most exciting parts of any assignment, opening the sealed orders to discover where Supreme Soviet High Command was sending the men and boat on their mission.

Captain Kobzar, accompanied by the *zampolit*, Captain Third Rank Fedor Lobas, quickly walked from the control room to the captain's cabin. From a safe, the commander took a sealed package of orders, and the men returned to the control room. Seals were broken on the packet and the mission orders retrieved. First officer Zhuravin and Captain-Lieutenant Nikolai Pikulik, the senior navigator, joined them at the cramped navigator's station. Several other officers and sailors stood anxiously waiting to hear what mission Moscow had deemed so important that the K-129 had to return to sea on another seventy-day mission, months ahead of schedule.

The details of these patrol orders have never been publicly revealed. The orders were probably for the K-129 to proceed to one of its regular patrol stations in a mission box that extended from 650 miles to 850 miles northwest of Pearl Harbor in the Hawaiian Islands. The known course and performance of K-129 for the first days of the mission indicate that the submarine initially followed the regular protocol for any autonomous mission ordered by the Naval Main Staff through fleet headquarters in Vladivostok.

With the orders reviewed by the boat's command staff, K-129 had passed the point of no return and the submarine headed out to the open ocean. Captain Zhuravin provided the mission plan to Senior Navigator Pikulik, who quickly worked out a preliminary course. The navigator plotted a course using a great circle route—the shortest distance between two points on a globe—to take the K-129 to the mission station in the fastest possible time.

Just as the wind blows on land, water moves in a similar fashion through the oceans in the form of currents, a phenomenon known to sailors as drift. Though the course to the mission box near Hawaii would have been southeast on a bearing of 133°, Captain-Lieutenant Pikulik compensated for the prevailing 0.6-knot current flowing from the northeast. In order to achieve its southeasterly heading, the submarine had to be steered slightly into the current. During the entire journey, he would be constantly adjusting his course, as the currents changed and pushed the boat first in one direction, then another.

The ocean surrounding K-129 was a chilly 33°F. Except for the engine room, where the heat from the propulsion machinery warmed the surrounding area, the inside of the sub was cold and damp. The men worked in their bulky sweaters, as the boat's rudimentary heating system strained to keep living conditions tolerable. But at this busy time of departure, comfort was the last thing on the minds of the crew. They were chiefly preoccupied with avoiding detection.

The officers and sailors of K-129 were keenly aware that U.S. Navy intelligence had a formidable array of systems designed to track them when they left the relative security of Kamchatka Bay. The Americans had spy satellites orbiting overhead to photograph their departure, and fast-attack submarines lurking just offshore to monitor, and perhaps even follow them, as they began their mission. The Soviet navy suspected there was a hydroacoustical listening system strung along the course their ships took as they traveled to and from their home ports. But in 1968, they had no information on how extensive or how effective that system was. They knew the Americans listened to their radio transmissions, but did not know the Americans were able to pinpoint the exact location of their submarines every time they communicated with headquarters.

Captains Kobzar and Zhuravin, like all senior officers of Soviet missile submarines, spent a considerable part of each mission trying to keep their location secret. They had to achieve stealth if their covert mission was to be effective.

But stealth had to be balanced with speed, especially in the first part of their journey, where they were most likely to encounter American submarines.

In an effort to confuse any American sub that might be lurking nearby, Captain Zhuravin changed headings and depths several times in the first hours after leaving the peninsula. He may have come to a full stop, dead in the water, letting the submarine drift while he listened with K-129's passive sonar for any American submarine that might be trailing behind. To determine if they were being followed, Zhuravin would maneuver from side to side in a butterfly pattern using the hydroa-coustical equipment to listen to the surrounding water. At times, K-129 was driven by two of its electric motors; at other times it was switched to the small silent motor, to operate at a quieter speed of not more than two or three knots. Depths and direction were controlled using stern and bow diving planes.

The submarine had sailed at a time when Soviet intelligence knew no satellite was passing overhead to record their departure, but this window of opportunity did not allow them to escape unnoticed by the Americans. Neither the precisely timed sailing nor their evasive maneuvers were effective, because the U.S. Navy's technical intelligence systems were multilayered and quite sophisticated.

The first surveillance system K-129 encountered was called SOSUS by the Americans, an acronym for Sound Surveillance System. This system was a vast array of passive hydroacoustical listening devices called hydrophones, placed strategically around the Atlantic and Pacific oceans. It consisted of cable-connected, underwater phones planted along the bottom of the oceans to collect sounds generated from any source. These sounds were transmitted to shore stations where they were recorded in lines on continuous rolls of graph paper. Acoustic experts were able to read these sound patterns to distinguish between natural ocean sounds, ships, and submarines. The hydrophones were so sensitive that even aircraft noise from planes flying above the ocean and the sound of falling rain could be monitored.

K-129, like all the Soviet Pacific Fleet submarines

leaving the Kamchatka Peninsula in the 1960s, was tracked by the SOSUS on this specific mission, from the time it left the protective waters of the bay.

The U.S. Navy had begun installation of a SOSUS network of hydrophones in the Atlantic as early as the 1950s. Installation in the Pacific began in the early 1960s. By 1968, Navy facility (NAVFAC) listening stations were already in place on Adak in the Aleutians; Midway Island; the Hawaiian Islands; all along the Pacific coast of the United States, from Alaska to the Baja Peninsula; and at "choke points" traveled by Soviet subs leaving and returning to port. The U.S. Pacific coast system was code-named Colossus; the central Pacific network surrounding Pearl Harbor and the Hawaiian Islands was code-named Sea Spider. One of the extended arrays that was instrumental in tracking the K-129 ran along the Aleutian Islands. Another array extended on the western side of the Kuril Islands to detect submarine activity in the Sea of Okhostk.

The network that would follow K-129 for most of its voyage was strung along the Emperor Seamount, and covered the Soviets' Kamchatka Peninsula bases. Captains Kobzar and Zhuravin did not know it, but their submarine was sailing directly toward that SOSUS array.

No matter how hard Soviet designers had worked to make their subs run silent, they still made noise, and the Americans were expert in detecting the slightest sound emitted by the boats.

Even though K-129, as a diesel-electric boat, was somewhat quieter than the early nuclear-propelled Soviet missile submarines, it radiated noise from hull vibrations, power plant equipment, and propellers. Its very movement through the ocean depths created flow or hydrodynamic noise that could be monitored by hydrophones and sensitive sonars aboard American attack submarines, stationed off the exit channels from Soviet submarine bases.

Fifteen miles from the exit of Avachinskaya Bay, Captain Zhuravin knew the mission was "good to go," as K-129 approached open ocean. He ordered the submarine up to periscope depth to transmit the first of a series of mandatory mission reports to Naval Main Staff at fleet headquarters at Vladivostok.

Radio officer Senior Lieutenant Alexander Zarnakov dispatched a message notifying headquarters that the boat was entering deep water and the mission was underway. This transmission, which was sent in a millisecond microburst signal, could be picked up, but not deciphered by the U.S. Navy. It was the first of several mandatory radio reports that all Soviet missile submarines made at fixed points to report the progress and security of their missions. Submarine commanders were permitted to disregard these periodic reports only if they thought they were under active surveillance by antisubmarine warfare units of the U.S. Navy or were being tailed by American submarines.

While the instantaneous radio burst could not be decoded by the Americans at that time, it provided highly valuable intelligence to the ever-listening U.S. technical spy network. Radio signal monitoring was the second layer of the Americans' elaborate surveillance system.

The Soviets were unaware that the real purpose of

the American radio communications eavesdropping system was to locate the submarines, not to try to read their coded messages. The Americans had not yet broken the Soviet naval codes. A radio-monitoring network, code-named Boresight, had been deployed to cover the oceans of the world from the early 1960s. In the Pacific, Boresight consisted of an array of powerful, radio-signal listening stations strategically positioned around the rim of the ocean. Huge antenna frames, nicknamed elephant cages, were positioned in 360° arrays at listening posts in the Aleutian Islands, Japan, the U.S. West Coast, and the Hawaiian Islands chain from Pearl Harbor to Midway. The elephant-cage antennas were ten stories tall and one thousand feet across. The computer-controlled receivers were tuned to all frequencies used by the Soviets; whenever a submarine transmitted even the briefest message, these sensitive listening posts snatched the message from the airways.

The transmissions were recorded by Navy operators at the antenna sites and relayed to huge central computers operated by the National Security Agency in the United States. When stations in two or three locations—for example, Midway, Adak, and Hawaii—picked up a radio transmission signal from a submarine, it was fed into a computer and the bearings triangulated. The intersection of these lines marked the exact location of the transmission. U.S. Navy intelligence was immediately notified of the location, and the Americans' extensive antisubmarine warfare system had another accurate fix on the submarine it was tracking.

Immediately after radio officer Zarnakov sent the message, K-129 returned to its cruising depth of two hundred feet. Just as it reached this operating depth, the sub left the area above the Asian continental shelf and entered the first deep waters of the ocean. The bottom of the sea was 3,250 feet below.

Silently waiting at the edge of those deep waters, American attack submarines, assigned to monitor the comings and goings of Soviet submarines, were constantly recording the class and capacity of the Soviet missile submarines stationed at the Rybachiy Naval Base.

When K-129 reached the deep ocean beyond the Kuril Trench, the Soviet submarine came under surveillance by one of these silent U.S. picket boats. Despite K-129's best efforts to evade detection by sailing in silent-running mode under cover of darkness, the Soviet submarine was no match for a Permit-class, nuclear attack submarine patrolling the Russian coast from Vladivostok to the Kamchatka Peninsula. As the Soviet boat leveled off and powered up to its cruising speed of seven knots, it may have seemed like a silent shadow moving in the deep, but the hunter submarine had a vivid picture that told the Americans everything they wanted to know about it.

The U.S. Navy Permit-class hunter subs had been commissioned in the early 1960s. They were a new line of "super sub," which had evolved from the prototype Thresher submarine. Equipped with the latest sensor gear, the submarine stalking K-129 boasted a BQQ-2 bow-mounted sonar and a veritable arsenal of the latest American torpedoes and mines. However, a U.S. attack submarine's primary job in peacetime was to monitor the Soviet boats as they left port, identify them, and radio the intelligence back to Pearl Harbor as quickly as the enemy boats hit the Pacific. The Permit-class submarine was well suited for the job, because the modern American boat was far quieter than the best of the Soviet submarines. This stationary stalker was virtually undetectable to the K-129's passive sonar.

The sonar operator of the U.S. surveillance sub reported that a Golf II–class submarine was heading out to deep sea. Later, the sonar recordings would be entered into the Navy's powerful Cray computers and the Soviet boat identified as the ballistic missile submarine K-129. Every missile submarine in the Soviet navy had its own dossier in the electronic records of the United States Navy. K-129's unique acoustical fingerprint was already on file.

Navy intelligence casually noted that K-129 was sailing much earlier than expected, having returned only recently from a regular patrol. They had closely monitored that patrol, too. Even though K-129 was one of the older-type ballistic missile subs of the Soviet North Pacific Fleet, the boat was still considered a dangerous weapon. The Americans, fully aware of the three one-megaton ballistic missiles ready in a row behind the conning tower, would record every movement of the Soviet sub, to the best of their technological ability.

Even though the Soviets had chosen their sailing time to avoid detection by satellite, it did them no good. The Americans had other satellites that covered the vast expanses of the open seas.

The U.S. Air Force had an orbiting network of spy satellites with infrared sensors that could track submarines in midocean by the slight variation of water temperature in their trailing wake. The primary mission of these satellites was to spot missile launch tests anywhere on earth. But they also covered the Pacific Ocean looking for the thermal wakes of submarines, particularly the heated water discharged by nuclear-powered subs. With a lesser degree of accuracy, they could detect the warmed wakes from diesel submarines.

The Americans had not yet perfected their surveillance systems to the point where they could continuously track a Soviet missile sub on its entire mission. However, they did know when the Soviet submarines sailed, when and where they called headquarters, when they came near the surface to recharge their batteries, and when they returned to port.

Unaware of the extent of U.S. surveillance, the commanding officers of K-129 carefully followed every procedure they knew, in hopes that their departure on this mission would go unnoticed.

The two Soviet captains were likewise unaware that the Americans were not the only observers surreptitiously watching the sailing of their sub. A shadowy group of men in Moscow, who would normally have little interest in the routine mission of a diesel-electric submarine, was also keenly tracking their progress.

7

THE FIRST DAYS OF THE VOYAGE of K-129 to an assigned patrol station in the mid-Pacific appeared to be routine, if such a dangerous undertaking could ever truly be routine. After leaving the safety of Avachinskaya Bay, K-129 set out upon a voyage across the expanse of the Pacific that would normally have taken two weeks' sailing time for a submarine of this type.

K-129 was capable of cruising at depths exceeding eight hundred feet. But during daylight and under noncombat conditions, Soviet diesel-electric submarines usually sailed submerged at depths between one hundred and two hundred feet, using electric motors run off the power provided by massive banks of batteries.

Living conditions during a long sea voyage were dramatically affected by changes in sea climate in the regions the submarine traveled. In the extreme climes of the North Pacific where K-129 sailed for the first few days after departing base, the crew endured bitter cold inside the hull, because outside waters were just above freezing. Small radiators were used to bring the near-freezing temperatures in the hull to more comfortable levels. As the boat continued into warmer waters, almost to the Tropic of Cancer, external temperatures rose into the sixties. When an older submarine like K-129 entered near-tropical waters, conditions inside the submarine became almost intolerable. Heat from the huge electric motors could raise the engine-room temperature to as high as 120 degrees. The heat, along with the foul air created by gases and unbathed bodies crowded into the small living area for many days, made the environment almost septic.

The ship's doctor, Major Sergey Cherepanov, and his assistants constantly checked the compartments for carbon dioxide, hydrogen, and other gases. Even under normal conditions, air in the living space was odorous. The air became increasingly foul following each snorkel to recharge the batteries. Soviet commanders in the Pacific rarely surfaced—even for brief periods, which would have flushed out the bad air—because they tried to avoid giving the Americans' spy technology a clear footprint of their location.

During daylight hours, K-129 ran on its main electric motors, maintaining an average submerged speed of seven to eight knots. Each night the sub ascended to within forty feet of the surface to snorkel and recharge its batteries, using a giant generator driven by one of its diesel engines. The snorkel drew in air for the diesel engines and exhausted carbon monoxide produced by the engine combustion. The smell of diesel oil seeped into everything; before long, the clothing, bedding, and even the skin of the mariners was saturated with a permanent oily odor.

During the snorkeling operation, the submarine ran on two of its diesels, while the third was coupled to generators to charge the 448 two-volt batteries. The massive arrays of batteries, located below decks in compartments two and five, were also a source of gases. The discharging batteries produced explosive hydrogen gas, which sometimes rose from the bowels of the submarine to add to the dangerous environment.

It took eight to ten hours to build a full charge. While near the surface, the submarine's two navigators used radio signals from land-based transmitters to take readings of their position. It was during these periods of snorkeling and the start-up of the diesel engines that K-129 was most vulnerable to detection by American antisubmarine warfare systems—infrared sensors on spy satellites, the hydrophone network, and patrolling ASW aircraft.

Because of the crowded conditions, sleep and toilet facilities were strictly regulated. But if living space was at a premium, the Red Navy compensated for the hardship by giving their submarine crews the best food the Soviet Union had to offer. The lowest-ranked Soviet submariner typically dined on meals that were usually available to the highest party officials or to regular Russians only at holiday feasts. On K-129, officers and enlisted men all enjoyed the same menu. They were fed four meals a day, including breakfast, dinner, supper, and tea, which was a late-night snack. In addition to meat or fish, vegetables, and dessert, all members of the crew were provided caviar, wine, and chocolate bars with their meals. Perishables were kept fresh during the first several weeks of the voyage in large refrigerators located beneath the living decks.

It is possible to chart the last voyage of K-129 with a reasonable degree of accuracy. The distances the submarine traveled, and the dates of departure and arrival at its approximate last location are known. From K-129's sailing on February 24, to its last known location on March 7, the Golf II submarine's final journey took slightly less than fourteen days. The great circle route from Rybachiy Naval Base on the Kamchatka Peninsula to a site between 350 and 400 miles northwest of Honolulu, Hawaii, was a voyage of just under 2,400 nautical miles.

When the records of the prevailing currents and wind conditions for that part of the ocean, on those dates, are factored into the charting, along with the boat's operational characteristics—such as speed capability and required time for snorkeling—a day-by-day account of the trip can be reconstructed.

FEBRUARY 24 (Departure from Rybachiy Naval Base)
K-129 leaves in the early morning hours, before daybreak. It runs on the surface, to get as far from port as possible before the next pass by an American satellite. Five million pounds of machinery cut through the water at a brisk sixteen knots. Although Pearl Harbor lies to the southeast, the K-129 steers a more northerly course into the prevailing 0.6-knot current flowing down from the

Bering Sea. This compensates for the sideward push cre-
ated by the currents (drift).

The wind is blowing from the northeast at a speed of
seventeen to twenty knots. Waves are moderate at six to
eight feet, with numerous whitecaps and some spray. The
water temperature is 33°F and air temperature is below
freezing.

Fifteen miles from the mouth of the bay into open seas,
the Asian continental shelf lies 750 feet below the keel,
then sharply drops away to waters 3,250 feet deep. The
submarine runs parallel to the drop-off for the next
twenty-five miles. K-129 radios headquarters that they
have entered deep water. The early run on the surface has
given the sub a good start on its voyage.

K-129 has traveled approximately 175 nautical miles.

FEBRUARY 25 (Day Two)

The prevailing current is from the northeast at 0.6 knots;
wind and sea action remain steady. The water temperature
is still 33°F, but the average air temperature has dropped
several degrees below freezing. The navigator makes adjust-
ments as the current changes, pushing the boat off its in-
tended course. Each time the boat rises near the surface for
navigational fixes and snorkeling, it risks colliding with
calved icebergs, commonly adrift in the area.

North of the course is the Meizi Seamount, a minor
ridge running from northwest to southeast, and rising to
within 9,500 feet of the surface. Just beyond the
seamount is Ostrov Beringa, the last island in the Aleutian chain, which forms an almost perfect arch from Kamchatka Peninsula to the Alaska Peninsula. The valleys of
that trench reach depths to 24,000 feet below sea level.

Deprived of daylight, the crew settles into an "at-sea" routine—sleeping, working, eating, and standing watch. The submarine is snorkeling at night, running at nine knots and cruising submerged at seven knots during the day. It will operate in this manner for most of the voyage. Occasionally, if seas are calm, and the electronic surveillance measure (ESM) shows they are alone in the vast openness of the North Pacific, the submarine will surface and run at a higher speed, between twelve and fifteen knots. Here in the open ocean, K-129's missiles are worthless; the faster it is on station, the sooner its deterrent value will be realized.

Captain Kobzar orders a series of drills that train the men for disaster response to flooding, fire, and hydraulic leaks. These drills will be continued—partly to hone skills and partly to relieve the boredom—two, three, and four times a day until they reach the patrol box.

K-129 has traveled approximately 369 nautical miles.

FEBRUARY 26 (Day Three)

For most of the day the submarine glides above a deep, broad ocean plain three miles below. It is heading directly for the Northwest Pacific Seamount chain. The boat's course is now running almost parallel to the angled slope of the International Date Line.

The 0.6-knot current shifts from the northwest, giving the submarine a "tail current" and an extra 0.5-knot boost in speed.

K-129 has traveled approximately 563 nautical miles.

FEBRUARY 27 (Day Four)

K-129 moves in a southeasterly direction, pushed by fol-

lowing currents of 0.6 knots. The ocean temperature has risen to 37°F and the air temperature has climbed above freezing for the first time since leaving Kamchatka. Sonar contacts increase as the submarine enters the great circle route taken by freighters traveling the sea-lanes between San Francisco and Yokohama, and between San Francisco and the Luzon Strait in the Philippines. At any time, hundreds of merchant ships are engaged in the transportation of goods vital to the economies of the Free World traders.

K-129 has traveled approximately 757 nautical miles.

FEBRUARY 28 (Day Five)

As the day passes, the following current begins a slow turn to the west and K-129 loses some of its added drift. The navigator increases the frequency of course corrections, compensating again for the sideward motion of the current. The ocean temperature has risen to 39°F and the air on the surface has risen 2 degrees. Sonar contacts drop off as the submarine leaves behind the well-traveled sea-lanes.

K-129 has covered approximately 951 nautical miles.

FEBRUARY 29 (Day Six)

To the northwest of the submarine's course is the Emperor Trough, 4.6 miles deep. Ocean currents, temperatures, and wind force remain unchanged. The ocean floor is 19,500 feet below sea level.

K-129 has traveled approximately 1,145 nautical miles.

MARCH 1 (Day Seven—West of the International Date Line)
*Early in the morning the submarine passes the halfway
mark between Rybachiy and Pearl Harbor. The milestone
goes unnoticed, except by the navigator and duty officer.
Currents and winds remain constant, but the temperature of the water and surface air has risen to 43°F. Frequency of sonar contacts again increases as the
submarine crosses another major Pacific sea-lane, the
great circle route between Los Angeles and San
Bernardino Strait in the Philippines.*

*Sometime during the day the submarine crosses the
180th meridian—the International Date Line, where
today becomes yesterday for eastbound sailors. Tradition-
ally, the captain would announce the event, which
would occasion some mariner merriment and jokes about
getting to live the day all over again. But today is different.*

*The first indication that something is amiss aboard
the submarine comes at the end of the day, when the
submarine fails to dispatch a routine signal to headquarters that the International Date Line has been
crossed.*

*K-129 has covered approximately 1,339 nautical
miles since sailing.*

MARCH 1 (Day Eight—East of the International Date Line)
*Again, it is March 1. Below is a flat, featureless expanse
of ocean bottom. By the end of the day, K-129 is nearing
an underwater volcano that sharply rises ten thousand
feet from the ocean floor. But there is no danger. Even at
maximum depth, the highest peak will pass 3,800 feet
below the submarine.*

K-129 has traveled approximately 1,533 nautical miles.

MARCH 2 (Day Nine)

The currents pushing K-129 to the northwest begin to change course. The submarine is on the edge of a giant underwater cyclone—a swirling mass of water three thousand miles wide—moving at a leisurely .5 knots. The vortex, which prevails in the North Pacific, is centered seven hundred nautical miles north-northwest of Oahu at this time of year. The temperature of both the air and surface water has risen to 53°F. Sonar contacts increase toward the end of the day, as the sub approaches the passage between San Bernardino Strait and Mexico.

K-129 has traveled approximately 1,727 nautical miles.

MARCH 3 (Day Ten)

The submarine begins the day crossing another of the seemingly endless underwater volcanoes, and then enters a zone of flat, featureless ocean floor.

K-129 has traveled approximately 1,921 nautical miles.

MARCH 4 (Day Eleven)

There is another indication that something is wrong aboard the submarine. Instead of slowing down to begin the usual silent patrolling in the mission box, K-129 keeps sailing toward Pearl Harbor. The water and air temperatures continue to rise, reaching the low sixties. Sweaters have been stowed and the boat's heating units are shut off.

K-129 has traveled approximately 2,115 nautical miles.

MARCH 5 (Day Twelve)

There is now no doubt that the submarine has departed from a routine mission schedule. For the second time K-129 fails to send a scheduled report to fleet headquarters. This signal is the mandatory announcement that the missile boat is on station and patrolling in range of its assigned target.

The submarine is checking its baffles more frequently now. On occasion, it rises and sinks through the ocean thermoclines, trying to catch any trailing American attack sub off its guard.

K-129 is traveling a course that lies between two converging seamount chains. To the northeast lies the Musicians Seamount, one of the largest collections of underwater mountains in all the oceans. Here are submerged massifs bearing such names as Hammerstein, Mahler, Rachmaninoff, Paganini, Ravel, Haydn, Chopin, and Mendelssohn. To the southeast lies the Hawaiian Ridge.

Sonar contacts from shipping and fishing activity are frequent. Surface vessels are identified by their unique sounds as freighters, tankers, and the occasional American warship (destroyers or light cruisers traveling fast out of Pearl Harbor for Southeast Asia, Japan, or Korea).

K-129 has traveled approximately 2,309 nautical miles.

MARCH 6 (Day Thirteen)

K-129 rigs for silent running, engaging its single electric auxiliary motor. It creeps along at two knots. All unnecessary equipment is secured. By late in the day, the sub is approximately seventy miles north of the Hawaiian Leeward Islands. To the east lies the western edge of Blackfin Ridge, a long, narrow, and steep plateau that runs east to west in the Northern Hawaiian Seamounts. K-129 frequently checks for trailers, often changing depth and course.

The submarine has traveled a total 2,363 nautical miles.

MARCH 7 (Day Fourteen)
The submarine is quiet as it continues slowly toward its secret destination. The air in the boat is becoming stale. Cruising at two knots draws a minimum of power from the massive batteries, extending the time between snorkeling cycles and the intake of fresh air.

On the surface, five hundred feet above, a beautiful sunset ends the tropical day. Below, in the darkness, men hurry about their tasks, readying the submarine for its mission. During the night, the order is finally given to surface the submarine.

K-129 has traveled approximately 2,396 nautical miles.

Exactly what occurred aboard K-129 after sailing from Rybachiy Naval Base can never be known to a certainty, unless American intelligence officials recovered written documents from the wreck and someday declassify them for public release. But an examination of what can be pieced together about the final journey reveals at least three major clues that something indeed went terribly awry aboard the submarine. First, the K-129 missed sending a routine, but expected, message to fleet headquarters that it had safely crossed the International Date Line on March 1. Then, on March 4, the eleventh day of the voyage, K-129 trespassed outside the boundary of its normal mission box and proceeded on a dangerous course that would take it closer to enemy waters than a normal assignment allowed. Finally, on March 7, a more ominous harbinger of trouble came with the submarine's failure to transmit the mandatory message to headquarters that it was on regular station and prepared to carry out its patrol.

It is also known that the submarine's commanders, Captains Kobzar and Zhuravin, in their long careers in the Soviet submarine service, had never before failed to follow all procedures to the letter. The K-129's *zampolit*, Captain Lobas, who was central to any decision to divert from an assigned mission, likewise had always been a model of Communist discipline. Yet these key command officers aboard K-129 did not follow standard procedures, whether by choice, coercion, or incapacitation.

Had K-129 been seized while en route to the mission box? The inexplicable presence of the extra men who were placed aboard the submarine a short time before sailing takes on new significance when the missed radio communications and deviant maneuvers of the boat are considered.

Later, the presence of these strange crew members became a key part of the mystery of K-129. Had these mysterious figures taken over the submarine? If so, was the takeover an outright mutiny? Or was control usurped with convincing orders from some higher command? In the latter case, these bogus orders would have had to originate in Moscow, because admirals of the Pacific Fleet and Kamchatka Flotilla later claimed they had no knowledge that K-129's mission was anything other than a regular combat patrol.

By the end of March 5, K-129 had sailed out of its regular patrol box and was heading toward Oahu Island, Hawaii. With no indication that orders for a special mission had been given by fleet headquarters, and failure to transmit periodic and mandatory radio signals to home base, the submarine had become a rogue boat.

Another baffling fact about K-129's journey is the absence of reaction to its aberrant behavior. At that moment, no one in either the Soviet fleet headquarters in Vladivostok or the U.S. Navy Pacific Fleet headquarters at Pearl Harbor raised the slightest concern over the missed signals or the deviation from course. It seems that K-129 had slipped through the cracks in the security systems of both navies.

The only sign that something terrible had happened aboard K-129 was not in the form of hard evidence at all, but rather in the premonition of a person thousands of miles away, on the other side of the Date Line, at Vladivostok.

Irina Zhuravina, wife of the submarine's deputy commander, had taken their young son, Misha, to her office at the Ministry of Economics. It was March 8 in Vladivostok (March 7 in Hawaii) and one of the most festive days in Soviet society—International Women's

Day. This was the day the Russian-style socialist system honored the role of women in the proletarian revolution. The office party was filled with celebrating professional women, most with their children. Irina was feeling especially good, with the party taking her mind off the troubling departure of her husband two weeks before.

Years later, Irina recalled what happened next, and despite the cynical realism that came with her Communist education, claimed that she experienced a once-in-a-lifetime, extrasensory perception of doom.

"I know exactly the day and the hour they died," Irina Zhuravina said. "We were celebrating International Women's Day at work. I was there with my son, and we were having a good time. All of a sudden, I went into hysterics. I broke down, went crazy—I didn't know what was happening to me."

Irina's coworkers put her in a car and drove her home. Several friends remained with her throughout the night, but she was inconsolable. The following day she quit her job, left Misha with her mother, and took the next available flight to Kamchatka and the Rybachiy Naval Base.

The submarine was not due to return to port for another two months. No word that anything was awry with K-129 had been received by any of the other wives of the submarine's crew. Irina could not explain her overwhelming grief and physical breakdown to the families she stayed with near the base. She recalled that the friends and wives of the sub's officers stayed up with her, looked after her.

"My friends did not leave my side, day or night," she

said. "They were always with me. What the other wives thought about it, I do not know."

Irina was eventually told by Soviet navy officials that her husband's submarine had been lost on the very day she experienced her premonition. As odd as it seems, Irina's foreboding may have coincided with real events aboard the submarine.

8

Soviet submarine commanders needed to become as adept at circumventing the Americans' superiority in antisubmarine detection technology as they were at compensating for the flaws built into their own equipment. Veteran captains had learned a few tricks to help even the odds.

The ocean contains layers of water with different temperatures and salinity called thermoclines. Using sonar or other acoustical gear in one layer to detect a target submarine in another layer could be difficult. The layers act like screens, deflecting noise that might otherwise be picked up hundreds of miles away. Soviet submariners learned to use the thermoclines as audio camouflage by skimming from one layer to another, then cutting their engines to "ultraquiet." By drifting silently through a new layer, a Soviet submarine could also increase its chances of detecting any U.S. sub lurking in the area.

By March 6, K-129 was nearing the end of its journey. It made the last leg entirely on its auxiliary electric motor. With the sub in this silent mode, Americans monitoring the SOSUS listening devices were having difficulty tracking the submarine as it left its normal mission box.

K-129 continued slowly until late into the night on a direct course toward Pearl Harbor at a speed of two knots. To avoid being followed, the boat's operators swung to starboard, then to port, allowing the butterfly pattern of its sonar to bear on the blind spot directly aft of the boat. The sonar detected nothing.

On March 7, fourteen days after sailing from Rybachiy, the Soviet submarine arrived at an area north of the Hawaiian Ridge. To the east was the westernmost edge of Blackfin Ridge. Still moving at approximately two knots, the submarine neared its final destination, just to the north of 24° N latitude and 163° W longitude. It had traveled a total distance of 2,396 nautical miles since leaving the base on February 24.

In the dead of night, this mechanical predator prowled six hundred feet beneath the surface of the North Pacific, unseen and unheard by its prey. It moved at a deceptively slow speed toward an exact confluence of invisible lines appearing only on a navigational chart. The boat's destination had neither name nor tangible features. It was, however, a fateful place in the vast sea that was to take on huge significance in the grand schemes of the Cold War superpowers.

K-129 was longer than an American football field and weighed more than six million pounds. Despite its mass, the high torque of its 180-horsepower, silent electric motor connected to a single five-blade propeller was more than enough to push the submarine smoothly through the water. The deliberate, unhurried forward momentum seemed almost leisurely, but whoever was in command of the boat was determined to reach a specific destination at an appointed time, without being detected.

No visible land above sea level lay in its path for more than three hundred miles. The submarine was maneuvering at its most efficient operational depth above a broad, deep plain more than three miles below. It could have safely dived a couple of hundred feet deeper if an enemy challenged. But there was no need to put such strain on the pressure hull, since there appeared to be no other warships of any navy for miles around.

The submarine's charts revealed that the only terrain breaking the monotonous sea floor ahead was a pearl-like string of submerged islets known as the Northwestern Hawaiian Islands and called the Leewards by local mariners. Two of these, Nihoa and Necker islands, lay less than seventy-five miles to the south. Rock masses formed the islets' subterranean bases, making them natural barriers between the submarine and the main islands of Hawaii to the southeast. These submerged islets were only a marker on the boat's charted course—they were not its destination.

K-129 moved forward as silently as a living sea creature, until suddenly the boat's commanding officer broke the carefully maintained quiet with an order: *Prepare to surface*. That order, barked over the intercom, pierced every compartment of the submarine and every heart of the ninety-eight men aboard.

The steps required to surface a diesel submarine, which had not changed in the navies of the world since the beginning of the century, were certainly followed

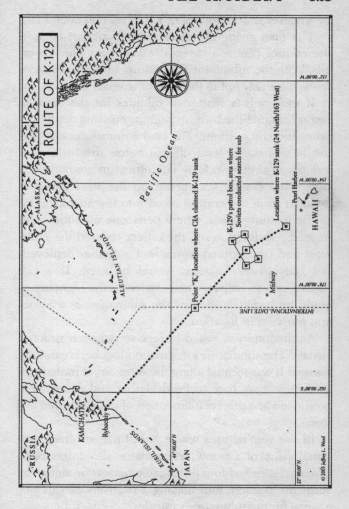

ROUTE OF K-129

RUSSIA

KAMCHATKA

JAPAN

KURIL ISLANDS

Rybachiy

ALASKA

ALEUTIAN ISLANDS

Pacific Ocean

HAWAII

Pearl Harbor

Midway

Point "K," location where CIA claimed K-129 sank

K-129's patrol box, area where Soviets conducted search for sub

Location where K-129 sank (24 North/163 West)

INTERNATIONAL DATE LINE

44°00'.00" N

22°00'.00" N

162°00'.00" E

176°00'.00" W

154°00'.00" W

132°00'.00" W

© 2005 Jeffrey L. Ward

by whoever was in control of K-129 on that fateful day.

The man giving the order stood at a chart table in the control center in sweat-streaked, navy-blue coveralls. With the submarine now sailing in tropical waters, it was miserably hot in the confining vessel.

It took only a matter of minutes for the crew to begin bringing the boat up from its cruising depth to a precautionary position. The boat commander directed the helmsman to level off just below the surface, at a depth of thirty-two feet. The officer in charge and a designated deputy scampered up the steel rungs of a ladder from the control room into the attack center in the conning tower, where periscope monitors were housed. On the way up, the officer ordered the ESM mast and navigational equipment antennas deployed, but only passive systems would be used. If K-129 turned on its active radar systems, the Americans could immediately identify the submarine as a Soviet and pinpoint its location.

An antenna was raised to receive radio-navigational signals. The submarine's destination had been carefully chosen. It was located along the most direct route from a Chinese navy base to Pearl Harbor and deliberately positioned at a precise intersection of longitude and latitude.

In the general area where K-129 maneuvered, four signal pairs of Loran-C coordinates also intersected. The navigator had four direct radio-navigation signals to verify his location, thus making it relatively easy to plot a target for the submarine's missiles.

By 1968, Soviet submarines in the Pacific were equipped with Loran-C and Omega radio-navigation receivers. With this much data coming into the command center, it did not require a navigator with advanced skills at working out complicated formulas to get an accurate fix on a target within the approximate eight-hundred-mile range of the boat's Serb missiles.

The advanced missile fire-control system, installed when K-129 was upgraded to a Golf II, allowed the submarine to target and launch its missiles accurately while traveling at low speeds, and without having to pause at an exact intersection of latitude and longitude. The older-model Golf I submarines, like the ones in the Chinese navy, still relied on earlier navigational systems. They *did* have to be positioned at exact longitudinal and latitudinal coordinates to accurately target their missiles.

As K-129 cruised just beneath the surface, the two officers in the action center above the control room scanned the dark horizons through the attack periscope and the navigational periscope. The officer on the navigational periscope elevated the instrument to search the night skies for antisubmarine aircraft. The periscopes visually confirmed the reports by the electronic receivers and passive sonar: The boat was alone in that vast, empty part of the Pacific Ocean.

The senior officer was satisfied by his personal reconnoitering of the waters immediately surrounding the conning tower. He slapped shut the handles of the periscope and slid down the ladder to return to the control center. Only the top edges of the fin were protruding above the surface at that point.

The next order was to "full surface," which, when relayed to the engine control room, created a stir of activity. Two crewmen began systematically turning levers to blow ballast tanks with compressed exhaust air from stored cylinders. Normally, K-129 would start up its massive diesel engines and use the exhaust to blow the ballast tanks. The precious reserve of compressed air was hoarded for emergency use. Since, to avoid detection, the commander had not started the diesel engines, the compressed air was the only source of pressure to force water from the ballast tanks and provide the buoyancy needed to surface.

The boat's bow broke the surface, rising in a geyser of sea foam. Before completely surfacing, the officer in charge had ordered the crew to prepare everything for an emergency dive. The commander would have had another reason not to engage the big diesel engines. He probably planned to spend only a few minutes on the surface, to avoid a retaliatory strike by any American ASW craft in the area.

Since the diesels were not being used, the sweltering crew had to wait for the cherished first blast of fresh air the diesels usually sucked into the boat through the snorkel tube.

The wait for fresh air was not long. Once the submarine was riding smoothly on the surface, the duty officer and a sailor wearing an officer's storm raglan sheepskin jacket, quilted pants, and heavy fleece-lined boots scaled the last ladder through the conning tower to open the hatch leading from the action center to the bridge. Some residual seawater sloshing on the bridge floor always poured through the opening into the living space. The splash of cold water dripping down two levels was a minor discomfort. To the men in the control room, after two weeks submerged in increasingly foul air, the rush of clean ocean air was exhilarating.

The dozens of officers and crewmen confined behind the guarded hatch separating the control room from the forward two compartments could not have felt the splash of fresh air. Even if they had, their anger or fear would have eclipsed any feeling of relief. After the intention of their captors had become clear from the staccato orders crackling over the intercom, a state of near-bedlam must have raged in the tightly packed compartments one and two.

These veteran submariners knew, from years of missile-launch drills, exactly what such deadly orders portended. The senior seaman and officers could also estimate from time elapsed, direction of turns, and speed of the boat, that their commandeered craft was dangerously close to the huge naval base at Pearl Harbor.

Soviet men who, just days before, might never have dared display any hint of religious feeling came to that place nearly all men in combat confront at such a time. Some likely prayed aloud, without regard for what their comrades would think. Those who had sailed away leaving wives, children, and sweethearts near the bases that would now most likely become ground zero for American retaliation would have loudly lamented the fate of their loved ones.

If K-129's top officers remained true to their rigorous naval academy training, they kept cooler heads and tried to maintain discipline, as long as there was any chance to change the situation unfolding on the other side of the metal bulkhead from their improvised prison. These officers probably clung to a last hope that intruders dressed in sailor attire were not technically expert enough to carry off such a doomsday act.

A rigidly enforced protocol was imposed on Soviet missile submarine commanders, which was designed to prevent accidental or unauthorized launch of a nuclear missile. The Soviet General Staff in Moscow had to transmit orders to a submarine that a red-alert situation existed. A transmitted order to prepare for missile launch implied that a nuclear strike against the motherland was imminent or in progress, and the Soviet sailors were trained to obey without further question.

Under the protocol, only at that point would the submarine commander open a prepackaged set of orders directing the sub to a target. These sealed instructions would define the course to coordinates at an appropriate launch site located near the sub's general patrol area.

Once the submarine had been positioned near the proper location for a launch, the captain and political officer normally waited for the confirmation order from fleet headquarters to launch the missiles. This final signal from headquarters included a set of codes to be added to the captain's codes, thereby completing the information required to conduct the launch sequence.

Another package kept in the safe of the submarine commander would then be opened. This package contained the codes to be entered into the nuclear missile control and guidance systems. The combined codes would also unlock the missile's fail-safe system.

The next critical step in the launch procedure required close coordination among the three ranking members of the submarine crew—the submarine commander, the deputy commander, and the *zampolit*. This step was to be taken only after each of these officers independently verified that the General Staff transmission was authentic and produced an individual key to the launch console.

On that night, this carefully designed procedure was not followed. But how could this have occurred when the stakes were so high? Had the first captain and second captain been overpowered, or were they obeying forged orders? Could lower-level regular officers assigned to the boat have been induced to participate in some mad scheme?

Despite its ability to launch while submerged, K-129 surfaced in the darkness, where it rolled in the ocean swells at a near crawl, approximately 360 miles from Honolulu. It had been positioned at a location—probably near 24° N latitude and 163° W longitude—which enabled even a minimally trained crew to program the guidance and control system to perfectly match the computerized, programmed target coordinates.

They were just north and west of the Hawaiian Ridge and due north of a smaller escarpment called Necker Ridge, where these reefs and shoals cross the imaginary earth-girding line called the Tropic of Cancer. It was an area usually shunned by mariners because of its confused jumble of subsurface islets and atolls. Nautical charts of this region are clearly marked "area to be avoided." The seabed drops sharply from these reefs to depths ranging from fourteen thousand to sixteen thousand feet.

In the final minutes of K-129's voyage, a small number of men aboard the boat began a fateful series of actions. The commander gave orders. The others crisply confirmed when each separate task was done. Hearts pounding. This is not a drill. Compartments sealed. Coordinates confirmed. Prepare for launch.

The hatch covering missile tube one was opened. The young missile technician in the heavy coat, padded trousers, and sea boots climbed out into the night, against the whipping winds and sea spray lashing the foredeck, and confirmed the launch tube was clear of debris. He huddled behind a protective shield in the conning tower, to await the launch.

Below, in the command center, the countdown was nearing conclusion: "... *shyest, pyat, chetyre* ..."

To the southwest, less than half the missile's range away, a large part of the U.S. Navy Pacific Fleet was resting in historic Pearl Harbor. Key units of the fleet were always out to sea, in obedience to a doctrine that ensured there would never be another surprise like that of December 7, 1941.

"... *tri* ... *dva* ... *odin* ..."

On the count of zero, the forty-two-foot-long missile with a one-megaton nuclear warhead should have stirred awake. The men in the control center had braced for the huge jolt of compressed air they expected would hurl the missile out of its tube before its liquid fuel ignited for a short, powerful run to the target. The target was easily within range of the Serb-type missile ready in tube number one.

At the instant of liftoff, every member of the crew, from one end of the boat to the other, heard a sound far louder and more terrifying than the roar of a missile leaving the launch tube.

The K-129 was wracked by a shock wave and then, almost as quickly, pushed downward from the force of a tremendous blast.

The conventional explosives in the warhead were packed tightly around the plutonium core in a spherical cover like a thick skin. It was segmented like a soccer ball, with detonators precisely placed in each segment of the explosives cover, to ignite in unison. This sphere of plastic explosives was designed in perfect balance for a powerful implosion, intended to compress the powdered plutonium core into a highly dense ball of fissionable material. The triggered compression was supposed to occur just as the warhead was delivered over its target.

A fail-safe device, hardwired beneath the warhead, had been designed as a last resort to prevent an unauthorized nuclear attack. The device was probably intended to render the warhead useless, not to create a major explosion. Mechanically disengaging the fail-safe device, even for a skilled technician, was practically impossible. In order to disarm it, the submarine had to be brought to the surface and the work done on the warhead from the top of the launch tube. Physically disconnecting the fail-safe device would then have been a task requiring several technical manuals and skills not readily available in the Soviet navy.

Thus, the launch crew must have had some confidence that it already possessed the proper disarming codes to override the fail-safe device. Unlocking the fail-safe mechanism was an essential first step for a missile launch. If the perfect balance required to trigger a nuclear warhead were interrupted by a partial detonation anywhere around the outer sphere, the force would blow outward. Within a millisecond, the plastic explosives would ignite, spreading out from the original point of detonation to create a directional blast that would destroy the warhead.

Apparently, this is what happened on board K-129.

The ignition series was set off by the operator at the control panel initiating the final launch signal. While it created a serious mishap, it was, in fact, no accident. Instead of waiting for the missile to arrive over its target, the warhead was blown apart at the instant the launch signal was sent. The explosion scattered powdered radioactive material throughout the area.

The exploding warhead rent the walls of the launch tube. The shock wave from the blast traveled along the axis of the launch tube and smashed the two fuel tanks of the missile together. The highly volatile fuels confined in the narrow tube exploded in a massive flash of energy that blew out both the top and bottom of the tube. It tore through the domed launch tube deck and the outer part of the submarine's hull, blasting a ten-foot-wide gap through the rear of the conning tower. At the top of the open launch tube, the explosion erupted into the night in a spectacular fireball.

The plastic explosives and missile fuel turned tube number one into a huge bomb, planted in the middle of the submarine. When the bomb went off, the boat was doomed. The force of the explosion at the bottom of the tube had torn a hole through the protective pressure hull to the open seas, severing the submarine's keel. K-129's back had been broken.

The explosion in missile tube one slammed into the adjoining tube, rupturing the fuel tanks in the second rocket. The two fuels ignited, causing a rapid buildup of pressure. Within a fraction of a second, the pressure had exceeded the design limits of the launch tube. Stressed beyond capacity, the heavy steel hatch, the missile's nuclear warhead, and shredded pieces of missile were blasted into the sky in a second fireball.

Tears in the two missile tubes spewed fire and hot gas into compartment four, compartment five, the inner conning tower, and the command center. Under tremendous pressure, the fiery gas filled the adjoining compartments.

All the crewman in the nearby compartments under the conning tower—including the command staff and the mystery men who had boarded the boat just before sailing—were most likely killed instantly, or died within a few seconds.

As crewmen in the outer forward and aft compartments rushed to seal connecting passage doors, the air supply throughout the submarine was quickly exhausted, feeding the raging inferno in the center of the boat. The hatch to the bridge was engulfed in flames from the first explosion and, thus, useless as an escape route. Some men in the engine rooms and aft torpedo room rushed to the only other exit, an escape hatch located on the back deck. A few may have tried to don their exposure suits, designed to protect them against the freezing elements of the open sea outside. It happened too fast. There was no time to seal off compartments, or even think of attacking the flames. Welds in the pressure hull, already weak from years of corrosion, split apart from the intense heat of burning, high-octane rocket fuel.

The sea outside the submarine, lighted for a moment by the two huge orange balls of flame from the explosions in the missile tubes, began immediately to pour into the ripped seams. High seas washed over the low deck and poured into the gaping hole in the conning tower and into the rear hatch, opened by a desperate sailor trying to escape or reach breathable air. Most of the flooding probably came from the huge breach in the bottom of the boat.

In less than five minutes the ocean was black again, with only a few fires from still-burning patches of radiated diesel fuel floating on the surface. The fires inside the now-dead ship were quickly hissed into steam, as cold ocean waters doused them.

Only a top-secret U.S. military satellite orbiting high above the Pacific Ocean was witness to the disaster. Its infrared heat sensors were designed to detect and distinguish heat patterns of burning Soviet rocket fuel from other heat sources, such as house fires. The fireballs from the exploding missile were recorded; then all else was dark, as the satellite swept over the night sea.

In minutes, K-129 took on enough water to lose its already precarious buoyancy. Still, a desperate few submariners in the aft torpedo compartment battled for survival in the eerie glow of the emergency lights. Unable to help those few men in compartments closer to the center who might have survived the heat and gas, these last submariners undoubtedly tried to work their way out against ice-cold seas, spilling into the after escape hatch opening. They tried to assist unconscious buddies who had been rendered helpless when their bodies were tossed into machinery by the violently heaving submarine. But the torrents surging into the submarine soon had them pinned down, too.

If any of the ninety-eight sailors aboard survived the initial blast, whirlwind hot fires, toxic fumes, and oxygen deprivation, they were quickly drowned while the submarine was still barely afloat on the angry surface of the Pacific Ocean. All the universal fears of the ways death may come that haunt the heart of every submariner were realized in those moments. They died from concussion, burns, asphyxiation, and drowning. The scene was every submariner's worst nightmare; the destruction was methodically unstoppable and complete.

Even if a few men had managed to escape from the flooding hatches, they would have perished from hypothermia, treading in black seas covered in oil made radioactive by the disintegrated plutonium core of the missile warheads.

K-129 heaved for a few minutes in the angry sea before beginning its last journey—an uncontrolled, three-mile dive to the bottom of the Pacific, somewhere between the Musicians Seamount and the Hawaiian Ridge in the Leeward Islands.

The submarine gained speed as it turned bow downward in an almost vertical dive. Before it reached crush depth, it had filled completely with water, thus avoiding implosion from the great pressure. K-129 was traveling faster than sixty miles an hour before it reached the ocean floor. When the submarine hit the seabed at a thirty-five-degree angle, it was wrenched apart by the impact and broke at several of the weakest points in the superstructure where the compartments were joined together.

A cloud of primordial silt billowed for hundreds of yards around the wreck. The force of the impact tossed the lifeless, burned body of the young sailor in the raglan coat from his shelter in the conning tower. As the silt settled, the body came to final rest beside the submarine on the ocean floor.

9

THE CATASTROPHIC EVENT that sank the missile submarine went unnoticed in the nearby Hawaiian Islands. Once it was discovered, the larger significance of the fiery explosions and sinking of Soviet submarine K-129 was deliberately hidden from the public by the United States government. Two American presidents, several heads of the Central Intelligence Agency and the Defense Intelligence Agency, National Security Council advisors, and a substantial number of admirals of the U.S. Navy participated in a massive cover-up to make sure the American people, and thus the world, remained unaware of the incident.

Among the several plausible reasons the public was denied access to the truth about what happened on March 7, 1968, in the Pacific, is the sheer panic that such a close brush with nuclear catastrophe would have evoked. The threat of a nuclear Armageddon at this stage in the Cold War was very real, and a jittery world had already begun to challenge the wisdom of continued Soviet-American brinkmanship.

The explosion and sinking of K-129 approximately 360 miles northwest of Pearl Harbor was recorded on the continuous printout at a Navy SOSUS listening post. The naval station monitoring the hydrophones actually picked up the sound of three blasts. Recordings from hydrophones arrayed along the Hawaiian Leeward Islands produced three blips, probably resulting from the discharge of the plastic explosives in the warhead trigger on the first missile, the ignition of its volatile rocket fuel, and the explosion of the second missile. These minor blips may have roused the curiosity of a petty officer at the SOSUS monitoring station, but when nothing suspicious followed, they were ignored at the time.

The sprawling U.S. Pacific base slept peacefully, unaware that a nuclear missile launch by a Soviet submarine had been attempted and failed, less than four hundred miles to the northwest.

Adjacent to Pearl Harbor, the half-million residents and visitors of Honolulu never knew how close they had come to the largest man-made catastrophe in history. Most would have been killed by the initial blast and fireball, or died within days from direct radiation fallout.

Instead of an unspeakable disaster, there was only a pattern of spikes in the rhythmic wavy lines printing out in continuous sheets from the Sound Surveillance System (SOSUS) monitor. The night watch between midnight and 6:00 A.M. was the loneliest and least popular shift. But since these were the hours known for sneak attacks, the sailors assigned were the best. Had the expert technicians been aware of any aggressive behavior from the K-129 explosion, or suspected an accident involving a Soviet warship, they would have instantly alerted higher authorities. The warning would have set off alarms all around the Pacific Rim and in Washington. During this tense period, such an alarm would have put strategic forces on a high state of alert worldwide.

Every sailor and marine on Pearl Harbor would have been awake and running to stations in minutes. Antisubmarine warfare units, both at sea and in the air, would have immediately headed for the submarine, even before it entered the defensive zone surrounding Pearl Harbor and the Hawaiian Islands. Clearly, the incident did not attract any special attention at Pearl Harbor.

The little pops from explosions hundreds of miles away that were captured on the sensitive instruments were not menacing enough to cause a stir. The spikes on the monitoring tape could have been caused by any number of natural or man-made events. Since the missile did not leave the submarine's launch tube, none of the other tracking equipment at the base sent out alerts, either.

The Pacific SOSUS system had been equipped with a modification that allowed it to filter out "nonsubmarine" noises, and conventional explosions at sea were not among the normal sounds made by submarines. In fact, the Pacific was a very noisy place, and the sounds of conventional explosions—legal and illegal—were quite common. Thus, this event went undetected at the time it happened. The Navy's hydroacoustical equipment could not identify the source of the noise as a malfunction in a nuclear missile launch. There certainly was no way, with the limited amount of information the SOSUS provided, to tell that, only seconds before, a one-megaton warhead had been electronically targeted to launch.

Pearl Harbor, America's fortress in the Pacific since the early 1900s, bristled with warships in that fourth year of America's involvement in the Vietnam War. The United States had other bases supporting the war effort and general defense of the Pacific Ocean. Major naval and air force bases were situated throughout the Japanese Islands and in the Philippines, as well as on the Asian mainland in Vietnam. None was as important to America's forward defense structure as Pearl Harbor.

The base provided port and repair facilities for all northern, central, and southern Pacific naval operations. It was a working combat base for U.S. Navy operations in the entire Pacific Ocean. Several squadrons of nuclear submarines, a large contingent of the surface battle fleet assigned in the Pacific, and sophisticated spy operations of the Joint Intelligence Center Pacific and the Space and Naval Warfare Systems Center were based there.

On March 7, marine sentries paced the perimeters of the giant base, guarding a huge cache of nuclear warheads to be deployed on naval warships. The base warehoused the nuclear weapons stockpile for the surface and submarine fleets of the entire Pacific, because other countries hosting American warships would not allow nuclear weapons on their territories. Nearby, additional nuclear bombs of the U.S. Air Force were stored for ready access. There was also a huge assembly of fissionable material other than weaponry in the armada of nuclear-reactor-powered submarines and surface warships that silently rode anchor in the militarized harbor.

The metropolitan area of Honolulu abuts the military complex. That night, half a million civilians went about their lives, secure in the knowledge they were under the watchful guard of their U.S. military neighbors. It was prime winter tourist season in Hawaii, and the luxury hotels were packed with snowbirds from all over the more frigid cities of North America.

Not one of the residents of Honolulu knew then, nor would they later be told, that their city, along with the military bases, was the target of the first attempted nuclear strike against America. It was only because Pearl Harbor was located there that the citizens of this American paradise were targets in the first place. Even though they would far outnumber the military personnel on the bases, the civilian casualties would be considered collateral damage by military strategists.

There is little doubt that had the rogue Soviet submarine successfully launched the Serb missile with its one-megaton warhead, Pearl Harbor, Hickam Field, and a large part of the Honolulu metropolitan area would have vanished in a mushroom cloud on March 7, 1968.

The casualty figures—including blast and radiation deaths and severe injuries—would have easily exceeded a half million people. The high degree of accuracy of Soviet rocketry, and the efficiency of Soviet nuclear warheads of the simple type carried by K-129, would have assured obliteration for that capital city and Oahu Island. The fallout would have blanketed the rest of the Hawaiian Islands with intolerable levels of radiation for at least the next two decades, rendering the fiftieth American state virtually uninhabitable.

The explosive yield of the one-megaton warhead, equivalent to one thousand tons of TNT, was nearly one hundred times greater than the 12.5-kiloton yield from the atomic bomb dropped on Hiroshima, Japan, in 1945.

The initial burst would have been especially damaging, because Pearl Harbor sits in a natural bowl surrounded by the low mountains of the Koolau Range on the east and the Waianae Range on the west. The bowl shape tilts toward Honolulu, thus assuring that the initial nuclear blast would have been deflected outward along the coast and into the heart of the city.

A one-megaton explosion at ground level over Pearl Harbor would have vaporized everything within a radius of six-tenths of a mile from the center, and killed 90 percent of the military and civilian inhabitants within a radius of 1.7 miles. Nothing would have been recognizable in that initial area of destruction. The blast would have created a crater two hundred feet deep and one thousand feet in diameter.

Only a few buildings, constructed from reinforced steel and poured concrete, would have been left standing within a radius of 2.5 miles. Pearl Harbor, Hickam Field, Pearl City, and Waipahu would have all been totally destroyed. The shock waves extending over most of Honolulu would have destroyed most residential houses. Buildings in the north and western edges of the city would have been reduced to structural skeletons. More than 50 percent of the people caught in that area would have died instantly, with another 40 percent suffering serious injury.

In the center of Honolulu, the contents of the taller buildings, including people, would have been blown out, littering the streets with debris and bodies. Thirty percent of the residents in downtown Honolulu would have been killed and another 50 percent severely injured. In the eastern section of Honolulu, farthest from the blast, only 5 percent of the people would have been killed, and approximately 40 percent injured.

Within an eight-mile radius, the damage from this blast would have inflicted instant death on a quarter of the population. For a distance of thirty miles downwind of the blast, with the prevailing winds blowing out of the mountains toward the city, lethal radiation would have killed everyone after a few hours of exposure.

In a period of two days to two weeks, lethal radiation would have begun killing people as far as ninety miles from the blast site. This deadly radiation cloud would have covered much of the island of Oahu. Because the municipal airport and commercial ports were also located adjacent to the military complexes, there would have been no facilities for mass evacuation from the island.

Experts say it is unlikely the initial blast would have caused secondary nuclear explosions from the hundreds of bombs and missile warheads stored in depots at Pearl Harbor and Hickam Field. However, the plutonium in these weapons and the nuclear fuel in the reactors in ships and subs destroyed by the initial blast would have spread widely with the radiation cloud. The Hawaiian Islands and large swathes of the Pacific Ocean would have been contaminated for at least the next decade. There is no calculation of the permanent effects such a nuclear attack on Hawaii would have had on Pacific Ocean fisheries for generations to come.

But it did not happen.

On that day in 1968, this nuclear cataclysm was prevented, and only a submarine with ninety-eight men aboard was lost.

The sinking of K-129 would become the center of a raging, behind-the-scenes controversy between the American and Russian naval and diplomatic communities that was to last for more than three decades. Each side has its own official and unofficial versions of what caused the Soviet missile boat to sink. Yet, the intelligence communities and inner sanctums of the respective governments at the highest levels have never trusted their military leaders with enough information to settle the arguments. As a result, neither the American nor the Russian military leadership has ever publicly acknowledged the true cause of the sea disaster.

While propounding a half-dozen theories for why the submarine sank, no authority in either the American or Russian navy has ever dared to propose publicly that an explosion resulting from an attempted nuclear missile launch was the primary source of the submarine's demise. But for years, there has been widespread, well-based speculation in both navies that an exploding warhead was the only possible explanation for the type of damage that sank K-129.

Ironically, the relatively simple fail-safe device that may have prevented doomsday was probably supplied by the Americans. In the 1960s, small groups of military science and technology specialists in the United States and the Soviet Union had secretly cooperated in a program to prevent an accidental or rogue nuclear war from breaking out. Even as the leadership of both states belligerently rattled their nuclear sabers in public, there was quiet cooperation to prevent the deliberate misuse of nuclear weapons. Of particular concern was the theft or unauthorized appropriation of one or more nuclear weapons by terrorists, a lone madman, or a rogue air force or naval crew.

In the case of the K-129 incident, a small group of American scientists—and a highly secret decision by President Lyndon Johnson to share classified, nuclear fail-safe technology with Soviet leaders—may well have prevented the obliteration of an American city and a potential third world war.

The United States had been sharing fail-safe technology with the Soviets as early as the Eisenhower administration. The sensitivity of giving technology to the enemy was referenced in an obscure, recently declassified memorandum from the hottest point of the Cold War era, when President Johnson was rapidly accelerating the war against the Communist forces in Vietnam. The memo was sent by then NSC staffer Spurgeon Keeny to President Johnson's special national security advisor, Walt W. Rostow. Excerpts from that secret 1966 memo are revealing.

"I think you should be aware of the proposal discussed in the attached correspondence for reciprocal exchange with the Soviets of information on procedures for insuring control of nuclear weapons," Keeny wrote. "This is a subject on which the President is very sensitive for obvious reasons, and about which the less said the better. At the same time, I think there may be merit in the idea of reassuring the Soviets about our control procedures and informing them of some of the specific equipment, such as Permissive Action Links (PALs), that we might wish to encourage them to incorporate in their own weapons. If we decide to go ahead with this project, I would recommend that we simply give the Soviets the specific information that we think they should have."

The Americans may have been willing to entrust their secret fail-safe technology to the Soviets, but the Soviet leadership inherently mistrusted the very men who had sworn to defend the Communist system with their lives.

Because Soviet missile submarines operated far from home with little direct control after leaving port, it is certain that special precautions were taken to prevent unauthorized or accidental launch of nuclear weapons. In the case of K-129, an extra safeguard in the form of a mechanical fail-safe system was likely installed by Soviet nuclear weapons scientists.

The PAL fail-safe system had been invented at the Atomic Energy Commission (AEC) labs at Sandia, New Mexico, in 1960. Not only was this system widely used to safeguard U.S. nuclear weapons from unintended uses, but the system was evidently provided to the Soviets. While the secret Keeny memorandum indicates the technology was to be shared with the Russians, there is no follow-up notation to indicate when the actual transfer was made.

Select technicians were designated by the top ranks of the Soviet military to install the extra safeguard devices in all nuclear weapons carried by strategic bombers and sea-launch warships. Codes to the fail-safe devices, in both the U.S. and Soviet military, were assembled in sets, with no one person having the complete set until final, verified orders were given to attack. Each set of codes opened a door to the next segment of the code. While the KGB maintained operational control of nuclear warheads, it did not have access to all segments of the code to disarm the fail-safe device. For example, one segment of the code might be held by the KGB, the second by the missile officers on the plane or ship carrying the weapon, and the final sequence by Soviet supreme headquarters.

There was no reason for many in the military and other government agencies to even know about the fail-safe devices, because unless someone attempted to circumvent strict procedures and controls, the fail-safe device would never be needed.

The device, literally a little black box, was typically buried deep inside the missile or warhead in such a way that it could not be easily identified or tampered with.

Submarine commanders and the missile officers responsible for actually launching nuclear weapons were aware that safeguards against unauthorized release of weapons were in place. Therefore, if the men who attempted to launch the K-129's missiles knew about the fail-safe system, they must have believed they had the knowledge to override it. Otherwise, they never would have attempted to launch.

Under the regular protocol, had an actual preemptive or retaliatory strike been ordered, the supreme Soviet military command would have radioed the codes necessary to disengage the safety system before initiating the launch sequence.

Later PAL systems used on American nuclear weapons were designed to lock up the electronic arming system of the warhead, thus freezing the mechanism and rendering the weapon useless.

However, in the 1960s, more lethal fail-safe systems were used to prevent unintended deployment of nuclear weapons. The early fail-safe systems included "emergency destruction devices" designed to destroy nuclear weapons without producing a nuclear yield. The crude devices could be set off if a sophisticated, but unauthorized, person tried to wire around or otherwise thwart the protective device.

The Soviets, whether because of less-advanced technical expertise or a darker paranoia, most likely installed devices that detected any attempt to hot-wire around the PAL system. Such a device would trigger a small explosion, which would permanently damage the weapon itself.

Unless properly disarmed, the PAL-type system quite simply would cause a nonnuclear explosion to destroy the warhead before the missile was launched. Certainly this added safeguard was not meant to be powerful enough to destroy the aircraft or submarine carrying the weapons. But Soviet technology, particularly electronics, was notoriously flawed, and the device designed to disable the weapons could have ended up destroying both the weapon and its carrier.

On the other hand, it is not too far-fetched to suggest

that the Soviet fail-safe device installed on K-129 did exactly what it was designed to do. It may have been intended to cause a catastrophic explosion when it detected an unauthorized launch attempt. After all, the fail-safe system on a nuclear weapon was a final precaution to prevent an accidental or unauthorized nuclear incident that could have led to global war. The top leadership on each side wanted to avoid an accidental or rogue attack on the other. Even an unauthorized attack risked a response of unlimited retaliation.

Fortunately, on March 7, 1968, Pearl Harbor was allowed to sleep in peace. Unlike the first sneak attack on Pearl Harbor, in 1941, no one would have survived this intended strike. Instead, K-129 went quickly to a watery grave in the deep, nearly three miles down and more than three hundred miles west-northwest of its intended target.

PART TWO

THE INTELLIGENCE

10

SOVIET PACIFIC FLEET HEADQUARTERS in Vladivostok failed to notice that missile submarine K-129 had not reported its arrival at the designated patrol area. It was several days past the sub's scheduled arrival before a duty officer in command central realized that one of its nuclear-armed submarines on a mission in the North Pacific had not communicated with headquarters in almost two weeks.

The submarine had reported entering deep water off the Kamchatka Peninsula after departure from Rybachiy Naval Base on February 24, but had missed its next two routine transmissions.

When the duty officer finally discovered that the contacts were long overdue, the initial reaction was routine. A coded radio signal was dispatched, ordering K-129 to reply by March 12. When no reply was received another, more urgent, dispatch was sent on March 17. Still, there was no response.

When the admiralty was informed there had been no communications with the missile sub for more than three weeks, panic seized the Pacific Fleet headquarters. As a routine matter, an admiral pulled the file on the tardy submarine, and was surprised to find that something besides the submarine was missing. The required manifest listing all crew members aboard the submarine could not be found, either at fleet headquarters or at the Kamchatka Flotilla headquarters. In the Soviet navy the failure of a submarine commander to file a complete and verified roster of officers and enlisted sailors on a combat mission was a serious criminal offense.

First Captain Kobzar, with years of outstanding service to his credit and a promotion to admiral at hand, was not the kind of officer who would make a careless mistake—especially when it came to compliance with mandatory procedures. His deputy commander, Captain Zhuravin, was also unlikely to be so sloppy when he was about to receive command of his first submarine. One of these conscientious officers would have certainly filed the report; the other probably would have double-checked it as well.

On this particular mission, the crew manifest would have received extraordinary attention, due to the replacement crew members from other submarines in the flotilla and the eleven extra men assigned to the boat. This focus on personnel matters would certainly have prompted the sub's officers to file the required roster—most likely in duplicate, at several layers of the command structure. Its disappearance from the files at fleet headquarters in Vladivostok and flotilla headquarters at Rybachiy was not accidental. Someone did not want information about the members of this patchwork crew discovered. The theft of this critical document added another layer of mystery to the already strange circumstances surrounding the composition of the final crew manning the sub.

There would have been no reason to hide the names of the regular crew members of K-129. Likewise, there was no secret about the identity of the replacement crew members from other submarines in the Kamchatka Flotilla. All these men would have been known by their peers at the relatively small naval outpost. The only reasonable explanation for the roster to disappear would be to hide temporarily the fact that the submarine sailed with ninety-eight men aboard, rather than the normal complement of eighty-three.

The identities of the extra eleven who had inexplicably been added to an already overcrowded submarine at the last minute were not significant, since their names would probably have been fictitious, anyway. The KGB was no less adept at creating legends for their operatives than was its CIA counterpart. But the extra number might have raised an alarm.

The missing crew manifest is evidence that a major and well-designed plot involving this submarine was underway. Communist bureaucrats were efficient to a fault when it came to keeping lists of names. Even if technical equipment and other systems were prone to break down, certain procedures did not. Soviet submarine commanders were particularly careful about filing this document before sailing. Thus, no other conclusion can be drawn than that someone with extraordinary power had deliberately circumvented important personnel procedures that were sacrosanct to the Soviet submarine service.

By the middle of March, Soviet naval officials at

both the Kamchatka Flotilla and Soviet fleet headquarters became alarmed that K-129 had met with some type of mishap. A check of the one recorded radio message that *had* been received revealed nothing unusual. All recorded radio transmissions for the rest of the fleet were carefully examined, to determine if any unidentified message or distress signals had been picked up between March 1 and March 15. All Soviet naval, merchant, and fishing vessels operating in the North Pacific for the previous two weeks were contacted. There had been no undocumented signals or unusual sightings at sea.

On or about March 21 the Soviets launched a huge flotilla to search for their lost boat. Submarines were sent from the northern bases, and surface vessels and naval aircraft were dispatched from Vladivostok. Sailors of the American attack submarine USS *Barb*, patrolling off Vladivostok, were startled when this armada of warships and submarines suddenly streamed from Soviet ports with their radios broadcasting in the clear.

The Soviet search boats covered a wide arc of the ocean as far north as latitude 65°, well into the Bering Sea, and to within 750 miles northwest of the U.S. Navy base at Pearl Harbor.

The center of the search was located in the North Pacific, the first location where K-129 had missed its position report—latitude 40° N by longitude 180°, on the International Date Line. This location, which was approximately seventeen hundred miles northwest of Pearl Harbor, came to be known as K-Point. It would be a site of major confusion and disinformation in the K-129 incident for years to come.

The North Pacific was in the throes of a winter storm when the search force of approximately forty vessels reached the area where the Soviets believed the lost submarine's last signal should have originated. Soviet officers aboard submarines from K-129's base at Rybachiy exhausted their crews, ordering their boats to dive, surface, dive, surface, and dive again, all the time pinging away with active sonars. Nobody seemed concerned that American surveillance ships might be listening. This major search effort continued for more than a month before the Russian sailors were ordered to cancel the operation and return to their bases.

Finally, in the last week of April 1968, the Soviet high command in Moscow officially listed K-129 as lost at sea, cause unknown.

The following week, K-129 wives who were living in the area of the submarine's home port on the Kamchatka Peninsula or near fleet headquarters at Vladivostok were notified that their husbands were lost at sea and probably dead.

Irina Zhuravina, who had flown to the Rybachiy base after having suffered the strange emotional breakdown at her office on March 8, was back at her job with the Economics Ministry in Vladivostok.

"I didn't believe they were gone," Captain Zhuravin's wife recalled. "I did not yet relate my strange illness on International Women's Day with the loss of my husband. We waited for them to return. We could not accept they were dead."

On May 5, the scheduled date for the return of K-129 to home port, the families became more convinced that their husbands and fathers were really gone.

"A government commissioner came from Moscow and asked us to put together documents," Irina said. "They gave us one thousand rubles apiece, and another five hundred for each child. I never spent the money. I put it in the bank. Then came devaluation and it just burned up. That was what my husband's life was worth to them."

The subject was likewise treated as a nonevent in terms of what the public knew in Russia. There were no announcements that a submarine had been lost at sea. The families of the officers and the seamen were never given an explanation for the fate of their sailors. They were told only that K-129 was lost, with all hands presumed dead. Strangely, because the Soviets had no physical proof the men were actually dead, they did not provide full pension benefits to the widows.

Meanwhile, on the American side of the Pacific, the U.S. Navy's curiosity about the huge Soviet search for the lost submarine became a priority project.

The Navy was notified by the North American Aerospace Defense Command that one of its satellites had identified and recorded an event in the North Pacific as having some of the characteristics of a Soviet missile launch. A satellite sensor had recorded two massive surges of radiant energy when the missile fuel in K-129's launch tubes one and two exploded. The camera's sensors were tuned to record the light spectrum created by the burning of specific chemicals known to be used in Soviet rocket fuel.

At first, the image did not raise concerns at NORAD,

because the fireballs had quickly disappeared without the follow-on trail of a missile in flight.

U.S. Navy intelligence had already concluded that the Soviets had lost a submarine, because of the massive sea search. After the satellite images provided by NORAD revealed a more specific location for the accident, the American intelligence operators realized that the Soviet search was centered hundred of miles from the actual site.

Armed with a more precise location, the Navy began scanning SOSUS recordings from the previous weeks. These records, along with other intelligence gathered from the Boresight radio-tracking system and eavesdropping by American submarines off Kamchatka, soon revealed that the lost submarine was a diesel-electric missile boat. However, nothing in the Americans' intelligence-gathering arsenal could provide clues to the actual cause of the explosion and sinking.

The hydrophonic screen employed in the SOSUS network was designed to track submarines sailing beneath the surface of the ocean. The system was not meant to locate surface explosions. SOSUS was designed to identify the general area where a submarine might be operating, so that ASW assets could be employed to visually and audibly pinpoint and track the Soviet submarines. The SOSUS system filtered out most man-made sounds, homing in on acoustical waves from submarine engines and propellers.

The Americans knew where the accident had happened, but not much more.

Because of the open hostility between the two navies, the Soviets were not about to ask the Americans for help, or even to admit they had lost one of their submarines. Eventually, the Soviets' vague inquiries about whether the Americans in the Pacific had seen or heard anything unusual were met with even vaguer responses. While the Americans knew the Soviets were looking in the wrong area, correcting them would have revealed too much about U.S. surveillance technology.

The Americans may have even actively hindered the Soviet effort to locate their lost boat. There have been reports that the Americans did, at one point during the search, suggest that the Soviets examine an oil slick far to the north of where the U.S. Navy believed the submarine had sunk. Soviet investigators have alluded to this mysterious oil slick, but its location and source have never been explained.

Admiral Anatoliy Shtyrov, a Soviet intelligence officer from Pacific Fleet headquarters who was primarily responsible for the investigation of the K-129 incident, mentioned this oil slick years later. He said the Americans advised the "Soviets to examine the oil spill they spotted. The analysis of the oil from the spill confirmed that its composition matched the type of diesel oil used to fuel Soviet submarines." According to his account, the U.S. Navy was not very cooperative in the search for K-129 and shared no specific intelligence data about the sinking.

"The Americans only informed the Russians about the fact of the disaster, but did not mention its [true] location," Admiral Shtyrov said.

The oil spill to which the Americans directed the Soviets may have been a decoy. There was speculation among American submariners that the Navy flew out to a site near the Soviet search area and dropped into the sea several open drums of diesel oil of the type known to be used in Soviet missile submarines.

After the U.S. Navy realized the Soviets were searching hundreds of miles from the wreck site, the Defense Intelligence Agency (DIA) saw a golden opportunity to examine an enemy ballistic missile submarine, up close and unhampered.

In the beginning, the American hunt for K-129 was a quest for military intelligence, and to determine the reason for the submarine's unusual maneuvers before it sank. The project to find and closely examine the wreck was kept top-secret for two reasons. First, in peacetime, locating another country's shipwreck without informing them of the discovery was legally questionable behavior under international law. The world would not look favorably upon any country that robbed the grave of another's lost sailors. At this point in history, world opinion mattered as much as military strategy in efforts to win the Cold War. Second, the Americans did not want the Soviet Union to learn about the technology used to locate and exploit the wreck.

Thus, from the outset, the K-129 incident was wrapped in a cloak of secrecy.

The job of conducting the search and exploitation of the lost Soviet sub went to America's relatively new military spy organization, the Defense Intelligence Agency. The DIA had been founded on October 1, 1961, drawing on existing military intelligence units from each of the service branches, to become the nation's primary producer of operational military intelligence. Five years before the K-129 incident, the DIA had created the Scientific and Technical Intelligence Directorate. This

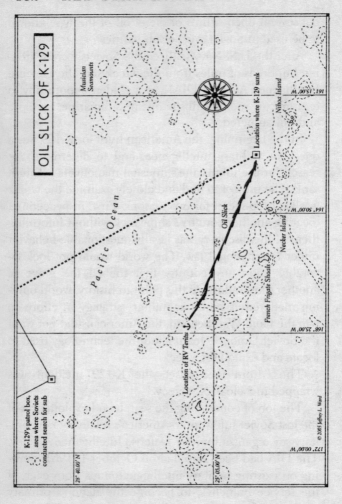

clandestine think tank could call on the nation's best and brightest scientific and technical brains, as needed. When this directorate was given primary responsibility for the K-129 project, a special task force of submarine intelligence experts and civilian scientists was quickly assembled to handle the assignment.

The Navy's spy-scientists were already involved in a deep-sea intelligence project, code-named Sand Dollar, with the mission of finding and recovering Soviet technology that routinely crashed into the oceans during missile tests, shipwrecks, and plane crashes.

The search for K-129 thus began as a small operation assigned to a highly specialized group of submarine officers and civilians.

Before the investigation could get underway, another incident involving the lost submarine came close to exposing the secret operation to the public. Soon after the sinking, a University of Hawaii oceanographic research ship accidentally came upon an oil slick hundreds of miles south of the Soviet search site. This large pool of pollution was floating on the surface and drifting slowly away from any landmass as it dispersed.

The oceanographic research vessel the university operated in early 1968 was the R/V *Teritu*, a ninety-foot converted yacht, with a rounded bottom that restricted it to working close to land. The *Teritu* was not suited for deep oceanographic work, which required carrying a considerable amount of heavy equipment on the upper deck. A much older research ship at the university, the *Neptune*, was past its time for retirement from service, and in 1968 was probably used only for minor projects in the immediate vicinity of the main islands.

At the time the *Teritu* discovered the oil slick, it was conducting studies along the Hawaiian Leeward Islands. The university research ship was operating in an area north of Necker Island, Gardner Pinnacles, and French Frigate Shoals. The *Teritu*, because of its limited size, stayed fairly close to the long chain of low and submerged islands that runs from Oahu to Midway Island. The chain consists of more than a hundred volcanic islets, atolls, and coral reefs. The uninhabited islands, some less than two hundred acres in area, and others completely submerged beneath the ocean surface, contain one of the world's richest ecosystems.

In the midst of a routine expedition in March, the research boat accidentally sailed into the large oil slick, probably in the vicinity of the Gardner Pinnacles. Quickly taking samples and testing them in the boat's small chemical laboratory, the scientists on board were horrified to discover the oil slick was heavily radiated. Later analysis of the oil slick identified Chinese fissile material and light diesel oil. The oil was of a type used by submarines to lessen the amount of smoke exhausted during snorkeling. The diesel engines of Golf submarines used a high-grade, nearly smokeless fuel called D-37. Attack submarines burned a different grade fuel called solar oil.

The scientific crew aboard the research boat was so disturbed by the discovery of radioactive waste that it radioed its finding to the university's research center before returning to Honolulu. The alarm was relayed to the head of the university's oceanographic and geophysics department, Dr. George P. Woollard. Dr. Woollard, who was working with the U.S. Navy on securing a number of research grants, called his contacts at Pearl Harbor to determine if the military was aware of a radiation-laced oil spill in the Leeward Islands.

Before anyone could make the information public, "government representatives" (probably from the Office of Naval Intelligence) moved in. Mysteriously, *Teritu's* deck logs for that period of time—the legal documents normally kept as a routine part of a ship's history—were lost, deliberately misplaced, or seized by the DIA.

The records and eyewitness accounts had to be immediately embargoed, otherwise the exact location of the sinking of K-129 could have been quickly pinpointed by anyone reviewing the widely available charts of winds and currents in the vicinity at that time. If an announcement about the discovery and location of an oil slick had been made public, the Soviets could have easily linked it to their lost boat and determined the site of the sinking.

The general location of this oil slick, carried by ocean waters to a point near the Leeward Islands, proved that K-129 had gone down close to the islands and approximately three to four hundred miles northwest of Honolulu. Sea charts of this area for March 1968 revealed that the prevailing currents and winds would have carried the oil spill in a southwesterly direction almost parallel to the islands. Had K-129 sunk farther to the north, where the Soviets were centering their search, or where American intelligence falsely claimed the sub had sunk, the currents would have carried the oil spill into open ocean waters in a northerly direction.

It can also be determined that the *Teritu* crew discovered the oil spill soon after the submarine sank, because the light D-37 diesel fuel carried by K-129 would have been broken up by sea surface motion and evaporated in a few days. The heavy plutonium particles mixed in the oil would have then dropped to the seabed. Thus, the oil slick had not moved far from the wreck site when it was discovered.

This dangerous radioactive waste would have completely dissipated from the surface into the ocean before making landfall. There probably never was a great risk of contamination from the oil and fissile material, because the fishery in that area was inhabited by schools of pelagic fish that did not feed or spawn on the ocean floor. The long-term effects of radioactive contamination were not as well documented in 1968 as they are today. The University of Hawaii probably believed the contamination posed no health risk to the local human population or the ecology of this pristine wildlife area. Moreover, it is unlikely the oil slick could have been contained, even if its presence had been known by the public.

However, there is evidence that the U.S. government appreciated the university's cooperation. Almost immediately after the incident, the university's oceanographic programs began receiving Navy research grants and contracts it had long sought. Within two months of discovering the oil spill, the school had acquired the kind of research ship it had always wanted. A remodeled Admiral-class Navy minesweeper was outfitted as a research ship and rechristened the R/V *Mahi*. The 184-foot ship, twice the size of the university's small research yacht, was leased from the Dillingham Corporation. Dillingham Corporation, with extensive facilities in the Hawaiian Islands, had performed work under numerous contracts for the Navy and other government agencies. Within three years, the university's oceanographic research program was able to acquire, again through a charter with a private company, the modern 156-foot research vessel *Kana Keoki*. This deep-sea research ship was specially designed for ocean expeditionary work.

It was imperative that the *Teritu*'s discovery of the oil slick be kept secret for the DIA's clandestine search and exploitation of the Soviet submarine. It was equally important that the location of the Soviet submarine's wreckage remain hidden from the searching Soviet navy. The research vessel's sampling of the radioactive oil slick, if publicized, would have jeopardized the secret recovery operations before they were launched.

This vital piece of intelligence proved that the K-129 sank far closer to Hawaii than the government was ever to reveal. The oil slick sample returned by the *Teritu* proved that the source of the radiation could only have been from a smashed Soviet ballistic missile warhead. Thus, the boat's logs had to be suppressed, and its crew sworn to secrecy.

More than thirty years after the incident, spokespersons for the University of Hawaii claim they have no idea what happened to the ship's deck logs. The *Teritu*'s crew and scientists who were aboard at the time refused to be interviewed about their discovery. The crew members of the research ship were compelled by federal agents to sign confidentiality agreements, never to discuss the voyage that discovered the radiated oil slick off the Hawaiian Islands.

11

IN THE EARLY MONTHS OF 1968, the U.S. Defense Intelligence Agency was already reeling under crushing caseloads resulting from North Korea's seizure of the USS *Pueblo* on January 23, and North Vietnam's unexpected massive Tet Offensive launched at the end of February. The new K-129 assignment was added to its intelligence-gathering burden because the mysterious behavior and sinking of the Soviet missile submarine near Pearl Harbor set off alarm bells in Washington.

The Pentagon wanted to know why a Soviet submarine went missing so close to America's strongest Pacific asset, and the DIA was tasked with providing answers without delay. With its operatives and analysts already overextended, the agency reached into the U.S. Navy's pool of scientific talent to draft a small team of deep-sea experts for the job. The man named to head the team was one of the Navy's best and most experienced civilian underseas experts, Dr. John Piña Craven.

The Navy had recently established a special unit known as the Deep Submergence Systems Project (DSSP). The unit's mission was to develop underseas surveillance equipment and systems for the exploration and exploitation of the deepest parts of the sea. Dr. Craven, an oceanographer and engineer who had served as chief scientist on the highly successful Polaris submarine missile program, was the unit's director.

The expertise of the DSSP members selected for the K-129 project was tailor-made for the challenge at hand. Dr. Craven was immediately called to Washington for a consultation. The project would be coordinated by Admiral Philip A. Beshany, one of the Navy's top submarine sailors.

The team's first task was to find the wrecked K-129 without the Russians or anyone else knowing that the U.S. Navy was even looking for it. When a quick review of the scanty information about the submarine revealed its peculiar behavior before sinking, U.S. naval intelligence had reason to be concerned about its mission. The ballistic missile submarine had been operating far too close to vital American defense facilities. This latest incident was too similar to some aspects of the sneak attack on Pearl Harbor to be ignored.

The fact that the Soviet search-and-rescue ships were in the wrong place—coming no closer than four hundred miles from the general vicinity where the U.S. Navy believed the submarine had sunk—only added to the Americans' worries. In the atomic age, a navy with nuclear warships was supposed to know exactly where its submarines were operating at all times. The very idea that a nuclear-armed submarine was lost was cause enough for an urgent response.

As the Soviets' futile search stretched into weeks, the admirals of two great navies grew increasingly worried, but apparently did not notify each other or ask for assistance. The Soviets in Vladivostok and Moscow were heartsick at the prospect that one of their submarines might have carried nearly one hundred sailors and officers to their deaths. Beleaguered American admirals feared the worst about the odd behavior of an enemy missile carrier in their own backyard.

But the American and Soviet admirals' unease and frustration over the fate of K-129 were no doubt dwarfed in comparison to the rising fears of a small group of men in the Kremlin with no obvious connection to naval matters. The lost submarine had not done what it was expected to do, and a monstrous scheme with potentially earth-shattering ramifications had begun to unravel on the day K-129 was reported missing.

Another incident, which at first seemed unrelated to the K-129 loss, further complicated the developing life-and-death drama unfolding in the North Pacific. A Japanese spy, operating undercover near a U.S. Navy facility on Honshu Island, observed a damaged American submarine put into port on March 17. The American attack submarine USS *Swordfish* sailed into the huge U.S. Navy base at Yokosuka, needing repairs. The submarine was apparently not attempting to hide the damage to its conning tower, since it entered the navy yards at the mouth of Tokyo Bay, on the surface, in broad daylight.

At first, the spy's report to his KGB handlers in the Soviet embassy in Tokyo was passed off as another piece of routine intel. The Soviets received reams of daily reports from spies working the scores of American bases and camps in the Japanese Islands. Japan's openly democratic society provided a plethora of intelligence opportunities for the Soviets during the years of the Cold War. A large Communist Party organization flourished in Japan, fueled by growing anger with the American occupation since the end of World War II. While it was no longer billed as an occupation, America maintained a huge army, navy, and air force presence throughout the island nation.

What finally grabbed the attention of the Soviet intelligence agents about the *Swordfish* report was the timing: The American submarine had entered port only a few days after K-129 went missing. Soviet naval intelligence quickly seized on this tidbit to make the erroneous assumption that the Americans were complicit in the loss of their submarine. This fallacious interpretation of human intelligence became one of the enduring myths of the K-129 incident and may have led to a horrific act by the Soviet navy—the revenge sinking of an American submarine two months later, in another part of the world.

Retired admiral Ivan Amelko, commander of the Soviet Pacific Fleet in the late 1960s and early 1970s, was the first high-ranking Soviet naval officer to make the charge that the U.S. Navy had caused the sinking of K-129 and the deaths of ninety-eight Soviet seamen. He claimed an American submarine had crashed into the Soviet sub while shadowing it in the North Pacific. He said he had learned that the American attack submarine *Swordfish* had made "entry to the Japanese naval base at Yokosuka for cosmetic repairs" from a local Japanese newspaper. This was obviously a clumsy attempt to hide the fact that Japanese spies were active in the area.

The widely held theory that K-129 was sunk by an American submarine became gospel for Soviet mariners, who still cling to this story today. Another former Soviet officer, Admiral Viktor A. Dygalo, claimed to have seen wreckage photographs showing an opening in the bottom of the doomed Soviet boat that could only have been caused by the *Swordfish's* conning tower ramming and punching a hole in its hull.

In reality, the ramming of K-129 by the American submarine as the cause of the sinking is not only implausible, but technically impossible.

Had the conning tower of a submerged submarine come in forceful contact with the hull of a Soviet Golf-type submarine, both boats would have suffered severe damage. When 12.5 million pounds of steel—the approximate combined weight of the two submerged submarines—crashed together in the high-pressure environment of the sea, the damage would have been catastrophic to both boats.

The Golf's hull along the central section of the boat was heavily reinforced with a huge steel keel to support the weak section created by extending the design of the German U-boat to accommodate the missile tubes. The reinforced bottom of the K-129 was its strongest area.

On the other hand, the conning tower on the USS *Swordfish* was the weakest and most vulnerable part of that submarine. It was not designed to take the force of an impact. Such a collision would have caused far more damage to the *Swordfish* than was reported by the Japanese spy.

A second fact refutes the Soviet theory about the involvement of the American boat in the K-129 disaster. The USS *Swordfish*, which was based at Pearl Harbor, would certainly not have sailed thousands of miles from the site of the K-129 to Yokosuka, Japan, for emergency repairs, when its home port was less than four hundred miles away.

The *Swordfish*, commanded by Captain John T. Rigsbee, had slight damage to its periscope housing and upper conning tower. Captain Rigsbee had the repairs done at Yokosuka so he could quickly return to his mission. The U.S. Navy will not reveal exactly what that mission was, but it is reasonable to surmise it had something to do with surveillance of Communist activities surrounding the recently pirated intelligence ship, USS *Pueblo*. The Americans had assigned every available asset to determine what the North Koreans were doing with the captured ship.

The *Swordfish* was regularly assigned to monitor Soviet and North Korean naval activity in the Sea of Japan and Sea of Okhotsk north of Japan. The Americans claimed the damage to the submarine resulted when it struck a small iceberg during one of its routine patrols.

"While on patrol on March 2, 1968, the USS *Swordfish* collided with pack ice," an American diplomat informed the Russian government in an official communiqué, years later. "She returned to Yokosuka on March 16 and subsequently entered dry-dock for repairs. However, on the eleventh [sic] of March when the Golf class submarine sank, the *Swordfish* was over 2,000 miles away from the Golf's position."

At the time there was ample reason—beyond merely

looking for someone else to blame—for the Soviet admiralty to suspect U.S. Navy involvement in the disappearance of its boat. By the late 1960s, American and Soviet submarines routinely challenged one another for dominance of the deep in deadly games of hide-and-seek. Frequently the games turned more aggressive and became tag matches.

"There have been numerous near collisions involving ships of the U.S. Navy and the Soviet fleet," complained a CIA intelligence report, dated January 27, 1968. "The harassment tends to be more severe when U.S. ships are operating in areas the Soviets feel are 'their' waters, such as the Sea of Japan."

In a few cases, the games turned even more dangerous, when boats deliberately came too close and roughly collided. The American equipment was stealthier and the American crews more cocky. Their tactics enraged the Soviet submarine officers. At one point in the Cold War, the Soviet navy commander in chief, Admiral Sergey Georgievich Gorshkov, became so irate at a U.S. sub tailing one of his submarines that he reprimanded his boat's skipper for not ramming the brazen American. The incident took place in the Barents Sea between the K-19 and the USS *Nautilus*. The American boat was caught in a vulnerable position. It would have sunk if the captain of the K-19 had rammed it, while the Soviet boat would have only been damaged.

Admiral Gorshkov was a strong proponent of the underseas competition between American and Soviet submarine crews. The dangerous contests were not all games. These aggressive maneuvers were considered valuable practice for real underseas warfare when and if the Cold War turned hot. The admiral would not have hesitated to demand an eye for an eye if he believed that one of his submarines had actually been sunk by an American in the course of playing this deadly game.

A hard-line survivor of Stalin's purges of the military, Gorshkov was nevertheless a pragmatic naval disciplinarian, not a political fanatic. He would not have tolerated a submarine commander in his elite corps who dared make a decision to launch a sneak attack on an American city without authorization. Though the gruff-speaking admiral would have ordered a total launch against scores of American targets at once, he would never have conspired in or countenanced a rogue attack without specific and verifiable orders from his superiors in the Kremlin.

Gorshkov was in charge of General Secretary Brezhnev's massive naval buildup, particularly the rapid expansion and upgrading of the submarine force. Under the admiral's leadership, the Soviet navy built the largest submarine force in the world, with nearly five hundred underseas craft of all types.

Neither the Americans nor the Russians had forgotten the troubled months following the Cuban Missile Crisis. It had been fewer than six years since that near-nuclear confrontation. Many Soviet naval leaders believed their politicians had blinked and brought shame on the Red Fleet. Ballistic missile submarines, including Golf-type submarines, had been ordered to Cuba. But the crisis was resolved by Khrushchev's withdrawal of nuclear missiles from the Cuban island before the Soviet boats could leave their bases. Only attack submarines reached Cuban waters, and these crews were forced to the surface by constant American antisubmarine warfare harassment.

The Americans had won every encounter in the seas surrounding Cuba, and the Soviet submarine force—which consisted entirely of attack submarines—had tucked tail and run for home. Admiral Gorshkov never forgot or forgave the American Navy for this humiliation, and like many military leaders in the Soviet Union, he was particularly angry with Khrushchev for caving under American naval threats.

This lingering hostility toward the U.S. Navy in the top ranks of the Soviet admiralty was further inflamed by the loss of K-129. The growing animus could well have led to another maritime tragedy involving an American sub in the Atlantic, a few weeks after the K-129 disappeared.

Dr. Craven's team had barely begun the hunt for K-129, when they were ordered to shift attention from the Hawaiian waters to a more urgent priority—finding another submarine that had gone down without a trace. This time it was an American attack submarine, and the site of the disappearance was an ocean away.

The USS Scorpion had been sailing from a lengthy deployment in the Mediterranean to its home port at Norfolk when it was diverted to investigate a strange assembly of Soviet warships near the Azores in the eastern Atlantic. The Scorpion disappeared on May 24, 1968, while returning from that clandestine mission. Speculation was rampant among submariners in both the United States and the Soviet Union that the Scorpion had been sunk by a Soviet torpedo.

As U.S. intelligence pondered the best method to locate the K-129 in the Pacific, the Navy began a search for the *Scorpion* in the Atlantic. After Dr. Craven worked out the likely area where the *Scorpion* might have been lost, the oceanographic research ship *Mizar* was assigned to find it—an operation that was closely monitored by the Soviets. Dr. Craven did not wait for searchers to find the missing American sub, which would ultimately take five months. He returned to the Pacific and supervision of the search for K-129.

Even after the *Scorpion* wreckage was located, the cause remained a mystery, and officially the reason for the sinking was listed simply as "mechanical failure." To this day, articles in Russian publications and on Internet sites suggest that the Soviets deliberately sank the *Scorpion* in an act of revenge for the Americans' sinking of the K-129.

It was in this hostile environment of suspicion and intrigue that the K-129 incident unfolded. American and Soviet intelligence agencies joined in a clandestine competition to discover and hide the secrets of one of the greatest mysteries in maritime history.

12

THE DEFENSE INTELLIGENCE AGENCY was focused on Soviet naval secrets in its assignment to locate and exploit the wreck of the submarine K-129. The sunken submarine had carried valuable technology: a ballistic missile guidance system, nuclear warheads, and communications codes and encoding equipment. The DIA's ambition to score an intelligence success was driven by the bitterness over the North Koreans' high seas piracy of the USS *Pueblo* and plunder of that boat's secrets. The Americans also knew the Soviets had been the primary beneficiaries of that international crime because Soviet intelligence agents had been seen on satellite images swarming over the *Pueblo*.

The intelligence hunt for K-129 quickly became the most carefully guarded secret of the Cold War. Only those naval officers and civilians directly involved in the search were told of the operation, and then only on a need-to-know basis.

From the outset, U.S. military intelligence agents were fairly sure the missing Soviet boat was a Golf-type submarine. The U.S. Navy had intermittently tracked it since its departure from the Rybachiy base in late February. The mechanics of that upgraded World War II–style, diesel-electric submarine were of little or no intelligence value, but the submarine was known to have sophisticated missile weaponry aboard. The Navy needed to decide first if the project had a chance of succeeding, then if the weapons secrets were worth the cost and commitment of scarce resources required to recover or photograph them.

As far as the Office of Naval Intelligence was concerned, the answer to both questions was a resounding yes.

A comment leaked to the *Washington Post* by someone in the naval intelligence community who worked on the K-129 project indicated how important it was to the Navy. The unidentified source told reporter Thomas O'Toole, "The lost submarine was a rare opportunity to get warheads and coding devices, either of which . . . would be in the gold mine category of an espionage find."

Captain James F. Bradley, Jr., the Office of Naval Intelligence's leading submarine expert, encouraged the Navy to commit resources for the project. He had worked closely with Dr. Craven and the DSSP group to retrieve dummy warheads and other paraphernalia dropped into the oceans from Soviet missile tests. The retrieval of operational missiles, complete with guidance and control systems like the three that were on the Golf submarine, could be a priceless intelligence coup. Captain Bradley and civilian scientist Dr. Craven easily convinced Admiral Paul H. Nitze, then secretary of the Navy, to support the recovery effort. The military phase of the K-129 hunt was launched in late April 1968.

A review of satellite and SOSUS recordings had identified a general area of ocean between 350 and 400 miles northwest of Pearl Harbor, but the exact location of the wreck was far from clear. The K-129 sank in deep water, more than three miles down. Because the submarine had been cruising on the surface at approximately two knots when the explosions took place, the doomed boat could have traveled miles on a descending angle before coming to rest on the seabed.

A deep-sea reconnaissance vessel could not begin the search until the wreck site was better defined. Even with a more precise location, it would require long days, even weeks, for a search vehicle to scan the murky depths for the wreck of a lone submarine. Dr. Craven and his team from the Deep Submergence Systems Project knew the difficulty from firsthand experience. They had experienced both successes and failures in locating Soviet hardware from missile tests. Success in such searches depended as much on interpreting the monitoring records as on the search itself.

There were gaps in the SOSUS tracking records the Navy had produced for the K-129's journey to the mission box. The submarine had gone silent after its last snorkeling maneuver on March 6 was recorded. It disappeared from the SOSUS track for a time; then the tapes showed two small and one large blip on the continuous paper printout. The disturbances had come during the night of March 7. The area where the blips occurred covered as much as thirty square miles.

The team secured SOSUS printouts from listening stations at Midway Island and Adak in the Aleutians, to compare data with the record from Hawaii. Intercepts from Hawaii and Midway would have been strong, while the Adak recordings would have been faint. Dr. Craven had created a hydrophone data triangulation methodology to narrow down the location of a sound emitted from vast areas of the ocean.

Next, the U.S. Navy team asked for assistance from other entities involved in some of the most clandestine intelligence work in the American spy arsenal. In the mid to late 1960s, the U.S. Air Force and National Security Agency were already covering much of the earth's surface with satellite-borne surveillance equipment. Though sky spying is still very much a vital part of U.S. national defense efforts, American satellite intelligence remains among the nation's most guarded secrets. Little information of significance has ever been declassified.

However, there have been published acknowledgments that satellite spy photography was used in the search for the K-129 site. A number of U.S. Air Force and intelligence spy satellites were operational in that period. The hyper-secret spy camera orbiter, code-named Corona, was at its prime from May 1966 to February 1971. During that time, the Corona covered 750 million square miles of earth with precision photographs that could identify, on land and sea, objects as small as five feet in diameter.

Another, and probably the most likely, source of satellite intelligence that could have been used to pinpoint K-129's location at the time of the explosion was a dual-purpose program that disguised orbital spies as part of the Defense Meteorological Satellite Program—ostensibly for weather forecasting. This system, code-named TIROS, began in 1965, and employed heat-reading infrared, multispectral scanners that could both track the heat in storms and pinpoint the heat trails of missile launches, from ignition and liftoff through the complete flight of the missile. The TIROS, which employed a television infrared observation satellite, eventually led to the development of today's civilian weather satellites.

These satellites were in constant orbit over the earth's oceans, as well as the landmasses of Europe and Asia. In 1968, a Pacific Ocean–orbiting TIROS would have easily spotted and recorded the heat generated by the missile explosion in the middle of the cool waters of the northern Pacific. The Soviet submarine would have had to be riding on the surface at the time of the mishap for the infrared television camera to detect the heat image.

There were other specialized satellite spy programs during the height of the Cold War, and any one of these could have been the source of satellite intelligence the team used to pinpoint where the K-129 sank. The Discoverer and SAMOS programs conducted continuous photo-reconnaissance missions during this period. The MIDAS program was designed specifically to detect missile launches and provide early warning that Soviet or Chinese missiles had left their launch pads. The MIDAS sensors picked up the specific spectrum of light given off by the combustion of the liquid fuel that propelled Soviet rockets. If the K-129 explosion were spotted by a MIDAS satellite, there would have been no doubt that a Soviet missile was involved.

While there has been no official confirmation that a spy satellite was used in locating K-129, there have been a number of clues in recent publications that a final location was determined by the glow on a satellite photograph. Satellite imagery, along with SOSUS data, and the site of the oil slick discovered by the University of Hawaii research vessel *Teritu*, provided Dr. Craven's team with enough information to make an educated estimate about the location of the Soviet submarine when it started its death journey to the bottom of the sea.

The bottom of the sea was where the wreck would have to be found, and the U.S. Navy had several ways to go down and take a look.

Navy intelligence was reasonably sure that K-129 had sunk approximately sixty to seventy miles north of a large reef that ran between the barren Necker and Nihoa islands in the Hawaiian Leewards. Still, secrecy was imperative. Even though the area was not on any regular shipping lanes and was approximately 360 miles from Honolulu—considerably closer to the inhabited Hawaiian islands of Niihau and Kauai—Soviet commercial freighters and spy ships disguised as fishing trawlers were always on the prowl. They spied as close to American territory as they dared without creating confrontations with Navy ships from Pearl Harbor.

The presence of these Soviet ships prevented the Navy from calling on its workhorse oceanographic ship for the search. The Navy's premier deep-sea research ship, the surface vessel USNS *Mizar*, was not considered an option by the DIA because of this overriding requirement to keep the K-129 operation a secret from the Soviets. The Americans also operated two small deep-sea submersibles, the *Alvin* and *Trieste*, but these had to be controlled from a mother ship riding on the surface.

The 266-foot *Mizar* had been converted from an ice-breaker/cargo ship to a research ship with deep-submergence support capability in 1963. Later, in order to provide a cover story for the method used to find the K-129, the Navy leaked a story that the *Mizar* had actually located K-129. That never happened, because the DIA knew all too well that the Soviets kept a particularly close eye on *Mizar*, and any operation in which it was involved was bound to draw attention.

Dr. Craven's Deep Submergence Systems Project had recently acquired just the right boat for the K-129 mission. It was a converted guided-missile submarine that had been conducting covert operations, including locating and recovering Soviet test missile parts from the seabed in the Pacific.

The boat was the USS *Halibut* (SSGN-587). Before it was converted to serve as a spy vessel, *Halibut* was already a unique submarine. It was the first submarine to have been designed exclusively as a launch platform for guided missiles. The weapon was a cruise missile called the Regulus, which served as a primary sea-launch deterrence system in the early 1960s. The 350-foot submarine was commissioned in 1960, and as a warship had a regular complement of eighty men. It was propelled by a nuclear reactor.

When the Regulus short-range missile system became obsolete because of the Navy's rapid deployment of the sea-launched Polaris ballistic missile system, the *Halibut* faced early retirement. Then Dr. Craven learned of the submarine's peculiar design characteristics and saw the boat not as a rusting candidate for the scrap-iron heap but as a thing of beauty.

The *Halibut* had a large, watertight bay—twenty-eight feet wide by fifty feet long by thirty feet high—built inside the hull to store the five Regulus cruise missiles it carried on war patrol. This area was accessible through a twenty-foot-wide deck hatch. Most submarines had tiny hatches designed for passage of men and small equipment. Everything that made the hump-backed boat noisy in the water and ugly to the combat submariner made it perfect for the deep-sea spies in Dr. Craven's squad.

The Navy's underseas scientists had leaped at the chance to have their own submarine. The *Halibut* was redesignated as an attack submarine to cover its true mission and sent to Pearl Harbor shipyards for major overhaul. At the shipyards, the conversion was conducted in complete secrecy. The submarine's large missile storage room was changed into a seagoing den for spies that became appropriately known as the "bat cave." It was so nicknamed because a pair of flarings used to streamline the large missile-room hatch resembled bat ears or horns, giving it the appearance of the secret entrance to Batman's headquarters in the popular comic book series.

The large bay was filled with scientific equipment, computers, a photographic darkroom, television monitoring screens, and a storage space for twelve-foot-long, deep-sea probes called "fish." In the center of the bat cave were giant spools and winches that could dispense seven miles of steel cable from which the fish were suspended. The fish had strobe lights and cameras, to explore deep holes in the ocean and televise and film objects with a high degree of quality. A watertight well in the room was designed to drop the fish beneath the submarine, while the mother boat cruised, unseen, hundreds of feet below the surface of the sea. The *Halibut* could operate at depths of approximately six hundred feet, but its fish tethered on a cable could roam miles deep, to the very bottom of the ocean.

The submarine was modified with side thrusters that could hold the boat motionless during tricky underseas operations, or maneuver the boat precisely above its target. The *Halibut*'s full capabilities remain top-secret. Its towed fish may have had grasping devices that could snatch small items and bring them up to the submarine. By the 1960s, the Navy was using small, deep-sea vehicles that could be towed or operated remotely from mother ships to retrieve almost anything from the sea floor. The robots could cut or blast through steel without damaging the contents of a sunken airplane or boat.

There were other devices mounted on small underseas rovers that could grasp and lift items from inside a wreck. It is not know if the *Halibut* had one or more of these sophisticated robots aboard at the time it exploited the K-129. However, had the crew been ordered to salvage some specific equipment from the wreck, the Navy's scientists could have quickly customized the required device and shipped it to the *Halibut*.

By early summer, USS *Halibut*, under the operational command of Captain Clarence Edward Moore, was ready to begin the hunt for the lost Soviet submarine. As special project officer, Lieutenant Commander John H. Cook III was in charge of the operations conducted from the bat cave. The submarine had a crew and scientific/spy staff of ninety-nine.

The *Halibut* finally set out from Pearl Harbor in the second week of July 1968. By then, K-129 had been down for more than four months, and the Soviets had given up on their major search activities far to the north of the search site where Dr. Craven sent the American spy submarine. It would have made little difference if a few Soviet search ships were in the area because they could not have detected what the *Halibut* was doing, anyway.

The Soviets did not learn that the United States had any submarines with such deep-sea espionage capabilities until near the end of the Cold War, in 1990. The Navy's spy-submarine operations, which would become extensive during the 1970s and 1980s under the clandestine Development Group One program, was one of the best-kept secrets of that era. The American public was also astonished when it first learned of the exploits of this silent service in the late 1990s. Sweeping revelations of a largely unknown branch of the U.S. Navy were made public for the first time in the book *Blind Man's Bluff: The Untold Story of American Submarine Espionage*, by Sherry Sontag, Christopher Drew, and Annette Lawrence Drew.

But in 1968, the deadly serious business of deep-ocean espionage that was already taking place would have seemed like science fiction to both the Soviets and most Americans, who were not privy to such operations. Submariners serving on boats such as *Halibut* were exploring and exploiting deep oceans, just as the astronauts and NASA's strange vehicles were exploring space. The biggest difference between the space program and the undersea program was that the space program was highly publicized, while no one would know about the exploits taking place in the oceans for another two decades.

Stealth was the most important asset of the *Halibut* as a spy sub. It could glide silently in a search area, then launch and recover its fish while still submerged. A complete operation could be performed successfully without the Soviets' knowing the Americans were even interested in their lost craft. Another advantage of this spy boat over the surface vessels was that it operated in calm underseas water, below the heaving, storm-tossed surface. This enabled the submarine to work for weeks without interruption from the weather.

The *Halibut* arrived on the search site in mid-July 1968 and deployed its fish through the well in the bat cave at the heart of the operations center. The search device was lowered three miles down, to begin the painstaking process of examining the ocean floor in quadrants. The area to be searched was between 16,191 and 16,381 feet deep. It was part of the vast abyssal plain that stretches between the Hawaiian Ridge of the Leeward Islands and the North Hawaiian Seamounts. This underseas terrain comprises the southwest range of the Musicians Seamount that K-129 had traversed on its way to the launch area months before.

The *Halibut's* special operations crew sat for hours that turned into days and then weeks, staring at the monitors as the probe's images of the primordial ocean floor were revealed in rhythmic flashes of the strobe light. One crewman on the *Halibut* mission said the assignment was like looking for a baseball in a large field at night, using a penlight. The customized submarine trolled back and forth across the target area, towing its camera at the end of miles of cable. The specially trained crews had to be rotated frequently from the hypnotic monotony of peering at the monitor screens, visually searching the ocean bottom for any man-made objects in a zone nearly devoid of natural life.

On this mission the *Halibut* had no limitations or time schedules, working continuously around the clock from the beginning of the assignment. The specialists operating the equipment were not told that their target was another submarine. There was very little to see in this lightless, cold world where pressures were so great that most man-made items would be crushed, and only the rarest biota could survive. The bright flashes of the strobes mounted on the *Halibut*'s fish were the first to light up the black gloom in the eons since sediment layers on the ocean floor had formed.

The USS *Halibut* found the Soviet sub in mid-August. The naval intelligence team working in the bat cave immediately focused its highly sophisticated cameras on gathering as many precise photographs as possible to help determine what had happened to the sunken boat.

The technicians' first views of K-129 came with an eerie discovery. Its effect on the *Halibut* crew, themselves all experienced submariners, can only be imagined. After weeks of staring at images of the empty ocean floor, the sailors were startled to see a skeletal human face. A corpse dressed in a raglan-style sheepskin coat and heavy storm boots came into focus on the monitors in the dark bat cave. His cold-weather gear indicated he had been outside when the disaster occurred. He had ridden the sinking submarine down to the bottom of the ocean, where his body was thrown clear of the wreckage.

A dramatic account of this discovery was written from an eyewitness interview in *Blind Man's Bluff*. That narration poses the question of why the figure had been reduced to a skeleton.

"Bones, a bare skeleton—by all accounts, that should have been impossible," the *Blind Man's Bluff* authors wrote. The authors further note that, although experts believed there was nothing to eat the flesh from a corpse at this depth, the eyewitness claimed to have seen "carnivorous worms" around the body.

Later, a number of sources pointed out that, because of a lack of oxygen at this great depth of more than three miles, the other bodies in the submarine were in such good condition that their ages and ethnic characteristics could be determined.

The fact that there was no skin on the face and hands of the sailor discovered lying outside the submarine's hulk became one small clue in solving the mystery of the submarine's demise. But at the time, the men staring at the monitors knew only that they were witness to the grotesque scene of a Russian sailor's final resting place.

Of greater significance to the *Halibut* crewmen monitoring the cameras at the wreck site was the visible damage to the aft section of the submarine's conning tower where it joined the deck. The eyewitnesses told the authors of *Blind Man's Bluff* what a number of other sources who later had access to photographs of the damage have confirmed: The Soviet submarine suffered a devastating wound behind the conning tower in the immediate proximity of missile tube number one.

The *Halibut* crew and intelligence team took more than twenty-two thousand photographs of the wreckage. They were able to gather such valuable intelligence because K-129 broke apart on impact, and its interior was exposed for the probe to explore. The myth later circulated by the CIA that K-129 lay intact on the ocean floor has been shattered by careful examination of bits and pieces of leaked information.

The submarine had broken into four or five large sections, most likely torn apart at the compartment joints where the hull structure was the weakest. It had hit the floor of the sea at very high speed, building forward momentum in its long descent. Since the compartments were torn open, the *Halibut*'s probe could easily be maneuvered to photograph far inside each section of the submarine. The fish was able to take close-up pictures of every operational aspect of the boat and get a firsthand look at the remains of the crew, to help analysts determine what happened in the last minutes of K-129's mission.

After nearly a month of photographing, probing, and possibly even plundering small items from the wreckage, the USS *Halibut* sailed back to Hawaii with a trove of intelligence about the boat, its equipment, and the fate of the crew.

The *Halibut*'s mission to find and recover intelligence from the Soviet sub succeeded beyond the wildest expectations of the DIA team assigned to the project. Somewhere amid the physical evidence recovered and the thousands of clear, close-up photographs taken was proof of the mysterious Soviet sub's clandestine, and probably rogue, mission. But everything the *Halibut* found, and the fact that it was even looking in the first place, remained among the top secrets of the Cold War.

Over the years, many facts about the *Halibut*'s mission to find K-129 have gradually been leaked to the press, but the man in charge, Dr. John Craven, still refuses to reveal exactly how the boat was found or what was discovered. The special project director for the recovery only generalized about some aspects of locating K-129 in his autobiography, *The Silent War*, published in 2001. In more recent interviews, whenever the subject of the exact location of the wreck is raised, he reminds the interviewer that he is under an official lifetime confidentiality oath regarding this operation. His silence, along with the silence of so many others who participated in locating the Soviet submarine, is evidence that the U.S. Navy, the Defense Intelligence Agency, and later the Central Intelligence Agency all had—and still have—some powerful reasons to keep the exact location and other details about the K-129 incident from ever being revealed.

Dr. Craven told a congressional hearing that the mission was completely successful, resulting in the "optimum recovery" of "significant intelligence information concerning the submarine, its mission and its equipment." He later told author William J. Broad (*The Universe Below*): "We milked the submarine dry of really meaningful information."

The evidence had to await analysis that would determine the true magnitude of the find. At the time, the CIA had not yet entered the picture, and the Navy's top priority—beyond learning all that could be known about Soviet submarine communications and ballistic missiles—was to keep the world from discovering the capabilities of their deep-sea research submarine, the USS *Halibut*. The Soviet boat contained largely obsolete equipment and systems, so other motives for exploiting the wreckage were obviously factored into the mission.

The mystery of the K-129 had not yet been solved by one of the most successful clandestine spy submarine missions in the history of the Cold War. The mystery, in fact, had only begun when the *Halibut* brought its treasure trove back to Pearl Harbor in early September 1968.

13

THE USS *HALIBUT* RETURNED to Pearl Harbor on September 9, 1968, triumphant from a harrowing, months-long mission to the bottom of the sea. In keeping with the clandestine nature of its assignment, there were no admirals waiting to shower the officers with laurels, no hula girls to bedeck the sailors with leis. But the success of this mission did not go unnoticed at the top echelons of the United States government.

In little more than a week, *Halibut*'s captain, Commander Clarence Moore, was summoned to Washington to receive the highest peacetime decoration a grateful nation could bestow.

"Commander Clarence Moore has been awarded the Distinguished Service Medal today by the Department of Navy. He will be brought over to the President's Office (the Oval Office) for a strictly off the record ceremony (no press announcement)," Walt W. Rostow, special assistant for national security affairs, told the president in a top-secret memorandum.

The boat and crew were also honored.

Rostow recommended that the USS *Halibut* and its

crew be given the Presidential Unit Citation. The coveted citation and numerous other individual medals and unit commendations were all to be privately awarded; the men receiving the honors were never to show them off. The memorandum recommending the citation stated: "I have been briefed on the substance of this mission. It is being held at the highest order of security in the government."

The Presidential Citation issued to the USS *Halibut* and signed by President Johnson contained a supplementary summary of the recommendation. This summary, which was partially declassified on April 25, 1994, with major details redacted, hinted at the significance of the mission. Portions of the citation read:

> *Recommended by Paul Nitze, the Secretary of the Navy, for the successful accomplishment of a mission of significant scientific and military value to the United States during July and August 1968. [CLASSIFIED].*
>
> *[CLASSIFIED] USS* Halibut *conducted a series of extended submarine operations resulting in successful accomplishment of missions of immeasurable scientific and great military value [CLASSIFIED].*
>
> *[CLASSIFIED] highly technical R&D project of inestimable value to National Interest.*
>
> *[CLASSIFIED] arduous and unrelenting schedule [CLASSIFIED] extraordinarily tenacious team effort [CLASSIFIED] achieved historical firsts of major importance which enhanced the defense capabilities of the United States.*

The demands placed on the men were extraordinary and required a great and sustained physical effort.

[CLASSIFIED] many complicated mechanical, electrical and electronic parts were designed, manufactured and installed.

[CLASSIFIED] required to and continue to maintain strict security cover on all aspects of their special project mission.

In addition to the anonymous commendation to the crew of the *Halibut*, President Johnson and the Navy Department, and later President Nixon, ordered a combined sixty-four secret commendations to Pacific units in the Integrated Underseas Surveillance System. These commendations went to units, officers, and men of the submarines *Halibut*, *Seawolf*, *Parche*, and *Russell*; the SOSUS network; the Boresight radio intercept system; and the spy satellite program. In addition, Dr. John Piña Craven was privately awarded the Navy's Distinguished Civilian Service Award.

Rarely, if ever, have so many meritorious service awards been issued in secret. These silent honors attest to the value of the intelligence that the American defense establishment placed on the coordinated effort to locate and exploit the Soviet submarine K-129. The early fruits of that search-and-recovery effort, while still hidden in the deepest chambers of the DIA and CIA, provided the evidence from which some startling conclusions were later drawn.

*   *   *

The final military intelligence product of this massive effort was a document called a Defense Intelligence Estimate (DIE), which is a military version of the more familiar National Intelligence Estimate (NIE) created today by the CIA.

CIA Director George Tenet described the important role these analyses play in shaping America's national security policy, in a statement issued to the *Washington Post* in August 2003.

"The National Intelligence Estimate remains the intelligence community's most authoritative product. The process by which we produce NIEs . . . has been honed over nearly thirty years. It is a process that is designed to provide policymakers in both the executive and legislative branches with our best judgments on the most crucial national security issues. This process is designed to produce coordinated judgments—but not to the exclusion of differing views or without exposing uncertainties."

Director Tenet pointed out that in recent years the intelligence estimates have been circulated for comment to all the agencies of the intelligence communities, including CIA, DIA, and NSA.

The original intelligence estimate prepared by the DIA on the K-129 sinking was not widely distributed. After it was shared with the White House, it was returned to the inner sanctums of naval intelligence. Subsequent distribution of any information about the K-129 incident, after the Central Intelligence Agency entered the case, was completely restricted to a very small, need-to-know list. Years later, attempts to have the files of the incident declassified were met by unusually intense efforts on the part of the government to keep everything secret. The CIA went to federal court twice to prevent acknowledging that an intelligence estimate even existed.

What was in the DIA's intelligence estimate that made this document such a hot potato? Certainly the intelligence gathered by the *Halibut's* clandestine dive on the wrecked boat was the primary source material. The estimate also contained the recordings and photography from America's most sensitive spy technology. These included submarine tracking reports from the boats that first picked up K-129's sailing from Kamchatka, satellite photography and infrared images from orbiting satellites, acoustical tracking records from the SOSUS network in the Pacific, and radio-signal intercepts monitored in the elephant cages hidden around the rim of the Pacific.

All this evidence, a large technological mosaic, still had to be woven together into some coherent pattern, a case made, and conclusions reached by human intelligence operatives in the Navy and DIA. One agent, who remains anonymous because of his security oath, and who worked on putting all these pieces together, confirmed that a comprehensive document about the K-129 operations accompanied the best of the thousands of photographic images taken by the USS *Halibut*.

The source would not reveal exactly what the intelligence estimate concluded, but he confirmed some of the elements in the document and the methodology used by the DIA investigators to prepare it.

The U.S. Navy and the Defense Intelligence Agency

conducted the initial inquiry into the K-129 as a military intelligence project, not realizing that their findings might have major geopolitical consequences as well. This being an older submarine and not one of the newer nuclear-powered boats, there was less technology of military value in the wreckage. Thus, the primary interest of the intelligence agents was to determine the cause of the submarine's destruction.

Any chance that the damage had resulted from an American action—intended or accidental—was quickly eliminated. Navy investigators knew no antisubmarine warfare assets had been patrolling from Pearl Harbor on that date, in the immediate area where K-129 had disappeared. So it was clear the damage had resulted from activity on board the boat itself.

The best evidence available to help determine the cause was in the photographs taken by the *Halibut*. The few people who have publicly admitted to having seen all or some of the photos agreed that the prints were extraordinarily good, considering they were made three miles deep in the ocean where only the light from strobes was available for exposure. The pictures covered much of the doomed submarine, including all the outside surfaces and some of the inside areas. It is easy to imagine the detail of photographic coverage of a 324-foot-long ship when twenty-two thousand precisely aimed shots were taken at point-blank range by cameras mounted on the submarine's towed fish. The *Halibut*'s advantage of being able to spend days on a site without interference by weather or snooping Soviet trawlers is clear.

Analysts focused attention on the gaping wound behind the conning tower. There was a ten-foot-wide hole apparently blasted outward from missile tube number one, just above where the sail joined the upper deck.

An eyewitness account of some of the images captured by the fish further describes the damage in the area of the missile tubes. The pipes and wiring inside the first tube were exposed, indicating the missile was completely destroyed. In the second missile tube the warhead was missing, but the missile itself was still intact. In the third tube, the missile and warhead were still in one piece. Considerable damage to the missile casings could have been expected as the submarine plunged into the extreme pressure of the deep. The thin-skinned missiles themselves would have been crushed like tin cans, forcing liquid fuel out in a volatile chemical mixture that might have blown the missile hatch covers off. But the type of damage seen in the photographs could not be explained by the crushing pressure.

If high pressure alone had caused the damage, all the missiles would have been uniformly crushed in the tubes, but the missile components would have remained intact. An explosion beginning in one of the missile tubes, before the submarine's final dive, was the only logical explanation for the type of damage to the missiles and the conning tower described by those who studied the photographs.

The experts had examined the possibility of other accidental causes for an internal explosion, such as an accumulation of gases from recharging batteries. This potential cause was assigned a low probability. If a hydrogen gas buildup from the batteries had been sparked, the resulting damage would not have been at the base of the submarine's conning tower in the vicinity of the launch tube.

Other photographs revealed additional damage to the center bottom of the submarine. In 1995, Admiral Viktor A. Dygalo, former commander of the division to which K-129 belonged, told American author and former U.S. Navy officer Peter Huchthausen that the Soviet investigators had seen photographs that revealed a tear in the bottom of the hull. Admiral Dygalo also served as technical consultant on a television documentary that graphically depicted an explosion in the bottom center of the hull. Photographs taken by the *Halibut* showed that this damage in the hull of the boat was also situated immediately adjacent to the bottom of missile tube one.

The only combustible material in the launch tubes was obviously contained in the missiles, where there was explosive material in the warhead and combustible fuel that propelled the rocket.

The damage seen in the area of the conning tower and hull provided enough evidence to narrow down the probable cause of the catastrophic explosion. Something had to have set off an initial explosion in the high-powered, nonnuclear material surrounding the nuclear core in the warhead. The blast in the warhead then ignited the highly volatile liquid rocket fuel. Since the door to missile tube one was clearly in an open position, an explosion originating in the fuel tanks at the bottom of the missile would have ejected the missile and the warhead out of the tube, thereby avoiding the superstructure damage seen in the photographs. Thus, the initial blast was followed by, not created by, the spontaneous ignition of the rocket fuel.

If the point of origin of the explosion was in the warhead, such an explosion had to have been electronically triggered. Years of missile testing by the Soviets and Americans had proven that most missile accidents ending in catastrophic failure or destruction occurred at or during launch.

The extensive damage in the area adjacent to the missile launch tube could only have been caused by the warhead exploding. The initial blast crushed the missile's fuel tanks, mixing the volatile rocket fuel and creating a massive explosion that tore through the steel walls of the missile tube and the reinforced steel of the outer plates.

The only conclusion that fit the physical evidence seen in the photographs was that missile number one had somehow exploded in the process of a launch attempt. That initial explosion set up a series of events that sank the submarine.

The determination that K-129 had sunk during a launch attempt left other, even more urgent questions unanswered. Had the launch mechanism been triggered accidentally or deliberately? Were the Soviets attempting to eject a malfunctioning missile from the tube, or was there something more sinister in the launch attempt? Considerably more analysis was needed.

During this time of high tension between the Americans and Soviets, any incident in which nuclear weapons were even marginally involved commanded immediate attention at the highest levels of the military. The more intelligence analysts learned from the *Halibut*'s photographs, the more ominous the picture became, and the more urgent their quest for answers.

14

ANALYSIS OF THE PHYSICAL DAMAGE TO K-129 was only the first step in the investigators' probe into the cause and circumstances surrounding its mysterious sinking. Beyond the stunning photographs supplied by the USS *Halibut*, the investigators had a considerable amount of satellite, radio, and electronic intelligence to reconstruct the Soviet submarine's fateful last journey and the possible intentions of those who commanded it.

The DIA analysts used a methodical approach to fill in the blanks where hard intelligence was lacking. The main purpose of the military intelligence document was to make a threat assessment of the K-129 incident. The method of evaluation applied "probability analysis" to each piece of evidence to form a bigger picture of several probable scenarios. For example, the fact that the Navy's radio eavesdroppers had not picked up normal radio dispatches when the submarine crossed the International Date Line, and again, when it entered the mission patrol box, became a weighted factor in the analysis. The absence of regular radio contacts indicated operations on the submarine were not normal; otherwise, the routine radio reports at designated points in the journey would have been sent. Investigators at both Soviet fleet headquarters and Pearl Harbor could therefore determine a starting point of trouble, based on the first missed communication when the submarine crossed the 180th meridian.

Pieces of evidence supporting one scenario or another, such as an accident on board, were assigned a percentage of probability, based on known behavior of a missile submarine operating in that theater. A matrix was created to weight each on a scale from zero to one hundred.

The methodology employed to assign probability was a complex analytical system known as the Bayes' Theorem. This system provides a means to apply quantitative thinking to what is normally called the "scientific method."

In dealing with raw intelligence data where the evidence is circumstantial, as much of it was in this incident, this process allowed the analysts to produce a quasiscientific conclusion on what the mysterious Soviet submarine was doing so near American territory.

The analysis was conducted by the DIA's team, assisted by scientists and military personnel from the submarine special operations unit. Since the only hard data came from the photographic and physical evidence gathered by USS *Halibut* from its dive on the K-129 wreckage, that package of information was central to the exercise.

Areas of inquiry covered in the analysis included: (1) the type and placement of the damage to the submarine's structure; (2) the geographical coordinates of the submarine at the time of sinking; (3) the proximity of that location to an exact longitude and latitude required to program launch data into a missile system; (4) the location and situation of the crew members' bodies found inside the wreckage; and (5) SOSUS tracking, radio interceptions, and satellite data on the maneuvers of the submarine before the sinking.

Since so little hard evidence was available on the K-129's last mission—no decoded communications between the boat and its home base, no human intelligence from the Soviet Union—U.S. analysts relied on this process to interpret the strange events surrounding the sinking of the Soviet submarine near Pearl Harbor.

When all the data came together, the intelligence officers were shocked. The analysis resulted in a finding of "high probability" that the ill-fated Soviet boat was a rogue, and, more stunning, that it was probably intending to launch a nuclear missile against Pearl Harbor at the time of its sinking.

Strong evidence for arguing that the submarine was a rogue was the lack of any follow-up hostile actions against the United States or its Allies by the Soviets in the Pacific or elsewhere. Everything was normal in the Soviet Union. Even if that normalcy included the usual saber rattling and angry bluster, no movement of troops, planes, or ships had been detected. The submarine appeared to be acting alone at the time it sank.

Satellite surveillance of the Soviet Pacific Fleet indicated no increased level of defensive preparations. Likewise, reports from around the world failed to detect increased defensive or offensive preparations anywhere in the Communist bloc.

K-129 was an older-type submarine with only three missiles, as opposed to one of the Soviet navy's newer nuclear-powered boats, which had a dozen or more missiles. This, too, made a sanctioned attack unlikely. An authorized strike by the Soviets would almost certainly have involved one of its more deadly nuclear submarines.

The Americans knew they had been tracking a Golf II missile boat that had sailed from Kamchatka to the general vicinity of the sinking. It was known that this type of boat could launch a missile while submerged— it did not need to surface. However, two pieces of evidence indicated it was on the surface at the time of the explosion. First, a spy satellite had recorded fireballs that could only have been seen if the submarine was on the surface. Second, the *Halibut*'s photography revealed that at least one of the crewmen had been fully clothed in foul-weather gear only worn by someone working outside the submarine. Inside, the submarine would have been uncomfortably hot.

The discovery that there was no skin on the face and hands of the sailor was initially explained as the work of sea creatures. But the skeletal condition of that sailor could just as easily have been caused by exposure to the heat from the fireball when the missile exploded. The fiery blast would certainly have engulfed the bridge area and burned all the exposed flesh in a flash of intense heat.

The boat's location was another enigma.

The fact that K-129 sank several hundred miles closer to Hawaii than the regular Soviet patrol area was considered especially significant and bolstered the case that the boat was operating in an aggressive mode. The submarine was approximately 350 miles northwest of Hawaii, much closer than it needed to be for its missiles to reach Pearl Harbor. The U.S. Navy knew the Golf II's missile range was between 700 and 800 miles.

The location was key to the rogue theory and was supported by the Soviet search area being so far off the mark. The search was concentrated hundreds of miles north of where the Americans knew the boat had sunk, indicating the submarine had been far off its authorized mission course. Along with these known discrepancies in location, the lack of routine radio communications led the investigators to reach a high-probability finding that K-129 was not acting on official orders. Therefore, it had to be classified as a rogue boat.

If it was a rogue, then what was the intent of the crew? Were the captain and crew attempting an unauthorized attack or could they possibly have only been planning to defect? The defection scenario was quickly abandoned because of the explosion in the missile area.

The answer seemed to lie in the submarine's behavior at the time of the explosions and the location of the wreckage. The submarine surfaced and sank at an exact intersection of longitude and latitude, which would indicate that it was necessary to be at such a precise position for a programmed launch to home in on a target.

The U.S. Navy had limited information of Soviet computer technology, but at the time, analysts believed that K-129 would have to travel to an exact, predetermined location to launch its missiles. In all the vast ocean, the likelihood that a submarine would arrive and sink at an exact intersection of longitude and latitude by chance alone was slim to none.

The only logical military target for thousands of miles in any direction was the U.S. Pacific Fleet at Pearl Harbor. The analysis rated the Hawaiian base as the "highly probable" target of the rogue submarine.

The analysis allowed Navy intelligence to be reasonably sure that a nuclear attack had been narrowly averted. The launch attempt could not have been an accident, even though the destruction of the boat itself was most likely an accident. It must have been chilling for the Navy's top intelligence minds to realize that there was absolutely nothing in the nation's arsenal that could have prevented a nuclear strike on American soil by a determined rogue. America had been spared the horror by luck, not by its superior defensive technology. Only a mistake by the would-be perpetrators had prevented a nuclear disaster.

The startling probability analysis, supported by ample photographic and technical evidence, created a new problem. Now that the DIA and Navy had their analysis of the K-129 incident, the question became what to do with such a sensitive document.

The timing of the completed report is important. Information fed into the analysis was not finally collected until late in 1968, more than six months after the submarine disappeared. It was September before the *Halibut* had completed its mission and returned the film and physical evidence to Pearl Harbor.

Though never officially confirmed, the existence of such a top-secret document on the K-129 incident is certain. What has not been revealed until now is that the document or documents concluded there was a "high" to "very high" probability that K-129 was destroyed while attempting to fire a nuclear missile at Pearl Harbor. This document, with its additional finding that the submarine was a rogue, has never been mentioned in any of the documents released by the U.S. Navy or the CIA, according to the anonymous source who worked on the report.

While, at the time, the knowledge that a rogue submarine might have destroyed itself in the act of firing a nuclear missile against an American naval facility and city was alarming, there was apparently no continuing threat perceived. No Code Red alerts were issued; no Strategic Air Command bombers were ordered into the skies.

That does not mean the White House and Pentagon simply ignored the intelligence team's findings. Other circumstances weighed on the official reaction, or lack of public reaction, at the highest levels of government.

The Democratic Party had been in control of the nation's defense for almost a decade, and expenditures for the war in Vietnam were exceeding all budget limits. Congress was in no mood for an expansion of military operations for any reason other than an attack on America itself. Of course, if the educated guesses of the intelligence community were correct, the K-129 incident qualified as such an attack. But there is no evidence that Congress was informed of the incident; at least there has never been a hint of a leak to indicate that any elected officials outside the White House were ever given details about the mysterious sinking of the Soviet submarine.

There are no records in the public domain to indicate when the Navy forwarded the findings to the secretary of defense or the Johnson White House. Certainly there were regular, off-the-record briefings of the White House while the analysis was in progress. The final analysis probably was not completed until very late in 1968, only weeks before Johnson relinquished office.

The Johnson administration had all it could handle in Vietnam, and had come under severe criticism from Republican leaders for failure to respond aggressively to the North Korean seizure of the *Pueblo* a few months earlier. With his war policies under attack from both the left and the right, the president certainly did not welcome the DIA's assessment that a Soviet rogue submarine may have come within seconds of launching an attack against a U.S. city and military installation.

Any rumor of such an attempted nuclear attack would have created extreme panic among an already jittery American public. The country was aflame with anti–Vietnam War sentiment, producing campus riots and huge demonstrations in New York City and Washington. The intelligence estimate concerning the K-129 had to be kept secret for military reasons and concealed from the public for political reasons. Mindful of his already precarious place in history because of the Vietnam War and massive increases in government spending, President Johnson, along with his supporters, wanted the information about K-129 hidden behind a curtain of classification for many years to come, if not forever.

The best way to keep the awful facts buried was to opt for scenarios from the probability analysis that were less dramatic. Thus was born what was to become a massive disinformation campaign by the major agencies of the U.S. government's intelligence community.

Initially there would be two lies permanently embedded in the early findings of U.S. military intelligence. First, the location of the wreckage of K-129 had to be obfuscated. If anything was ever leaked to the press about the incident itself, the site of the sinking had to be placed beyond the maximum range of the type of missiles carried by K-129.

At the time, there was a legitimate military reason to keep the location vague or even misstated: The Navy planned additional recovery trips to exploit the wreckage for more intelligence.

Other than the military men and intelligence agents, only the civilian scientists aboard the University of Hawaii research ship that discovered the oil slick knew there had been an accident involving nuclear material. The defense officials knew the importance of keeping the incident secret. As patriotic Americans in a time of war, the university research crew could also be counted on to keep quiet. They all agreed never to reveal their discovery.

"The captain [of R/V *Teritu*] was asked by our government not to speak of it and he is honoring their request," said an official in the University of Hawaii oceanography department. "The logs are also gone, so there is no record in our possession of the incident."

It must have appeared to the DIA that everything had been done to keep the location secret.

The second piece of disinformation needed for the cover story was the cause of the sinking. That was extracted from the probability analysis itself. While the intelligence team had ranked an attempted missile launch as the cause with highest probability, the second most likely cause was an internal explosion resulting from a buildup of volatile gases. The explosion might have been caused by equipment failure. After all, everyone knew that Soviet submarine technology was notoriously flawed.

If an accident could be blamed for the sinking, there would be few or no repercussions if the story leaked to the press. So the Navy brass and the political appointees in the Defense Department reached down into the probability analysis for a safer explanation: The boat sank from an accumulation of hydrogen, which built up while recharging its batteries. The hydrogen gas explosion became the U.S. Navy's official position on the cause of the sinking of K-129.

That cover story persisted for years, despite overwhelming evidence that submarine hulls, designed to withstand tons of ocean pressure in deep dives, were too strong for an explosive gas buildup to cause enough damage to sink the boat.

The amount of hydrogen gas buildup inside the submarine required to cause an explosion forceful enough to rip the hull open would have been detected long before an explosion of that magnitude could have resulted. That kind of buildup was impossible on this type of boat. Golf submarines were equipped with sensors to monitor just such a gas buildup. The environment in the living compartments was tested every thirty minutes for excess levels of carbon dioxide and hydrogen. Compartments two and five, located above the batteries, each had a flameless heating unit installed in the ceiling, which was designed to automatically vaporize excess hydrogen.

Former Soviet submarine commander and fleet admiral Rudolf Golosov, who commanded the squadron to which K-129 belonged, specifically debunked the gas explosion theory.

"The widely touted hypothesis of battery explosion caused by stored hydrogen can be refuted by the sad experience of such explosions aboard submarines of the world's navies," retired admiral Golosov wrote. "No damage of such magnitude could be inflicted by exploding battery or batteries even to a sub's hull that could operate at depths of 100 meters. The hull of K-129 was vastly stronger because it was designed to safely operate submerged at 300 meters."

Dr. John Craven, the U.S. Navy's former chief underseas scientist, also scoffs at this explanation in his autobiography, *The Silent War.*

"When I read this [hydrogen buildup as a cause of K-129 loss] I could not restrain my sardonic chuckle," Dr. Craven, who was also involved in the probability analysis, wrote about the incident. "I have never seen or heard of a submarine disaster that was not accompanied by the notion that the battery blew up and started it all."

During the years that diesel-electric U-boats and submarines were in operation, there had been countless instances of fires and explosions resulting from hydrogen gas accumulating during recharging of the batteries. It is true that batteries did not behave well when they came in contact with salty ocean water and might explode under some circumstances. However, in all these countless accidents there is no record of such an explosion being powerful enough to tear open the tough skin of a submarine. Submarine hulls, whether single- or double-walled, are built to withstand enormous pressure from diving beneath the weight of the seas.

The *Halibut*'s photographs of the damage, which have been seen by a number of witnesses and reported extensively, further refute the gas explosion theory. In the photographs, the severe damage aft of K-129's conning tower is nowhere near the compartment where the huge batteries were located. Gases leaking from the batteries beneath the decks in compartments two and five would have accumulated in those compartments. Any resulting explosion would have been in parts of the submarine much farther forward or back of the area where the real damage was located.

When the true location of the sinking is linked to the real cause of the K-129's destruction, there can be little doubt about what happened. A rogue submarine from the Soviet Union attempted an attack against the United States on March 7, 1968. Instead of succeeding, the submarine blew up in the process.

The startling and unthinkable conclusion of Defense Intelligence Agency analysts was suppressed in 1968, and has been kept from the public ever since.

15

A WAR-WEARY, LAME-DUCK JOHNSON administration had little time left in office to deal with the implications of an attempted rogue attack on a major American city. Still, the president's war cabinet could not ignore early reports that a lone Soviet submarine had been destroyed near American territory.

The reaction in Washington was swift, decisive, and secretive. A solution to such a threat would be enormously expensive and even then, would be only a stopgap measure. Nothing yet devised by the best technical brains in the land could completely defend against a lone submarine armed with nuclear weapons. But if it ever became public that such an attempt had been made, President Johnson needed to be on record as having done everything in his power to protect the country from such an eventuality. Some type of defense against this hole in America's shield had to be mounted quickly and without arousing congressional uproar or public panic. A ready-made set of plans for a partial missile defense system had been abandoned several years earlier and sat gathering dust on a Pentagon shelf.

The antiballistic missile defense plan, code-named

Sentinel, had been developed in the Pentagon planning offices and on the drawing boards of hopeful defense contractors during the early 1960s.

The limited ABM plan had been abandoned in 1966, because it was determined to be too thin to guard American cities from a long-range Soviet ICBM or massive sea-launch nuclear attack. By the time of the K-129 incident, American intelligence had also changed its threat estimates and concluded that China would not have a sea-launch ballistic missile capability until the 1970s. So in 1968, when the Sentinel program was suddenly reactivated, the China threat was of less concern in the Defense Department. However, DIA analysts then realized that earlier planning to address the threat of an attack by a lone Chinese submarine would also apply as a countermeasure against a rogue Soviet submarine attack. As it became increasingly apparent that K-129 was such a rogue, the China model was dusted off.

Even though the Navy did not know exactly what had occurred in the Pacific northwest of Pearl Harbor on the night of March 7, there was enough early intelligence to cause serious alarm. Analysis of bits and pieces of data from sonar, satellites, and eavesdropping American spy subs suggested that a Soviet submarine had met with disaster in waters far closer to Hawaii than it should have been. Furthermore, the incident involved ballistic missiles and nuclear warheads.

The DIA could have quickly put together enough information to make a reasonable assessment that a hostile action had occurred.

First, a review of the SOSUS network printouts

showed that the Navy had tracked and periodically lost contact with a Soviet ballistic missile submarine that had left Kamchatka late in February. The last SOSUS recordings placed the boat outside its normal mission box and much closer to Hawaii than the usual patrol of this type. Second, the NORAD satellites' late-night recordings on March 7 revealed flashes of radiant light that could have been caused only by burning missile fuel. Third, around the fifteenth or sixteenth of March, the University of Hawaii research ship *Teritu* reported finding an irradiated oil slick drifting off the Hawaiian Leewards. Tests showed the oil slick was composed of diesel fuel of a type used by Chinese and Soviet submarines and fissile material of a type used in Soviet, and possibly Chinese, nuclear warheads.

Finally, on March 21, the sudden sailing of the Soviet Pacific Fleet's search armada provided unambiguous evidence that a ship, probably a submarine, had been lost.

More startling was the fact that the search area was centered hundreds of miles from where the American intelligence placed the explosion. This suggested the Soviets had no idea where their lost submarine was or had been.

These early clues likely provided disturbing hints of an unauthorized, but nevertheless potentially deadly, attempt to launch a nuclear missile in waters near American territory. Under such circumstances the president of the United States would have been briefed immediately. No commander in chief could have failed to respond.

On March 29, 1968, President Johnson issued National Security Action Memorandum No. 369, declaring a national emergency. It read, in part: ". . . the President, under authority granted by the Defense Production Act of 1950, today established the Sentinel Program as being in the highest national priority category."

Ironically, the president had no intention of seeing the deployment of the Sentinel through to completion. He announced two days later, on March 31, that he would not seek reelection. The weight of the office, with its seemingly intractable wartime problems, had finally exhausted President Johnson.

The Sentinel program, which was to replace the Nike X system, called for deployment of ABMs and radar around key coastal cities and strategic missile silos, which could defend against limited nuclear strikes. The document justifying the system specifically cited the potential danger of an attack by the Red Chinese or, more pertinent to the issue at hand, "an unauthorized" submarine attack.

The suddenness of the president's emergency action caught senior congressmen, and even Pentagon officials, off balance. Defense experts have called the unexpected action "curious." The timing could not have been worse for Johnson. He was hoping, for the sake of his place in history, that a strategic arms control and limitation treaty could be signed with the Soviet Union as a parting gift from his lifetime of public service. His hopes of softening his "war president" image would certainly be dashed when the Soviets learned that the United States intended to ratchet up the Cold War by deploying a major new antiballistic missile program.

Strategic Arms Limitation Talks (SALT), in which the Americans and Soviets had been engaged since December 1966, soon collapsed anyway, but not because of the Sentinel initiative. The Soviets led a Warsaw Pact invasion of Czechoslovakia in August 1968. Secretary of State Dean Rusk had warned the Soviets as recently as July 23, 1968, that such an invasion would have a "harmful effect on U.S./Soviet relations," and it resulted in a complete breakdown of friendly exchanges for the rest of Johnson's term.

The declaration of a limited ABM initiative only weeks after defense intelligence detected K-129's strange behavior was powerful evidence of how seriously top leadership took the incident. At a time when inflation was already rampant due to the spiraling costs of the Vietnam War and attempts to roll out huge new domestic programs of the Great Society, the announcement of a costly new defense program was an outrage to the growing antiwar movement. Congress was fighting the White House over every requested increase in war costs, even as the president and his advisors called for the new 960-million-dollar Sentinel program.

The expensive Sentinel ABM system included long- and short-range radar facilities with Spartan and Sprint ground-to-air, antimissile missiles. Initial deployment included installations to protect Boston, Chicago, Dallas, Atlanta, Detroit, Fairbanks, Los Angeles, San Francisco, Seattle, Oahu, New York, and Washington. Other ABM facilities were to be located to protect ICBM silo complexes in Montana, North Dakota, Missouri, and Wyoming.

"The Sentinel System is designed to defend against a

possible deliberate ballistic missile attack by the Chinese Peoples Republic or the accidental launch of a nuclear armed intercontinental missile by any foreign power," explained a letter to a prominent senator from the president's defense planning office.

This letter, which was similar to letters sent to congressional representatives from other locations where the system was to be deployed, was clearly intended to cover up the possibility that a Soviet rogue submarine had come very close to successfully launching a missile against an American city.

Secretary of Defense Robert McNamara had earlier specifically insisted that the Sentinel program be immediately deployed to protect against a future *rogue* Chinese threat. This explanation had to be part of the cover-up, because by this time the U.S. government was reasonably sure that the rogue submarine attempting to launch against the United State's Pearl Harbor naval base was a Soviet Golf II.

Mao's China was widely held in some quarters to be the greatest threat to the United States in the Pacific. However, by 1968, the fear was not about a sneak attack on America, but that China threatened to widen the Vietnam War by land invasion, as it had done in the Korean War in 1950.

The Johnson administration's concern over a Chinese nuclear threat had originally been caused by Red China's test of its first nuclear device in 1964. The increasing frequency of Chinese thermonuclear and ballistic missile testing was closely observed by U.S. spy satellites, leading the Johnson administration to produce a flood of intelligence estimates during the mid-

1960s, warning of the potential for a Chinese sneak attack.

Much of the fear of an emerging new nuclear superpower in the Pacific resulted from a lack of good military intelligence about China's armaments program. This fear was exacerbated by the confusion in the streets of Chinese cities, resulting from the Cultural Revolution and the Red Guards' murderous rampages. The Americans knew the Chinese were rapidly developing the weapons, but did not know who, if anyone, in China had control of the nuclear button.

Initial arguments supporting the Sentinel program were almost all aimed at that specific China threat. A report from the U.S. Defense Research and Engineering Department described "the threat to American and world security posed by the emerging Chinese nuclear capability" as "extremely serious." The report revealed that the Department of Defense (DOD) had intensified efforts to counter short-range submarine-launched ballistic and air-breathing missiles that "may well be the initial Chinese nuclear strategic threat." The report noted that the Red Chinese had fission bombs, a Chinese copy of a Soviet missile submarine, short-range cruise missiles, and an active ballistic missile development program.

During this period, the research staff warned President Johnson that current defense systems were inadequate to cope with an initial Chinese capability composed of submarine-launched ballistic and air-breathing missiles.

President Johnson, early in his presidency, took the Chinese threat so seriously that a preemptive nuclear strike against warhead and missile manufacturing facili-

K-129 photographed off the Russian coast.
(Soviet Naval Archives)

Captain First Rank
Vladimir Kobzar, com-
mander of K-129. He was
in line to be promoted to
a command position at
Soviet fleet headquarters.
(Courtesy of Kobzar family)

Captain Second Rank Alexander Zhuravin, first officer of the K-129. Zhuravin was to assume command of the sub on its next mission.
(Courtesy of the Zhuravin family)

Captain Zhuravin (foreground, center) was a popular officer among his submariners.
(Courtesy of the Zhuravin family)

A Soviet Golf-class sub running on the ocean's surface.
(U.S. Navy photo)

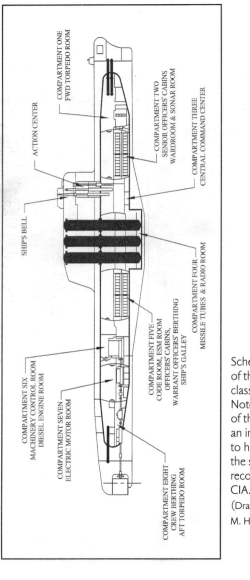

COMPARTMENT ONE
FWD TORPEDO ROOM

ACTION CENTER

COMPARTMENT TWO
SENIOR OFFICERS' CABINS
OFFICERS' WARDROOM & SONAR ROOM

COMPARTMENT THREE
CENTRAL COMMAND CENTER

SHIP'S BELL

COMPARTMENT FIVE
CODE ROOM, ESM ROOM
OFFICERS' CABINS,
WARRANT OFFICERS' BERTHING
SHIP'S GALLEY

COMPARTMENT FOUR
MISSILE TUBES & RADIO ROOM

COMPARTMENT SIX
MACHINERY CONTROL ROOM
DIESEL ENGINE ROOM

COMPARTMENT SEVEN
ELECTRIC MOTOR ROOM

COMPARTMENT EIGHT
CREW BERTHING
AFT TORPEDO ROOM

Schematic drawing
of the K-129, Golf-
class submarine.
Note the location
of the ship's bell,
an important clue
to how much of
the submarine was
recovered by the
CIA.
(Drawing by Christine
M. Haggy)

A submarine commander's view from the bridge of a Soviet sub.
(Soviet Navy photo)

Escape hatches on K-129 were located in the control room and aft torpedo room, as depicted here in a similar sub. (Photo by Frank Parker, with permission of Submarine Attractions Seattle, Inc.)

The forward torpedo room of K-129 was identical in design to the compartment in this Soviet Foxtrot attack submarine. (Photo by Frank Parker, with permission of Submarine Attractions Seattle, Inc.)

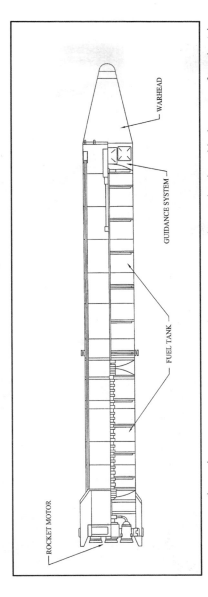

ROCKET MOTOR

FUEL TANK

GUIDANCE SYSTEM

WARHEAD

The Soviet R-21 (SS-N-5) missiles aboard K-129 carried one-megaton nuclear warheads and had a range of nearly eight hundred miles. The CIA most likely retrieved at least one of these missiles. (Drawing by Christine M. Haggy)

Open missile hatch on a Golf submarine.
(U.S. Navy photo)

U.S. Navy intelligence tracked Soviet submarines by intercepting communications between the subs and their headquarters using massive listening stations nicknamed "elephant cages."
(Photo courtesy of Lynn Lee)

The Soviets believed that the USS *Swordfish* sank the K-129 while trailing too closely in a deadly cat-and-mouse game common during the Cold War. But the U.S. attack submarine was two thousand miles away, spying on Soviet naval activity.

(U.S. Navy photo)

Three weeks after K-129 sank, President Lyndon Johnson issued National Security Action Memorandum No. 369, declaring a national emergency and establishing the Sentinel missile program as being "in the highest national priority category."

(U.S. Army photo)

Leonid Brezhnev (left) and Mikhail Suslov (right), who plotted to oust Khrushchev, later became bitter enemies.
(Soviet Archives photo)

Yuri Andropov, disciple of Suslov, was head of the KGB when the K-129 incident occurred. In that capacity, he controlled the special KGB *osnaz* commando units and had access to nuclear weapons.
(Soviet Archives photo)

USS *Halibut* found the wreckage of K-129 three miles deep in the Pacific Ocean.

(U.S. Navy photo)

President Nixon ordered the CIA to retrieve K-129 from the ocean floor. The super-secret *Glomar Explorer* was built especially for this daunting task.

(U.S. Navy photo)

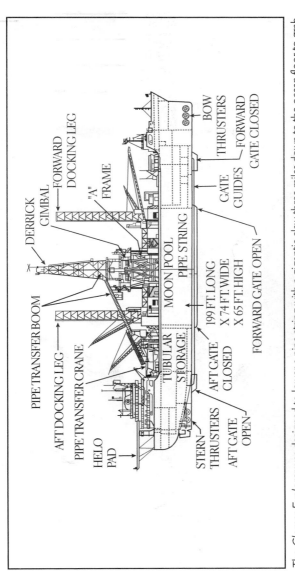

The *Glomar Explorer* was designed to lower a pipe string with a gigantic claw three miles down to the ocean floor to grab sections of the broken K-129 and lift them to the moon pool hidden in the center of the ship.

(Drawing courtesy of *Offshore* magazine)

This ID photo of a Soviet sailor is believed to have belonged to one of the eleven "extra" crewmen placed aboard K-129 shortly before it sailed on its last mission. The photograph was turned over to Soviet navy personnel by the Americans in the early 1990s. The sailor remains unidentified.

(Photo recovered from K-129 by CIA)

President Richard Nixon and Chairman Mao jointly proclaimed China's opening to the West in 1972. The Americans provided military secrets about the Soviets as part of the negotiations leading to this great diplomatic success.

(Courtesy of the Richard M. Nixon Library)

President Gerald Ford had to decide whether the recovery of K-129 should continue in the face of almost certain outrage from Leonid Brezhnev if the mission were exposed. (Photo courtesy of the Gerald R. Ford Library)

The final number of crewmen lost on K-129 was confirmed when the Russian Federation awarded medals to ninety-eight sailors at this memorial service.

(Photo courtesy of the Zhuravin family)

Captain Kobzar's widow, Irina Ivanova (center), and first officer Zhuravin's widow, Irina (right), attended the memorial service to accept their husbands' medals.

(Courtesy of the Zhuravin family)

In 1995, Rear Admiral Viktor Dygalo, K-129 division commander, told author Peter Huchthausen, "The true story of K-129 will never be known." (Soviet Naval Archives)

Irina Zhuravina at the grave of her son Mikhail. Captain Zhuravin's image also appears on the monument, although his body was never returned.

(Photo courtesy of the Zhuravin family)

ties in China was contemplated. A DOD office developed a "worst-case scenario" that envisioned a nuclear-armed China as such a serious threat that it would "be necessary to attack Chinese nuclear weapons facilities as a counter-proliferation measure."

The Pentagon not only feared China's general nuclear capacity, but also specifically expressed concerns that a Golf submarine could carry out an attack. A 1965 technical defense assessment cited the specific type of weapon thusly: "a 350 n.m. [nautical mile] missile, which is the normal armament of the Soviet G-class submarine of which the Chinese have produced one copy."

These intelligence estimates for the period 1964 to 1966 repeatedly warned of the Chinese nuclear threat, and particularly the potential for a sneak attack by a lone submarine on a U.S. city. Most of these intelligence estimates were prepared by advisory panels that included U.S. Navy technical intelligence specialists.

By late March 1967, a U.S. Navy warrant officer, John A. Walker, Jr., who later became infamously known as Johnny Walker Red, was pilfering top-secret defense files and selling them to the Soviets. Some of the plethora of classified documents warned of a sneak attack on America by a nuclear-missile-armed Chinese submarine. The gist of these documents—that the Americans had been obsessively concerned about a Chinese sneak attack—would have been a red flag to the KGB. This intelligence may very well have been the germ for a sinister plot involving the Soviet Golf submarine K-129.

Warrant officer John Walker, a submarine communications specialist working in a sensitive intelligence post at the Navy base in Norfolk, Virginia, had contacted the KGB at the Soviet embassy in Washington and offered to sell America's greatest secrets for cash. The story of the turncoat and his KGB spy ring did not surface until 1985, when the network was exposed. But during the critical period of 1967–68, the Soviets netted some of the most damaging information that Walker was to supply to the KGB. The scope of the spy operation was breathtaking. Not the least of the sensitive information given to the Soviets during this period were the U.S. naval codes used for clandestine communications.

It has been established that Walker provided information that led to the capture of the USS *Pueblo* and the stripping of that American espionage boat of its decoding machines. At first, the U.S. Navy was not too alarmed because the sophisticated equipment was useless without the all-important encryption information needed for the machines to break Navy codes. The U.S. Navy was not aware that Walker had previously supplied these keys to the ciphers, and that the Soviets were already monitoring and decoding communications between American submarines and their headquarters in the Atlantic and Pacific.

American submariners from the Cold War era are especially embittered about the Walker spy case. Many of them suspect that the traitor's stolen secrets resulted in the sinking of the USS *Scorpion*. It is widely believed that the Soviets used the code machines and encryption codes to zero in on and torpedo that boat.

Although the Navy has repeatedly denied that the *Scorpion* was the victim of a Soviet submarine attack, stories persist among both American submariners and former Soviet submariners that the U.S. boat was attacked in retaliation for the sinking of K-129 several weeks earlier. However, two official courts of inquiry have ruled that a malfunctioning torpedo from the *Scorpion* itself was the most likely cause of the sinking.

Walker began delivering classified information from the day he approached the KGB at the Soviet embassy in Washington in March 1967. After the end of the Cold War, his KGB handlers confirmed that the material he provided was particularly impressive because of its high level of secrecy, and that Walker was most prolific during the first months after he began spying, when he was trying to impress his handlers with the value of his services.

The KGB paid Walker millions of dollars for the information he provided. Former KGB general Boris Aleksandrovich Solomatin, who was Walker's handler in the Soviet embassy in Washington, said the American traitor was "the most important" spy the Soviets ever developed. John Walker "gave us the equivalent of a seat inside your Pentagon where we could read your most vital secrets," Solomatin told Court TV.

Oleg Kalugin, another former KGB official whose work with Walker was extensive, confirmed the importance of Walker's spy work. Kalugin, former chief of KGB foreign intelligence, was promoted to the rank of major general because of the extraordinary amount of intelligence gained from the American naval spy.

Kalugin, who became disillusioned with the Soviet system, and was forced out of the KGB in 1990, said in a CNN television documentary that Walker dropped "big brown bags filled with top-secret, classified information" into the hands of the KGB in Washington.

Among the thousands of classified documents Walker delivered to the KGB were certainly some of the extensive files produced from 1964 through 1966, which were replete with warnings about China. It has also been reported that Walker gained access to the U.S. strategic nuclear plan, known as Single Integrated Operational Plan, prepared in 1963 (SIOP 63). One of the scenarios in that supersecret war plan called for devastating nuclear retaliation for a limited sneak attack by a Chinese missile submarine.

This information would have been of great interest to some in the Kremlin who were equally alarmed about the Chinese nuclear threat to the Soviet Union. A Stalinist faction in the Kremlin had agitated for a nuclear attack on the Chinese since 1966, when Mao began a campaign to shift the leadership of world Communism from Moscow to Beijing.

The discovery, in documents turned over to the KGB, that the Americans feared a sneak attack against a U.S. city by a nuclear-missile-armed Chinese submarine was of particular interest to Moscow hard-liners. A radical element in the Kremlin controlled the KGB leadership. Yuri Andropov, who had become chairman of the KGB and a candidate member of the Politburo in 1967, was the most visibly powerful man in the clique. But there was another, more likely leader, operating in the shadows of this group. He was the power broker Mikhail Suslov, who had been behind every palace intrigue in the Kremlin since Stalin's death.

Andropov had all the credentials needed to recognize the significance of America's fear of a Chinese sneak attack. Before assuming the chairman's post in the KGB, Andropov had been one of the men leading the Kremlin's ideological campaign against the Chinese Communists.

This tiny cabal in the KGB was one of the most ruthless that the post-Stalin Soviet system produced. Despite the lessons of the Stalin purges, it was dedicated to returning the Communist state to the internal and international policies of the dead dictator.

"I think [if] we compare Hitler to Stalin, and the Gestapo to the KGB, the KGB was far more ruthless," former KGB general Kalugin told CNN. "Not because they killed far more people, but because they were indiscriminate in the selection of victims. The Soviet system was a lawless system, and the KGB was a tool of lawlessness," he said.

At the time the K-129 mysteriously disappeared only a short distance from America's greatest defense asset in the Pacific, the small KGB-centric group of reactionary Stalinists in Moscow was nearing the peak of its power in an otherwise weak central government headed by Leonid Brezhnev.

"After years of scorn and travails under Khrushchev, the security ministry once again was ascending to its rightful place at the heart of Soviet society," Kalugin wrote in his autobiography, *The First Directorate*. "And in 1967, when the forceful Yuri Andropov took over the KGB, our power would know no bounds."

This dangerous group of plotters had the will, the power, and the keys to the machinery necessary to cynically launch a devastating attack on any enemy, within or without, that stood in the way of restoring a hard-line, Stalin-like regime to accomplish world domination.

All this cabal needed was a foolproof plan that guaranteed its own survivability in the aftermath of its horrific deeds. Ironically, American intelligence—thanks to turncoat Johnny Walker Red's sacks of pilfered military secrets—may have supplied that perfect plan.

16

NAVAL INTELLIGENCE ANALYSTS and civilian scientists piecing together the puzzle surrounding the K-129 incident did not have access to important evidence that would have answered major questions about the boat's unusual final maneuvers. Without a well-placed mole at navy headquarters in Moscow or Vladivostok—such as the spy John Walker in Washington—the American investigators were unaware that K-129 had been manned by a suspicious contingent of seemingly extraneous personnel.

The highly unusual makeup of the crew, with fifteen more men aboard than were needed for normal operations, has never been addressed by former Soviet admirals in their published accounts of the K-129 incident. At least eleven of those extra crew members had no apparent reason for going on the mission. These men had no known operational assignments, and there is no record that they came from elsewhere in the fleet. Some of the other replacements assigned to the K-129 have been identified as submariners from boats in the Kamchatka Flotilla.

In all the interviews with former Soviet admirals from

the Pacific Fleet concerning the loss of the K-129, this obvious anomaly in the crew size has never even been acknowledged. Some of the headquarters officials, who were in the best position to know something was wrong with the composition of the crew, have been the most vocal in blaming the Americans for the sinking, rather than answering questions about the known violations of operational procedures. These same former admirals have repeatedly accused the U.S. government of hiding information about K-129. Yet they have shed no light on discrepancies in the K-129 account, such as the unusual orders to return to sea before the regular schedule, the failure of the officers to file a crew manifest, and the extra men on that last mission.

The oversized crew is thus a particularly strange part of the story—not just the fact of its existence, but the way it has been almost "officially" ignored. In every commentary on the K-129 incident by Cold War–era Soviet admirals and government statements by the new Russian Federation Navy, no one has attempted to explain why an always uncomfortably crowded submarine carried fifteen more men on a lengthy mission than the boat regularly required.

Two former Soviet submarine commanders, speaking off the record for fear of political retaliation under the new crackdown on press freedom in Russia, have recently confirmed that such overmanning of a submarine on a long combat patrol would never have been sanctioned by the Soviet navy. These retired officers stated that K-129's extra crew was a significant factor in understanding what went wrong on that mission. Both expressed amazement that no inquiry about the number of lost seamen has ever been conducted by the post-Soviet government.

One of these former commanders, who is now living in St. Petersburg, Russia, did respond to a published explanation that the extra men on the doomed submarine might have been trainees or cadets.

"The notion that cadets were sent on a regular autonomous patrol is wrong," said the retired captain. "Naval cadets used to serve on board submarines only for short training exercises at sea. They never served for patrol duty. So you can't find any cadets [trainees] on board the K-129 on her last patrol."

There is no question about the number of crewmen who served on this type of submarine. Several authoritative sources confirm that the Golf II submarine had a full crew complement of eighty-three, which included twelve to fourteen officers and sixty-nine to seventy-one sailors. The Golf I boat required even fewer crewmen, numbering only eighty.

The most definitive source on Cold War–era Soviet submarines, *Russian Strategic Nuclear Forces*, edited by Pavel Podvig, describes the crew as numbering eighty-three officers and enlisted men. That encyclopedic book was researched and written by top experts at the Center for Arms Control Studies at the Moscow Institute of Physics and Technology and other scholars in Russia, Canada, and the United States. The book, which is widely recognized as the most accurate account of Soviet nuclear weapons systems, was published by the Massachusetts Institute of Technology. In recent years, the book has been banned in Russia and its researchers harassed, as public access to information is once again being restricted by the Russian government, which is increasingly being run by former KGB officials.

Two other authorities with expertise in Soviet submarine technology also confirm that submarines such as K-129 had crews of no more than eighty-three men. These are the prestigious Federation of American Scientists (FAS) reports on Weapons of Mass Destruction, and the editors at *Chinese Defence Today*, an unofficial but well-regarded publication on Chinese military technology.

There is little doubt that ninety-eight men were aboard K-129 when it sank. No questions were raised in Russia in 1996, when President Boris Yeltsin posthumously awarded the Order of Valor to ninety-eight men who died aboard the submarine K-129. The names have been etched into a monument at the Kamchatka Peninsula headquarters of the Russian navy, and widely published in Russian newspapers, magazines, and books.

When the unusual number of men in the crew is coupled with the revelation that no crew manifest was found when Soviet Pacific Fleet headquarters first determined that the submarine was lost, it seems obvious that someone did not want the odd composition of K-129's crew to be known. The mission becomes even more suspect when the strange behavior of several officers of the regular crew on the eve of sailing is added to the mix.

Paul Neumann, a naval engineer and Soviet-era naval historian in Vancouver, British Columbia, who has studied the K-129 incident and conducted numerous interviews with former Soviet submarine commanders, was also curious about the makeup of the crew. In researching post-Soviet Russia, he uncovered a published statement by Rear Admiral (retired) Y. A. Krivoruchko, former commander of the 15th Submarine Squadron at Kamchatka, concerning the K-129 crew.

"A full list of the crew, signed and stamped by the division commander, had never [before departure] been made," according to Admiral Krivoruchko. "And it did not occur [was not noticed] until twelve days after K-129 was pronounced missing. From the point of view of the military regulations, it is not just negligence, it is a crime. The submarine did not go for training or target practice. It was a combat patrol in the times of the Cold War."

There are a few other tantalizing pieces of evidence that suggest something was not normal on board the K-129 on this last mission.

Author Clyde W. Burleson conducted scores of off-the-record interviews with government agents and civilians who worked on the K-129 inquiry. He was told a strange story about one of the bodies recovered from the submarine.

A "personal journal" belonging to a young missile officer was recovered along with the junior officer's dog tags, which were used to identify him. By cross-referencing a list of the officers aboard K-129, which was released after the end of the Cold War, it is possible to determine that this man was probably the assistant weapons officer, Captain-Lieutenant Victor Zuev. The diary was found alongside his body in a bunk in the officers' quarters in compartment two of the boat. The diary, along with other papers about his training, may have given the CIA some special insight into the last days of the submarine.

What makes that find significant is that the officer apparently thought K-129's mission was so unusual that he risked being sent to a gulag for keeping a forbidden diary. Operations aboard missile submarines at the height of the Cold War were top-secret, and both the U.S. and Soviet navies forbade crewmen from keeping unofficial records such as journals.

American intelligence was so interested in the young man's account of the sub's journey that the book was rushed to a NASA laboratory for restoration. An ultralow vacuum chamber and lasers were used for restoration, in a major effort to read whatever secrets the diary's author had recorded. This diary or trip record was reported as one of the most important pieces salvaged from the evidence later recovered.

Did this illicit diary, kept hidden under a mattress in the missile officer's cabin, tell the full story of what had happened on the submarine? Years later, U.S. intelligence officials made a point of letting the Soviets know that such a written account of the mission existed. But there is no record that the diary was ever returned with the other personal items from K-129 that were handed over to the Russians after the Cold War ended.

Diplomats, spies, and even U.S. intelligence agents involved in the K-129 investigation also appear to have, at some point, informed Soviet intelligence or the Soviet navy that a large number of bodies—estimates range from fifty to seventy—was discovered crowded into the forward two sections of the doomed submarine. Whether this information was derived from photographs taken inside the sunken boat by the USS *Halibut* or from later salvage efforts is not clear.

Officially, the U.S. government has never admitted to recovering more than six bodies, which the CIA claims were reburied in somber naval ceremonies at sea. However, several former Soviet admirals and a Soviet navy intelligence officer have written or told interviewers the Soviets learned from American sources that up to seventy bodies were found in the forward third of the submarine, which corresponds roughly with compartments one and two.

On a combat patrol, it would be inconceivable for more than a dozen men to have been in these two sections, if the submarine had been operating normally at the time of its destruction. The first compartment contained only the torpedo room, a tight space manned by a half-dozen sailors during battle stations. Compartment two housed the officers' quarters, the officers' wardroom, the sonar room, and the main battery controllers. Even at maximum normal usage, there should have been no more than ten officers and seamen in this section of the boat.

Since there were no exit hatches in this section, trained submariners would have fled *out* of these compartments in an emergency rather than *into* them, if they were seeking to exit the ship. The only logical explanation for so many men being jammed into such a tiny space is that they had been forced into the area and compelled to remain there.

Suspicions about the motives of the crew were first expressed by Dr. Craven, the U.S. Navy's original scientific investigator into the K-129 incident. He summed up the mystery in his autobiography *The Silent War* with these words: "The secret residing in the secret— the motivations of that Soviet captain and his crew— had remained intact and that, ironically, is the secret that ought to be revealed."

Dr. Craven confirmed in his memoirs that the investigators suspected the boat was a rogue, and that it had destroyed itself in an attempt to launch, or while launching, against Pearl Harbor. Under a lifetime confidentiality contract, Dr. Craven is quick to qualify that conclusion each time it is mentioned in his book.

Most likely, however, it was not the motives of Captain Kobzar or his senior commanders that should have been questioned. There are good reasons to believe now that the officers and senior sailors in the regular crew of K-129 had nothing to do with an attempted rogue attack on the United States. Once the longest leg of the journey to the mission box had been completed, only a small part of the regular crew would have been needed to divert the submarine from the mission box, position it near Hawaii, and attempt to launch a missile.

The key to this assumption may be found in the eleven-man unit that is known to have boarded K-129 at the last minute. Just as evidence about the inexplicable extra manning of the boat came to light after the end of the Cold War, other military information not available to U.S. agencies has recently surfaced that can explain a great deal about the incident.

The officers of K-129—particularly the submarine's commander, Captain First Rank Vladimir Kobzar, and its first officer, Captain Second Rank Alexander Zhuravin—were known to be devoted husbands and fathers, and they had unblemished service records. While these admirable traits would not necessarily have precluded their willing participation in a rogue operation, they do make these men unlikely suspects for leading a revolt against the homeland and defying orders by participating in a serious unauthorized activity. These top officers and other staff officers seemed to be no less loyal or patriotic to their homeland than their counterparts commanding American submarines with similar capacity to launch nuclear war. They were the best and brightest their countries had to offer, and the last people who would have contemplated a suicidal and terrorist attack that could have caused World War III.

The officers and crew were highly respected by the admirals and fellow submariners of the Soviet Pacific Fleet. We know this is true of Kobzar, Zhuravin, the senior missile officer, Captain Third Rank Gennady Panarin, and his assistant, Captain-Lieutenant Zuev. Rather than perpetrate an unauthorized sneak attack, it is reasonable to believe that these men would have fought against any rogue element attempting to take over their submarine. These men would certainly have known that any unauthorized attempt to launch a nuclear missile would have been thwarted by the fail-safe system. They probably went to their deaths with the knowledge that K-129 would be severely damaged or even destroyed in such a launch attempt. They may even have warned those attempting the launch of such a consequence, and been rebuffed. It is far more likely that they were unsung heroes than rogues.

If the launch was not attempted by the regular crew

of K-129, then who would have been qualified to do so? The evidence points to the mysterious strangers who boarded the submarine shortly before sailing.

What occurred aboard K-129 in its final days, beginning around the time the submarine first failed to report when it crossed the 180th meridian, will not likely ever be known. But an explanation based on new information coming out of Russia in the last decade can be used to fashion a reasonable hypothesis.

17

IN 1967–68, WHEN THE COLD WAR had reached its most dangerous phase, a number of drastic changes were occurring in the leadership hierarchy in Moscow. A behind-the-scenes power struggle, pitting progressive elements of the Kremlin against reactionary neo-Stalinists, was in full sway. A shadowy group with its power base in the KGB was silently scheming for control of the Politburo. The state security apparatus, employing more than a half-million people, had, for all practical purposes, become a parallel government. The KGB was engineering a plot to end the so-called Prague Spring, which led to the invasion of Czechoslovakia in August 1968. The secretive organization was conducting an undeclared war against the People's Republic of China and was sponsoring terrorist assaults on Western interests around the globe.

A new and cynical leadership in the KGB was ruthless enough to devise any scheme, no matter how horrific, to further its ambitions of world dominance and had the hard-core, handpicked specialists with the training and skills to carry out its assignments.

Kremlinologists have recently begun to gain access

to old Soviet archives and eyewitnesses that paint a far darker picture of what was occurring in Moscow than had previously been known in the West.

An example is a study by Anssi Kullberg, head of the editorial board of the *Eurasian Politician*, the Web-based journal of a European think tank that studies political and security issues in Eastern Europe.

Kullberg noted, "The beginning of modern terrorism could be traced back to a single date: On 18th May 1967, an exceptionally unscrupulous man, Yuri Andropov, became the head of the Soviet secret service KGB, and among his first actions was to return 'special' operations to KGB policy, in order to bring about a global wave of subversion against Western democracies."

Andropov, who earlier in his career had been the architect for the Kremlin's murderous suppression of the Hungarian Revolt, used GRU special operations troops known as *spetsnaz*, disguised as visitors arriving at airports, to seize government facilities before Soviet troops poured into the satellite country. The GRU was the intelligence agency of the Soviet military high command, and the army and navy each had special operations units.

The original Soviet special operations units, *spetsnaz*, were created by military intelligence, the GRU, in the late 1950s, in direct response to America's deploying tactical nuclear weapons in Europe. One of the primary missions of special operations was to penetrate behind enemy lines and disable missiles before they could be used on the battlefield. The *spetsnaz* units were specifically trained to handle all types of nuclear warheads and missiles. The brightest, most aggressive and fit young men in the Soviet army and navy were originally recruited for the *spetsnaz*. All recruits were athletic, and reports abound that many of the Soviet sports teams traveling abroad were made up of *spetsnaz* squads.

In addition to training in nuclear weaponry, the special operations units were also trained in operating all types of military equipment, including submarines. Some units of the GRU's naval *spetsnaz* actually were assigned their own minisubmarines. All *spetsnaz* units assigned to the navy wore regular submariner or naval infantry uniforms, with no special markings identifying them as covert warriors. There was one other requirement for membership in these special operations teams. The trainee was chosen for his political reliability, with each conscript taking an oath to die before divulging secrets about a mission.

The KGB, which had its own sizable force of uniformed units, recognized the value of the special operations troops deployed so effectively by the Red Army, and created a black ops capability for its purposes in the early 1960s. The KGB's version of the GRU *spetsnaz* had far more sinister and grizzly assignments than simply fighting enemy soldiers behind front lines. The special operations units from the state security organization were tasked with annihilating the civilian leadership of opponents.

The KGB "had its own terrorist apparatus, which includes an organization very similar to *spetsnaz*, known as *osnaz*," according to Viktor Suvorov, a former Soviet military intelligence officer. Their ruthlessness was later attested to by a particular mission in the early 1980s.

KGB *osnaz* agents opened the Soviet invasion of Afghanistan by storming the presidential palace in Kabul and assassinating all government officers, their families, and the civilian staff.

In 1968, as the new chairman of the KGB, Andropov was directly in charge of the *osnaz* units, which were reserved for only the highest-priority, most secret operations of the organization.

These special operations troops were drawn from the ranks of the army and navy *spetsnaz*. The units were slotted in the Third Chief Directorate, the large bureau with responsibility for ensuring the political reliability of the armed forces. But the KGB *osnaz* answered directly to a special arm of the KGB called the Executive Action Department, which handled what were known as "wet" operations—missions often involving kidnappings and murders.

In addition to having political officers and spies in every military unit, the KGB's Third Directorate, which carried out military counterintelligence and criminal investigation in the armed forces, had complete access to the files of every officer in the Soviet army, navy, and air force. Thus, it was an easy matter for the KGB to exert considerable control over military operations, even though the Soviet generals and admirals were open rivals for political power in the USSR structure.

The KGB recruited the toughest men whose files indicated, after special training in the *spetsnaz*, that they would be most likely to carry out any order, without question, no matter how ruthless or hazardous. Since the state security apparatus had the files, it was not hard for them to pick the men with the technical expertise and killer instinct for any mission the KGB leader needed to accomplish.

The *osnaz*, as well as the military intelligence teams of the GRU, were trained in nuclear missile technology and submarine operations, the skills required to run a submarine and launch a missile. All the special operations men were trained in the deadly arts of personal combat and functioned much like America's Green Berets, Rangers, and SEALS teams.

Both GRU *spetsnaz* and KBG *osnaz* teams disguised themselves as enlisted men and mingled on special assignments with regular military units, including submariners. The special operations units were broken into teams of eight to ten men with an officer, warrant officer, or senior petty officer in charge. This unit description corresponds to the odd group of sailors who boarded K-129 at the last minute. That group numbered ten men and a leader wearing the insignia of a senior petty officer. It was later reported that, while a number of crew replacements came from other submarines in the Kamchatka Flotilla, the origin of this last group of eleven men has never been determined—or at least never been reported by Russians authorities writing about the K-129 incident.

Why additional crewmen were needed for the mission has never been satisfactorily explained. The reason given by Soviet officials—that they were replacements for a large number of furloughed K-129 crewmen—does not stand up. Soviet submariners who served in the Pacific Fleet were given priority seating on regular flights between the Far East and European Russia whenever they were recalled to duty in emergencies. Regular crewmen probably could have been called back to their boat, had someone not intended to dilute the regular crew with substitutes on some sort of special assignment. There is also a confirmed record that the required replacements had already been assigned from other submarines at Rybachiy base. So the addition of these eleven extra men to the crew confounds all reason.

Based on information recently revealed about the clandestine *osnaz*, a strong case can be made that the extra men inserted on the K-129 fit the description of a KGB *osnaz* unit. A special operations unit would have had the skills needed to position and launch a missile, after coercing or incapacitating the K-129 officers and senior crew.

One other skill attributed to the special troops that would have been a factor in such an attempt is their training in defeating sophisticated locks and security systems. This training might have led the leaders of the takeover to overestimate their ability to bypass K-129's missile fail-safe system.

As far as taking over a Golf-type submarine and running it—while not a task for the untrained—a determined *osnaz* team could easily accomplish such a mission. No contingency plans for defense against a takeover existed for Cold War submarines, because it was highly unlikely that there would ever be an opportunity for a hostile force to gain entry to a ballistic missile submarine on the high seas. With the careful selection of crews and intensive training, the very idea that a fully manned missile submarine could be commandeered while at sea surely never entered the minds of Soviet or American submarine commanders.

Normally, the crew went about its duties without sidearms, except when a submarine was in a foreign port on a visit. In home port, a squad with arms remained on board as a security detail. The submarine was easy to guard because there were so few entrances. At sea, there was little possibility that an enemy could approach close enough to a submarine and board it, even when the boat was on the surface.

But a well-planned internal takeover of a submarine such as K-129—especially such an operation conducted by KGB agents, with all the authority invested in that dreaded state security organization—would be relatively easy.

The intruders would not necessarily have to take their own firearms on board. While regular crewmen were unarmed, there were ample weapons on the boat, kept under lock and key. An automatic pistol was furnished for each officer on board, which in this case would be fourteen pistols. A half-dozen Kalashnikov assault rifles were provided for security when the submarine was in foreign ports. The captain kept the key to the pistol locker and the first officer had the key to the assault rifles.

Nonetheless, it would have been a simple matter for the infiltrators to bring small, automatic weapons on board in their sea bags, if they wanted them. There was no reason to inspect the kits of new crew members, and contraband, such as vodka, was often smuggled aboard Soviet naval vessels.

Some basic assumptions about such a takeover of a submarine can be made.

A KGB unit would probably first attempt to persuade

the officers and crewmen that it had the authority to divert the submarine from its regular mission by producing documentation from some high-ranking and recognizable official. That ruse would likely have failed with veteran submarine officers such as Kobzar and Zhuravin, who were too well drilled in adhering closely to the chain of command to allow any change in official orders that could not be verified. The *zampolit*, Captain Third Rank Fedor Lobas, while being more susceptible to KGB pressure, would also insist that any change in orders be confirmed by radio contact with Pacific Fleet headquarters or a higher authority in Moscow.

Failing to accomplish its mission by bluff, an *osnaz* team was fully able and brutal enough to physically take over the boat. A trained team could either break into the weapons lockers or secure the keys by force. Making an example of a senior officer would impress the crew with the deadly serious intentions of the *osnaz* team.

Once the intruding party of eleven was armed and had arrested or otherwise incapacitated the key officers and senior petty officers, it would be a simple matter to keep the remaining crew in line. On a submarine, with strictly confined compartments accessible only through single hatches, any officers or crewmen unwilling to follow the commands of the KGB team could be forced out of the way into compartments one and two in the forward part of the boat. None of the equipment in those forward compartments was essential to the operation of the submarine or the launch of its missiles.

A single armed guard could control the one hatch

between these forward compartments and the operations center in compartment three. There was no other means of entrance or exit from these compartments to any other part of the submarine.

Some crew members, particularly the lower-ranking seamen, would cooperate with the KGB out of the fear instilled in the populace by the organization they represented. Others, particularly key personnel such as the navigator, might be made to cooperate by threats to the lives of their fellow officers and crew members. Thus, while there is practically no way a ballistic missile submarine could have been externally seized, it would not have been difficult for a KGB team to accomplish a seizure from within.

No hard proof of what happened aboard K-129 has ever been recounted in official documents. Unless the crewman's personal journal was actually recovered and restored, as the CIA's planted rumor contends, the last days of the K-129 can be only partially reconstructed from other known facts that have been revealed. If a legible journal exists, it has never been released. However, the extremely odd deviation from standard Soviet ballistic missile submarine operations, particularly in composition of the crew, points strongly to a takeover of the submarine as early as March 1, when the first mandatory contact with headquarters was missed.

It is also logical to assume that such a plot did not originate with a renegade band of low-ranking sailors, or even a small special operations team as capable of mayhem as a KGB *osnaz* team. A scheme of such terrifying magnitude would have had to originate at a much higher level, among men with powerful motivations.

There were such disgruntled men in high positions who were convinced the Soviet Union was about to collapse unless drastic actions were taken. These men bitterly opposed the modernizing influence of the leadership in the Kremlin and the army, and plotted behind the scenes of power in Moscow throughout the 1960s.

The Central Intelligence Agency was aware of this unrest, and vaguely knew some of the key plotters by name and reputation. KGB Chairman Andropov was among this group.

One former U.S. intelligence analyst, speaking in confidence about the K-129 incident, has agreed that it makes no sense that a commander such as Captain Kobzar, who was known to the U.S. Navy as a professional submarine officer with a bright future in the Soviet navy, would suddenly turn rogue on his own and try to attack an American port. To obtain that rank and control of a missile submarine, he would have had to be a dedicated Communist in good standing with the party.

The former analyst also agreed that no one man, or even a few officers on a submarine, could have planned and executed such an outrageous scheme without direction. Even the highest-ranking field officer was closely monitored by political officers working for the KGB. Therefore, the brutish agents who actually attempted the rogue attack had to have been acting on high authority from Moscow taskmasters to whom they owed great loyalty and whom they had vowed to follow blindly, even into the hellish fires of a nuclear war.

18

THE BUILDING AT NUMBER 26 KUTUZOVSKY
Prospekt on the west side of central Moscow would not
have been worthy of notice among the surrounding
gray monumentalist architecture, except for the unusually large number of KGB guards from the Ninth Directorate who were always lurking around it. The
multistory apartment building blended into the Or-
wellian cityscape of the Stalin-era neighborhood,
where residences of high officials purposely displayed
no distinguishing designs.

Located in a setting of parks and museums along the
Moskva River, the building was within walking distance
of the famous Kiev train station. And the broad Kutuzovsky avenue provided unimpeded travel by chauf-
feured limousine to the Kremlin, the Bolshoi Theater,
and KGB headquarters.

This drab apartment building housed the plainly
decorated flats of the three most powerful men in the
Soviet Union—Leonid Illyich Brezhnev, Yuri
Vladimirovich Andropov, and Mikhail Andreyevich
Suslov. Brezhnev was the general secretary of the Cen-
tral Committee and, in 1968, the titular head of Soviet

government. Andropov was the newly appointed chairman of the KGB and may have been the first member of the state security apparatus to become a member of the Politburo. Suslov, known as the Red Professor, was the chief ideologue of the Communist Party Soviet Union (CPSU), a shadowy man who eschewed titles of significance. He was, by reputation, the most feared man in the USSR.

The apartment building was important because, more telling than the titles of its occupants, it revealed a hidden hierarchical structure within the secretive sanctums of the Soviet government of that troubled era. Brezhnev's apartment was located below Andropov's. Suslov's apartment was on the top floor of the building, a lofty position, higher than the others.

Each of the three-bedroom flats was deceptively Spartan—only sixteen hundred square feet with one bath. The Soviet leadership could point to these modest living quarters as proof of their austerity, while lavishing the perks of position on their *dachas*, hidden in the forests just outside Moscow.

The building was important for another reason. It was most likely the location where the master scheme involving the rogue submarine attack on Pearl Harbor was conceived and developed.

To carry out and survive such an audacious sneak attack against the greatest superpower on earth, the plotters needed strong motives and a foolproof plan of deniability for themselves and the Soviet Union. The attack had to be executed in such a manner as to prevent overwhelming retaliation against them by the United States. One way to pull off such a ruse was to lay blame on the only other belligerent nation with both nuclear missile and submarine capabilities.

The radical Stalinists in Moscow had strong enough motivation to risk such a brazen act. The plot instigators knew better than anyone else in the Politburo that the Soviet economic system was near collapse under the financial burden of the Cold War arms race. In the mid-1960s, years before vast oil reserves were discovered in Siberia and the Black Sea regions, the Soviets were already secretly spending more than half of the Communist confederation's gross national product on their military. Additionally, the billions of rubles needed to support poverty-ridden client states such as Cuba and North Korea was fast driving the Soviet Union to bankruptcy. Only a few key leaders in the Politburo knew the USSR was about to be smothered by the Western Alliance's technological superiority in the arms race.

Some in the Kremlin held an almost paranoid belief that the imbalance of power could tempt the Americans to launch a first strike against the Soviet Union with virtual impunity. To compound these fears, China had become openly hostile.

This double threat was summed up in a U.S. national intelligence estimate issued in September 1969, which noted that increased Soviet military expenditures were "squeezing Moscow's ability to invest in the future growth of the economy. Events in the Far East and in Europe have posed new military requirements. Thus the perennial problem of resource allocation has sharpened, and promises to sharpen further."

The cabal also strongly believed that Mao's Red China had become a more dangerous threat to Soviet world dominion than the United States, and that a nuclear-armed Red China was an imminent military threat to Soviet territory in Asia.

Almost coincidentally, the American naval spy John Walker supplied stolen secrets revealing the Americans' fear of a solo Chinese nuclear attack delivered by submarine. This intelligence could have been a key factor in the plotters' scheme, if not providing the impetus for a plan. A plot was likely devised that, if successful, could eliminate the collapsing Soviet system's problems with one horrendous act. The outrageous scheme was worth great risk because the Soviet Union's two major enemies, China and the United States, would be dealt with in a single blow.

The plotters had to know that if Pearl Harbor were attacked, the Soviet Union would be the first to be suspected, and that the Americans would certainly retaliate with overwhelming nuclear force. The solution was to devise a plan that shielded the Soviet Union from blame for the attack. The only other country with the motive and capability to accomplish such a horrible deed was Red China. By tricking the United States into a massive retaliatory attack on China, the USSR could simultaneously weaken the Americans and eliminate Mao, without spending a dime from its depleted treasury.

The much-discussed deterrence policy of both the Soviet Union and the United States—known throughout the Cold War years as "mutual assured destruction" or MAD—was always an exaggeration. Certainly, by the mid-1960s, the United States had more than enough nuclear warheads and means of delivery to annihilate every major military, industrial, and population center in the Soviet Union. But the Soviets never had the capacity to completely destroy the United States. At most, they had enough thermonuclear capacity to wreck Europe. Even so, the possibility that a few bombers and missiles might get through to hit even one North American city was, in itself, a powerful deterrent for the Americans.

A sneak attack by a missile submarine firing a low-yield nuclear warhead on Pearl Harbor would immediately cripple the U.S. Navy in the Pacific and throw the Americans into a temporary state of confusion. The plotters rationalized that the source of such an attack would be impossible to determine immediately in the chaotic aftermath.

Mao had often provided a motive in his own anti-American screeds. And China had two Golf-type ballistic missile submarines. In order to successfully place the blame on the Chinese, the plotters relied on the efficiency of American intelligence. The Soviets knew U.S. spy satellites were regularly monitoring their naval facilities, and assumed they were looking down on Red China's bases, as well. The Americans, therefore, must certainly know about China's new Golf I submarine, which had been built and launched at Darien, China, in September 1966. Even though the Chinese boat was not as technically advanced as the Soviet Golf II submarine, it was this older version of the Golf, with its ballistic missile capability, that the plotters hoped the Americans would mistakenly blame for the sneak attack on Pearl Harbor.

Another piece of evidence the plotters could count

on to further implicate the Chinese in the attack was the fissile material in the warhead. Years earlier, China had provided uranium ores that were refined by the Soviets to make the plutonium in some of their warheads. That material was still used in Soviet nuclear weapons. Later testing of samples from the explosion at Pearl Harbor would reveal the Chinese origin of the nuclear material. The Americans would be unable to distinguish a one-megaton Chinese nuclear blast from a Soviet blast.

If neither General Secretary Brezhnev nor anyone else in the Soviet military leadership were made aware of the scheme, there would be no mobilization of forces for war or preparation for civilian defense anywhere in the Soviet Union to tip off Western spies that the Soviets were plotting a first strike. In fact, the always-nervous Brezhnev could be counted on to be near apoplectic when an angry President Johnson called him on the red phone.

The most reliably convincing culprit in this Machiavellian scheme was the one person that Suslov wanted to tar with the blame for the ruthless sneak attack, Chairman Mao Tse-tung himself. Mao had been hated by the ideological Stalinist element in Moscow since his address before the Fifth Congress of the Albanian Party in October 1966, when the Chinese leader directly challenged the Soviet party for world leadership.

"The revisionist leading clique of the Soviet Union, the Tito clique of Yugoslavia, and all the other cliques of renegades and scabs of various shades are mere dust heaps . . ." proclaimed Mao. "They are slaves and accomplices of imperialism, before which they prostrate themselves, while you are dauntless proletarian revolutionaries who dare to fight imperialism and its running dogs, fight the world's tyrannical enemies."

Mao, likewise, did not spare the Americans. His repeated bellicose threats to unleash a nuclear war against the United States provided blatant proof of Chinese animosity, and automatically pointed the evidence away from the Soviets, whose diplomats were seriously negotiating with the Johnson administration on a nuclear arms limitation treaty. Mao had even criticized the limitation of nuclear weapons and loudly proclaimed that China would never agree to relinquish any part of its growing nuclear arsenal.

In early 1968, Suslov and others in Moscow knew the USSR was not only losing the standoff with the United States and her allies, but was losing ground to Mao in the escalating ideological struggle to dominate the Communist cause in the Third World. Mao Tsetung had declared the Soviet-style Communism to be a "personality cult" that had deviated from the true Marxist course. The Chinese leader repeatedly and publicly called for the overthrow of the Soviet-style Communist system and the punishment of its current leaders.

The best solution for the survival and rejuvenation of the Soviet Union would clearly be the crippling of both enemies at once—the United States and Red China. But the USSR simply could not do that job, even if its leadership was of a mind to do it. And that leadership, under the weak General Secretary Brezhnev, could never have been persuaded to attempt so bold a move.

The next best thing would be for the United States

and Communist China to be tricked into fighting each other. Such a war could easily last many years and slowly drain the United States of its economic superiority. By 1968, the U.S. war in Vietnam, fought against a ragtag cadre of guerillas and a Third World army, had already destroyed the American public's will to invest any more lives and treasure.

Even if a nuclear war between China and the United States ended quickly, China's industrial and military centers would be laid waste. The plotters reasoned that the Americans would never attempt to occupy a land as vast as China. The Soviets were in a position to move into the chaos on the ground. At the time, more than half the Soviet army had already been positioned along the Sino-Soviet border.

Red China's rhetoric against the United States reached a fever pitch in 1967–68. Mao had repeatedly ridiculed U.S. nuclear might and dared the Americans to strike China with nuclear weapons. The Chairman told the world that nuclear war would be useless against his country of one billion people, scattered over the Asian landmass.

At the same time, China was in a state of upheaval, with so-called Red Guards rampaging throughout the vast country. The Americans could be expected to believe that this chaos was a factor in a Chinese sneak attack, since no one seemed to be in charge. Soviet and Red Chinese troops were in open skirmishes all along their common border.

The Soviet leadership was also engaged in low-grade confrontations on all fronts, with the wakening Red giant in China to the southeast, and the ever-stronger

European Allies controlling the regions west and south of the country, from Iran and Turkey to Norway.

Not only was there turmoil in the Soviet Union and China, but the United States was facing antiwar riots in many of its cities and universities. The Johnson administration's military leadership was focused on Southeast Asia and distracted by the escalating war in Vietnam.

Timing was right for heaping another massive burden on the weary Americans; conditions seemed perfect for such a scheme to succeed.

Placing the blame on the Chinese was central to the success of the plot. For that reason, K-129 had to mimic exactly the capabilities of the Chinese Golf I–type submarine by positioning itself within four hundred miles of the target and surfacing to launch the strike. The K-129 had the ability to launch its missiles while submerged and hit a target nearly 850 miles away—a much safer procedure. The difference in submarine missile capacity was critically important if the Americans were to be fooled into believing the attack had been from the PRC and not the USSR.

These slight differences posed no obstacle to the plotters. All the Soviet submarine had to do was move closer to the target and come to the surface to fire its missiles. U.S. satellite technology, while excellent, would not be able to distinguish the Soviet K-129 from a Chinese Golf, even if the submarine were photographed in the act by a satellite camera.

The plotters reasoned that the Americans knew the Chinese version of the Golf did not have the range or the capability of the Soviet Golf to fire while submerged. U.S. military analysts would assume that an attacking enemy would use the maximum technical capabilities of its weapons systems. Therefore, the Americans would conclude that a surfaced submarine attack on Pearl Harbor from 350 to 400 miles off the target was the best the submarine could deliver.

Official Soviet reaction following such an attack would also be a factor in shifting the blame to the Chinese. After a strike against Pearl Harbor, an outraged President Johnson would immediately call General Secretary Brezhnev and accuse the Soviets. The plotters were confident Brezhnev could be counted on to react in his usual hysterical way. He had actually once fainted when plotting with Suslov and a small group in the Kremlin to overthrow Nikita Khrushchev. Brezhnev's shocked response to the furious American president's call, and the lack of evidence that the Russians had prepared for a counterattack, would almost certainly convince the Americans that the Soviets were not to blame. They would be sent looking elsewhere for the perpetrators.

It would be imperative for Western spies to observe that everything was calm in Moscow on the day of the attack. There would be no military alerts underway anywhere in the USSR. All Politburo members and their families would remain in the cities, going about their normal lives. That aspect of the scheme required no planning. Since only the few closest members of the plot were even aware that a rogue strike was imminent, the citizens of Moscow and their leaders in the Kremlin would be observed conducting business as usual.

If not the Soviet Union, then only Red China was capable of such a sneak attack. Soviet intelligence agents kept track of the Chinese Golfs' sailing schedule. With careful timing by the plotters, the American satellites should discover that one of the Chinese ballistic missile submarines was somewhere at sea in the first week of March 1968.

It seemed a perfect plan to men who were evil enough to sacrifice tens of thousands, even millions, of lives to achieve their long-held and long-frustrated goal of world dominance by Soviet-style Communism.

The plotters' line of reasoning almost certainly set as its primary goal the complete obliteration of China's power structure by an immediate U.S. nuclear retaliation. With that terrible task accomplished by the Americans, Brezhnev would be forced to send the Soviet Union's million-soldier Far East Army into China. The Soviets would be seen by the rest of the world as marching to restore order in China, while the Americans would once again be branded as the only great power to employ nuclear weapons on an Asian populace.

With most of its ground forces tied up in Vietnam, there was little likelihood that the United States could occupy the vast territory of mainland China, with a hostile and reeling population of nearly one billion. China's key territories with rich natural resources and hegemony of the entire Communist world would fall to the Soviets.

Suslov, Andropov, and a select cadre in the KGB probably found little in such a plot that could go wrong. They certainly reasoned that their own cover was adequate, and the unfolding revelations on the ground would prevent the Americans from blaming the Soviet Union. But there was one small weakness in their plan that they could not have identified at the time. Like many of the proverbial best-laid plans, this one was doomed to failure from the outset.

The plotters had underestimated America's spy technology. Soviet intelligence was not yet fully aware of just how good the SOSUS hydrophones, radio intercepts, and satellite spy systems had become in tracking Soviet submarines. The DIA and NSA had been accurately tracking all Soviet submarines for more than a year, and had tracked K-129 from the time it sailed from Kamchatka Peninsula to its arrival in the patrol box northwest of Hawaii. The U.S. Navy knew they had a Soviet Golf II, not a Chinese Golf I submarine, in the vicinity of the Hawaiian Islands on March 7, 1968.

Had the attack on Pearl Harbor succeeded, the mighty American hammer of revenge would have fallen swiftly on the Soviet Union, dooming plotters and innocents alike. But the men in Moscow who sent K-129 on its ill-fated mission were unaware of this small, but fatal, flaw in their horrific plan and proceeded, oblivious to the potential consequences of their deed.

19

THERE WAS NO SHORTAGE OF CYNICAL MEN in Moscow who would have been perfectly willing to sacrifice a few million comrade citizens for world dominance, if a nuclear exchange could produce Soviet hegemony, or even stave off the impending economic collapse of the Communist system.

Central to the success of a plot of this magnitude was deniability. Even the most brazenly reckless men would know that a scheme to neutralize the United States had to be foolproof. If the plotters were caught, even by their peers in the Kremlin, the end would be swift and certain. If the strike succeeded but the ruse to blame China failed, U.S. nuclear superiority guaranteed that the Soviet population, themselves included, would be blasted back to the Middle Ages. Survivors would be reduced to a collection of nomads living on the fringes of radioactive ruins where the great gray cities once stood.

Still, they felt safe in their furtive meetings. The plotters, limited to a handful of key people, could gather unnoticed in the seclusion of their building at Number 26 Kutuzovsky Prospekt. Because of their high ranks and direct control over the security apparatus, no one dared spy on their activities. But in the paranoid environment of the Soviet Union, even high-ranking officials were careful not to be seen gathering for unexplained meetings too often. Under tight security by their KGB guards posted outside the building, no one in the Kremlin would be aware that Suslov came down from his top-floor apartment to his protégé's apartment immediately below for extensive planning sessions. Nothing in the scheme required they meet at their offices in the Kremlin, at KGB headquarters, or in any other public place where they might be noticed by rivals within the Politburo. Discussions on the state of the economy or a plan to launch a war between the United States and China could be held without anyone knowing the meetings took place.

The plotters held Brezhnev's circle in the Kremlin and the Soviet military in utter contempt, for their lack of nerve to take the necessary action against the Western alliance or Mao's China that would restore the Soviets to leadership of world Communism. Yet the plotters were not strong enough to purge Brezhnev from the Kremlin, nor close enough to penetrate his security to poison him, as some in the scheme had allegedly done to their old mentor, Stalin.

While party boss Brezhnev was indeed too cautious to take aggressive action against the West or China, the Soviet generals and admirals were not constrained by timidity. They were pragmatic and knew that their planes, missiles, and ships were already far outgunned by those of the United States. In the 1960s, the Red Army leaders knew the Soviet army and navy were no match for the nuclear forces of the Free World powers. Though they would have fought to the last tank, ship, or plane—not to mention their willingness to throw millions of soldiers into suicidal assault against any aggressor striking the motherland—they were certainly not about to do anything to cause a showdown between their forces and the Americans. Therefore, it is reasonable to conclude that such a preposterous scheme would have been overwhelmingly rejected by the designated leaders of the Soviet military and Politburo.

The only way to proceed was by guile. If their plot succeeded, the military leaders would be forced to come to their side. If it failed, no one would be the wiser.

What kind of men were ruthless enough and powerful enough to conceive and carry out such a horrendous plot?

Many hardened survivors of the Stalin era in the party leadership had no qualms about imposing suffering or massive loss of life on their own people. Many who still held leadership positions in the Communist Party and the military remembered—and some had even played a role in—Stalin's bloody purges and the murder or starvation of thirty million Soviet citizens in the 1930s. Others, particularly in the military, remembered the massive purges of the officer corps just before World War II. Some of these same generals had hurled human waves against the Nazi war machine, resulting in millions of additional deaths during World War II. An examination of the leadership structure, with its mix of old Stalinist and newly educated Red fanatics, reveals no lack of candidates who, without conscience, could kill a half-million Americans in a sneak attack and chance a nuclear holocaust.

Short of a deathbed confession or the secret diary of a remorseful participant, the identity of those who were involved in the mad scheme to send a rogue submarine to attack America will probably never be proven beyond a doubt. In all likelihood, most of the low-level facilitators of the plot either were quietly liquidated in the former Soviet Union or have long since died of old age.

However, some information from inside the old Soviet Union has recently come to light that provides reason to suspect key participants in such a plot. One name seems to surface each time some new dastardly deed is revealed about the Kremlin during that era. Although rarely in the forefront of the leadership, over the years this man was linked to every coup d'état, purge, or liquidation. And he always seemed to have access to both the manpower and the tools necessary for special projects of the darker kind.

The American CIA was aware of this mysterious man and attempted, without much success, to understand his role each time he emerged from the shadows in unexpected power shifts in the Kremlin. Despite his appearance on the scene at key moments, he never took the highest office for himself, and soon disappeared again from public sight. Defectors and exiles to the West almost always mentioned his name with fear and reverence, but until the end of the Cold War the extent of this man's villainy was never clear.

A retired Cold War–era analyst specializing in Soviet affairs for an American intelligence agency was quick to suggest his name when discussing the K-129 incident.

"A good bet for the leader of such a ruthless plot would have to be a guy named Mikhail Suslov," the analyst whispered, "along with his hand-picked enforcer, Yuri Andropov."

Recently translated books by Russian dissidents, and newly released Soviet documents from the 1930s to the end of the Cold War, reveal that the relatively unknown Suslov was an evil genius who kept the Communist behemoth functioning for much of the seventy years of its brutal history, particularly since the end of World War II.

Suslov was almost a nonperson in the Soviet hierarchy from Stalin through Gorbachev. Yet every piece of infamy attributed to the Soviet system had his fingerprints all over it. He plotted against Stalin, even though the aging tyrant was his mentor. He was the power behind the emergence of Khrushchev after the death of Stalin, and led the plot in the subsequent ousting of Khrushchev. He manipulated the rise of Brezhnev, and then turned on him. He placed Andropov in all his positions of power, and even mentored Gorbachev before finally disappearing and dying in obscurity.

Suslov was born in 1902, in a small village in the middle Volga region, to peasant parents. He rose through the ranks from youth leader for the Communist League to chief ideologue of the Soviet Communist Party, with an astonishingly eclectic and often contradictory career in between. He was at times a grandfatherly teacher known as the Red Professor, and at other times the jackbooted leader of purges and deportations known as the Grand Inquisitor.

One of the most ardent Stalinist hard-liners, he had

survived all the purges from Stalin through Brezhnev, because he had been a participant, perpetrator, and mastermind in most of them. In 1967, at age sixty-five, he was already considered the gray eminence of the surviving original Bolsheviks, although his rise to power did not really begin until after World War II. While his name did not appear prominently in the Soviet government dossiers kept by the CIA, Suslov was one of the American spy agencies' most watched men in the Soviet Union for decades.

There were several mystery men such as Suslov in high government positions who could have been potential plotters. But Suslov was first among them. During the troubled post-Stalinist, post-Khrushchev era, intrigue was the key to survival. And Suslov was a master of the game.

Suslov was a brilliant, university-trained economist and one-time economics professor at the University of Moscow. While still a professor, he had come to the attention of Stalin himself, who began giving Suslov choice assignments as early as 1948. Although not a scientist, Suslov dabbled in the state secrets of military technology. He was the party liaison to the Third Directorate, the KGB department overseeing the loyalty of the Soviet army and navy.

Still, he was suspected of participating in the widely rumored plot to oust his mentor Stalin. Evidence has recently surfaced that a group of conspirators actually poisoned Stalin to prevent his starting a new purge that would have eliminated them. Suslov is believed to have been one of these conspirators. The men who masterminded that plot replaced the dictator with Khrushchev.

They later became enemies of Khrushchev when he launched an ambitious de-Stalinization plan. Suslov was especially angered by Khrushchev's efforts at economic reform, which aimed at saving the collapsing financial system by introducing privatization of state industries and collective farms. He then led the plot to oust Khrushchev.

Suslov knew, more than anyone else, how near the Communist system of the Soviet Socialist Republics was to complete economic collapse. As editor of *Pravda*, a position he held from 1949 to 1950, Suslov had become expert at hiding facts about the failing collective economy of the Soviet Union. He was not only the guardian of a rigid Marxist ideology, but was the leading expert on the collective-style economic system of the state.

In the 1960s, he was described as grandfatherly, though little is known about his personal or family life, except that he sometimes disappeared from Moscow for months on end. Suslov was a tall, gaunt, bespectacled man who would have stood out among the normally beefy Politburo *apparatchiks*, had he not routinely positioned himself on the shadowy edge of the crowd when it came time for group photographs. This penchant for anonymity may have been the key to his survival. He wore black horn-rimmed glasses, and in his ill-fitting, double-breasted suits and drab ties, usually went unnoticed among the boisterous, heavy-drinking Red leaders.

Suslov had other well-honed skills that were alien to his image as both a grandfather and a professor. He was described as careful and calculating by those subjected to his darker talents, particularly in the satellite Soviet states, where he was known as despotic and completely devoid of emotion.

Suslov had been one of the most murderous implementers of the Stalinist purges and deportations.

Early in his career, Suslov left his university teaching post to become an *apparatchik* in the party's Central Control Commission, which was in charge of party discipline and purges. As such, he became a key participant in what came to be known as the Great Purges of the 1930s. He was a staff director in Stalin's collectivization of the Kulaks, the wealthy peasant farmers of the Ukraine and western Russia. Well over one million farmers died in this ruthless pogrom.

As a regional functionary, he headed a commission that purged the party in the Urals and Chernigov region of Russia in 1933–34, sending hundreds of his Communist colleagues to their death or long imprisonment in frozen gulags. He later headed purges that amounted to ethnic cleansing of several of the indigenous peoples of the Crimean region, and during World War II conducted major purges in the Baltic States.

In 1937, as a chairman in the Central Control Commission, Suslov turned on many of his old comrades in the educated elite and led the Stalinist purges to eliminate all the educated and technical specialists throughout Soviet society who had been held over from the czarist era to keep the country running. Most of the original Bolsheviks were liquidated, to be replaced by the young "new Soviet men" from the peasantry, who had been educated for the first time under the Soviet system.

Until Stalin's death in 1953, Suslov was in charge of numerous smaller purges of military and governmental leaders who displeased the Red dictator. As long as Stalin was alive, Suslov held top posts as a member of the Central Committee and the Supreme Soviet. He was immediately demoted upon Stalin's death. But he took his schemes behind cover to become one of the most powerful movers and shakers in the USSR.

In 1956, Khrushchev, who had succeeded Stalin, brought Suslov out of the shadows and sent him to Hungary to suppress the uprising in Budapest. It was there that Suslov took a rising star, hard-liner Yuri Andropov, under his wing. Later he would use his influence to have Andropov named director of the KGB. Despite his key role in all the important intrigues, Suslov always managed to avoid the limelight and hover in anonymity in the dark corners of the Kremlin.

Suslov was the ringleader behind the plot to oust Khrushchev and place Leonid Brezhnev in the top Soviet leadership position. He was sure he could manipulate the plodding and supposedly cowardly Brezhnev. Suslov himself could never have been named to the top spot by the Communists because of his brutal past as one of Stalin's chief mass murderers.

His unseen hand in the affairs of Soviet politics made him a valuable player to the leadership. He was called back into service each time there was a problem that needed a fixer without a conscience.

One of the greatest problems to confront the international Communist community was the internecine feud between the Soviet Union and China, which broke out in the early 1960s.

Suslov had personally negotiated much of the Soviet military aid package to China when fraternal relations were at their rosiest. His close ties to Mao and the Red Chinese dated back to the negotiation of the 1950 Sino-Soviet Treaty of Friendship, Alliance, and Mutual Assistance. The small group of Soviets who had worked for years to establish the alliance with the Red Chinese was especially angered by China's ingratitude.

Suslov knew that the Soviets had provided China with one Golf submarine of the older type and, more important, with seven sea-launch ballistic missiles. He also knew that China had since developed and tested its own nuclear warheads and was perfectly capable of mounting such a weapon on the missiles. This intimate familiarity with the way the Chinese systems worked would be key to plotting a successful attack on America and carefully fabricating a trail that would lead straight to Mao's front door.

It was Suslov who headed the delegation that made a last-ditch effort to mend the rift with Red China in 1963. When it failed, it was Suslov who recommended the hard-line Soviet approach against Red China to the Central Committee Plenum in 1964.

More may have been at play than an ideological struggle for dominance of world Communism. Suslov harbored a visceral, personal hatred for Mao, who had publicly humiliated him before delegates at the fortieth anniversary celebration of the October Revolution in Moscow, in November 1957. American author Harrison Salisbury interviewed delegates to that plenum, who said Mao had openly boasted that his "little guy [Deng Xiaoping, who would become China's premier] . . . bested Mikhail Suslov, the tall ideologue." For years after, Mao took every opportunity to insult

Suslov on the international stage by reminding the world that the Soviets' ideological Red Eminence (Suslov) had lost the debate over who should lead international Communism. The incident has been described as the genesis of the Sino-Soviet rift. Suslov was not the kind of person to get angry over an insult; he had a personal history of getting even.

Suslov's clique was the prime force calling for the destruction of Mao by any means necessary. His insider experience dealing with the Chinese gave Suslov a unique depth of knowledge about the inner workings of the secretive government in Beijing. This special insight provided the plotters with all the intimate details necessary to carry out a scheme to frame the Chinese for the K-129 attack.

The plotters in the K-129 incident needed absolute command control of unquestionably loyal fanatics in the military structure. They had to have access to records that identified lower-echelon personnel who were willing to risk everything on one dangerous mission. In addition to finding the men needed to implement the plot, the ringleaders had to be able to get control of exactly the right equipment (submarine and missile), accomplish everything with precise timing, and be able to manage a master plan to avoid the American retaliation that would certainly follow such an attack.

This ability to recruit such a specialized crew willing to commandeer a submarine and risk death to start a nuclear war took someone in the highest ranks of the Soviet government. Logistically, carrying out such a plan required the steel nerves of a highly placed manager who was no stranger to life-and-death plots.

Suslov could not have carried out such a grand scheme alone. But the plot only required a few people—the fewer the better. Secrecy was of the essence. Suslov found willing allies in such insiders as Andropov, whose career he had engineered into the post of director of the KGB in 1968.

For years, Suslov had been the Kremlin's chief bureaucratic watchdog of the KGB. This position, while anonymous, gave him unquestioned access to officers and men skilled enough to take charge of a Soviet missile submarine and ruthless enough to launch a sneak attack. Suslov and Andropov had the necessary pipeline through the KGB to circumvent the regular Soviet navy and place the KGB's specially trained *osnaz* unit aboard K-129.

Had the mission succeeded, and the K-129 somehow eluded furious U.S. naval sub hunters from carriers in the Pacific Ocean, no medals would have awaited the surviving crew. Considering the villainy of Suslov and his associates, all of the common sailors and officers would certainly have been liquidated, probably including the *osnaz* team itself.

The plotters evidently believed that the dangerous risks to carry out the clandestine attack on the United States base in Hawaii would be worth taking. There was the whole world to be gained, and only human lives to be sacrificed. Such niceties had never deterred men such as these in their pursuit of ruthless ambition. This time their outrageous plot failed because of a technicality; their only concern then was to make sure no one in Moscow or Washington ever learned the whole truth.

PART THREE

THE COVER-UP

20

RICHARD M. NIXON WAS INAUGURATED as the thirty-seventh president of the United States on January 20, 1969. The Johnson administration turned over the reins of government after eight years of Democratic Party rule that had seen tensions with the Soviet Union intensified by the Cuban Missile Crisis and the escalating Vietnam War.

By all reckoning, the K-129 incident should have been packed away with the boxes of the outgoing administration, and the case closed. It was a chilling near-nuclear catastrophe, but fortunately it had somehow been averted. True, questions were left unanswered. But since no nuclear attack against America had actually succeeded, there was no residual emergency facing the incoming Republican team. The K-129 incident remained virtually unknown to the general populations of America and the Soviet Union. The public was not even aware that a submarine had sunk near Hawaii. The U.S. Navy was willing, officially at least, to chalk up the sinking of the Soviet submarine to an accident caused by battery gas combustion.

This should have been the end of the story of K-129,

another unexplained mystery of the Cold War to bury in storage boxes until some naval historian declassified the files for study at a future date.

But for some inexplicable reason, the strangest part of the saga of the aging submarine was only beginning, as the vanguard of the Nixon team took over the defense and intelligence agencies of government.

Instead of disappearing into bureaucratic obscurity, the ghost of K-129 resurfaced with a vengeance, and events were set in motion that would haunt the troubled waters of the Pacific for decades to come.

There has never been a satisfactory explanation for why some of the most powerful men on earth became so obsessed with raising, figuratively and literally, this aging submarine from its three-mile-deep grave. But that is exactly what they did, and the strange behavior of the world leaders involved in the K-129 incident from that point on posed an even greater Cold War mystery than the circumstances surrounding the sinking itself.

Even before the Nixon inauguration, a key figure in the new administration, who was destined to become one of the most enigmatic men of the Cold War era, took almost complete control of the diplomatic and intelligence affairs of the United States. Henry Alfred Kissinger, a forty-five-year-old Harvard University professor, was named assistant to the president for national security in December 1968, a month before Nixon took office. Kissinger quickly positioned himself between the president-elect and the heads of the government's intelligence agencies, so that all information would have to be funneled and filtered through him before it arrived on Nixon's desk.

While the Nixon transition team was still operating from suites at the Pierre Hotel in New York City, Kissinger took charge of the President's Daily Brief (PDB) given by the CIA. He decided what would be shown to the president—which items needed the president's attention and which did not. During this transition period, daily briefings for Kissinger were conducted by a career CIA agent, Paul Corscadden, in a secure room built in the basement at 450 Park Avenue, where the New York headquarters of the presidential campaign had been located. Kissinger established the pattern that kept CIA directors removed from personal contact with Nixon, who held grudges against the Agency from perceived past slights.

The haze of intrigue that would surround the Nixon administration was cast early in this preinauguration briefing center, established in the basement of an old office building. The door to the briefing room was, appropriately enough, black. The furtive comings and goings of government agents through the black door soon drew the attention of other building occupants. Whispers that some highly clandestine operation was being conducted from the location spread throughout the neighborhood. The setting was only a harbinger of the secrecy that would characterize the administration's conduct of foreign and intelligence dealings.

In mid-December, Kissinger directed that National Intelligence Estimates (NIE) also were to go to him personally. Kissinger culled the material and briefed Nixon on matters he deemed important. This practice continued after the move into the White House, where Kissinger remained in charge of all intelligence and sensitive international matters.

One of the first directives from the Oval Office was Nixon's announcement that he would personally conduct all foreign policy from the White House, rather than through the State Department. As the president's national security advisor, Kissinger became one of the most powerful men in Washington and, thus, the world. He ran the intelligence and foreign policy program through the National Security Council. Kissinger personally chaired six NSC subcommittees. One of the work groups under his direction was called the Forty Committee, which was responsible for approving all clandestine operations of the United States government. Kissinger was so secretive that he often advised his enemy counterparts sitting across the table in unpublicized negotiations to caution their diplomats against telling the U.S. State Department anything about the talks.

From his first day in office, Nixon's dealings, even between agencies of the government, were shrouded in mystery and intrigue. It was the way the administration worked, but few politicians or diplomats had any idea how global his schemes really were.

If the Johnson administration had been too exhausted to make use of the stunning Defense Intelligence Estimate and photographic packet on the K-129 incident, the top national security team in the incoming Nixon administration knew exactly what they had and what to do with it. In the new Nixon era of global intrigue, this was the kind of material on which grand strategies could be built, not to mention its potential value for geopolitical blackmail.

For President Nixon, the incriminating analysis and supporting photographs provided a ready-made tool to pry cracks in the Iron and Bamboo curtains. The president and his advisors were soon busily planning how to use this top-secret intelligence to maximum benefit. The K-129 incident was the linchpin for an aggressive, and sometimes bizarre, new foreign policy.

The DIA's findings on the rogue submarine came to the attention of the White House within a few days of Nixon's inauguration. A member of his inner circle of newly appointed advisors learned of the intelligence trove from the USS *Halibut*. General Alexander Haig, then assistant to National Security Advisor Kissinger, was the first of Nixon's men to see the photographs. He was impressed by the quality of the underwater photography, but more excited by the DIA's interpretation of what the photos revealed. The probability assessment, attached to the package of photographs and written catalogue of military secrets snatched from the rogue submarine, was a stunning document. Rogue or not, a finding that a Soviet submarine had actually tried to launch against America and had blown itself up in the act was priceless. Such a document, along with its supporting evidence, could have many uses—all of them good for the Americans, bad for the Soviets.

Haig insisted the photo package and naval intelligence analysis be delivered immediately to his boss. Kissinger, who was likewise impressed, wasted no time in sharing the stunning evidence with the president.

The K-129 matter was soon removed from the aegis

of U.S. Navy intelligence and deposited in Nixon's National Security Council. Whereas the Johnson administration had tried to gloss over the intelligence finding about the rogue attack with a quick fix and forget it, the incoming Nixon administration was excited about its potential geopolitical value.

Kissinger would become America's master of back-channel diplomacy, and this was the first intelligence plum to drop in his lap. The information regarding the K-129 incident was exactly the kind of enemy intelligence that lent itself to shadowy communications between adversaries that thrived in an environment of secrecy and black operations.

As a piece of military intelligence, the K-129 wreck had proven of limited value. As bait for a political trap, the sunken submarine suddenly had unlimited value.

The Navy's deep-sea intelligence operatives soon guessed that their prize was being snatched away by the spooks and politicians.

"The discovery of a high probability that the Soviet submarine was some sort of rogue, and that at the outset the Soviets had no idea that its loss was not just an accident, was a situation made to order for Kissinger," said Dr. John Craven in his autobiography. "Moreover, our disclosure to the Soviets of what we had learned about their submarine would likely raise an unanswerable question in Brezhnev's mind about his command and control of his armed forces."

Possibly a scheme was developed in the White House to use this material to blackmail the Soviets, since revelation of a sneak attack with nuclear missiles would have been a crushing embarrassment to Brezhnev and the Soviet military, regardless of who in Moscow had orchestrated it. Brezhnev was already reeling under world criticism over the Czechoslovakia invasion and the "Brezhnev Doctrine," which called for the armed invasion of any Communist satellite state that dared deviate from the Moscow line.

It was only a short time until the Soviets had been secretly apprised that the Americans had found their sunken submarine. A small, but tantalizing packet of classified material about the missing boat mysteriously fell into Russian hands. Reports that an unmarked packet of information on the K-129 had been left on the doorstep of the Soviet embassy were obviously part of an effort to hide the real source of the leak.

The KGB had covertly contacted Kissinger even before Nixon was elected. Oleg Kalugin, Washington station chief for the KGB, established a back channel to Nixon through Kissinger as early as August 1968, three months before the election. The KGB, at the time, was being run by Andropov and his mentor Suslov.

A high-ranking Soviet intelligence officer sent Kissinger a series of letters to be delivered to Nixon, stating that the Soviets would welcome his election. There were already signs of a growing rift in the Soviet leadership. This clandestine contact exemplified the aggressive plotting in Moscow because, concurrently, Soviet Ambassador Anatoly Dobrynin was secretly contacting the Democratic campaign of Hubert Humphrey. Dobrynin sent word that the Politburo supported the Democratic candidate's campaign. An offer of campaign contributions was refused by Humphrey.

Regardless of the origin of these clandestine contacts

and the appearance of Soviet meddling in American politics, Kissinger would use the opportunity to establish personal contacts that were to be the hallmark of American foreign policy for the next four years.

Kissinger almost certainly recognized the significance of the DIA's conclusions about the K-129 incident for another reason. He could see through the sinister plot of the schemers in Moscow because he had envisioned a similar scenario in his early writings. He had hypothesized a plot involving a sneak attack by a fledgling nuclear power against a superpower, with the goal of placing blame on a third superpower adversary. Kissinger wrote extensively about such an attack in his book *The Necessity for Choice* published in 1961, while he was still a professor at Harvard University. In his hypothetical case, the smaller nuclear power was called the Nth country.

"The Soviet Union cannot look with equanimity on the emergence of a powerful China armed with nuclear weapons," Kissinger wrote. "The unchecked diffusion of nuclear weapons is said also to raise the specter of what has been called catalytic war—a conflict started by an irresponsible smaller country with a nuclear attack on a major nuclear power. Since, in the missile age, the direction from which the blow comes may be difficult to determine, the attacked nation may react by an all-out blow against its chief opponent."

Kissinger pointed out that this idea of a sneak attack by a smaller country to induce two larger powers to destroy each other was the storyline of a popular 1960s nuclear holocaust movie. He wrote: "As described in *On the Beach*, a catalytic war starts with a nuclear attack by one of the Nth countries on a major power which, unable to discover the origin of the blow, retaliates against its chief opponent."

Of course, in the K-129 incident the scenario was reversed. A cabal in Moscow had planned a sneak attack against the United States, and had attempted to make the lesser nuclear power appear to be the attacker, so that the Americans would obliterate Red China.

If the plotters used the ideas of an unwitting Kissinger to help design their horrific scheme, they were somewhat selective in what they chose to plagiarize. Kissinger predicted, accurately, a few paragraphs later, that by the time the Nth countries had developed rudimentary nuclear missile technology, the major powers would have perfected systems for determining, with high accuracy, the point of origin of an attacking missile. In 1968, the United States was not quite at that point of perfection with its satellite and SOSUS surveillance systems, but it was much closer than the Soviet navy or the plotters in Moscow were aware.

With the KGB's recognition of the critical position Kissinger assumed in the administration, his earlier writings were most certainly scrutinized by KGB Chairman Andropov. Long before Kissinger became the most prominent foreign-affairs figure in the Nixon administration, his influence on Western defense policies was widely recognized and undoubtedly closely followed by the Kremlin and the KGB. His 1957 book, *Nuclear Weapons and Foreign Policy*, had established him as one of the West's leading authorities on strategies for dealing with the Soviet bloc's nuclear threat. He was director of Harvard University's defense studies program from 1958 to 1971, and served as an advisor on nuclear defense to every U.S. president during that period. Kissinger's prescient warning in *The Necessity for Choice* describing a duplicitous nuclear attack, coupled with John Walker's documentation of the Johnson administration's fear of a sneak attack by a lone Chinese submarine, seemed to provide a blueprint for the plot. The germ for the Kremlin plotters' idea, ironically, could have originated in American political books and U.S. intelligence documents.

The sunken Soviet submarine became the central focus for intrigues after Nixon assumed the presidency. Documentation of events that came to light after the end of the Cold War revealed that the Nixon administration purposefully delivered intelligence of Soviet military operations to the Communist Chinese leadership as leverage for opening dialogue. While there has been no direct mention of the K-129 incident in newly released transcripts of exchanges between the Americans and the Chinese, it is entirely plausible that Mao would have been especially grateful and interested in learning that the Soviets schemed to attack the United States and place the blame on China.

Central to Nixon's extraordinary success in bringing down the Bamboo Curtain, which has never been fully explained by historians, was Kissinger's ability to offer the Chinese key strategic information about their Soviet adversary. A growing body of information reveals that the path to rapprochement with the Chinese was paved with lavish gifts of American military intelligence. Kissinger was the chief bearer of these gifts to the grim Chinese leaders, and positioned himself as the indispensable conduit between China and the United States.

Kissinger clearly wanted to impress the Chinese with the high value of the military information about the Soviets that the United States would be able to provide. Information that the Soviets had schemed to implicate the Chinese in an attack against the United States would have been "golden" in the parlance of spydom.

It seems more than coincidental that, at the very time of these early meetings with the Chinese, the White House was launching a huge secret project centered on the sunken Soviet submarine. Many other sensitive topics relating to the Soviet's military activities were discussed, and highly secret intelligence was made available by Kissinger and his deputies, according to recently released documents about the Kissinger meetings with Chinese leaders.

Declassified transcripts of a meeting in New York between Kissinger and China's UN ambassador Huang Hua prove the Nixon administration was offering China military secrets about the Soviet Union months before any formal negotiations were launched. In one such meeting National Security Advisor Kissinger told Ambassador Huang, "We would be prepared at your request, and through whatever sources you wish, to give you whatever information we have about the disposition of Soviet forces."

Agence France Presse revealed, in January 1999, that top-secret documents showed Kissinger had been giving the Chinese intelligence on the Soviet military from the early days of the administration, as part of Nixon's "triangular diplomacy."

Triangulation of foreign policy involving the United States, the Soviet Union, and the People's Republic of China was an outgrowth of the realpolitik of the Cold War era. That policy reached its zenith in the early Nixon years under the skillful guidance of Henry Kissinger. Previous U.S. administrations had treated both the Soviets and the Red Chinese as adversaries. In the Pacific and eastern Asia, the power struggle had reached its most dangerous impasse by the end of the 1960s. International relations centered on strategic competition among these three powers, and Kissinger was able to masterfully manipulate the two Communist adversaries by pitting each against the other in a series of early behind-the-scenes meetings.

"When one of three states perceives at least one of the other two as a threat, that state tries to avoid having simultaneously poor relations with the other two and endeavors at all cost to prevent collusion between them," concludes a major study of this triangular diplomacy and the Cold War period. "The aim of each is to avoid collusion of the two others, and to blackmail one's main enemy by threatening collusion with the third."

Kissinger became the master implementer of this strategy. The intelligence package on the K-129 almost certainly was one of the valuable weapons in his arsenal. It could be used effectively either to blackmail Soviet negotiators or to bribe Chinese representatives.

Although Kissinger had been contacted directly by the KGB, most likely on behalf of the Suslov-

Andropov faction before Nixon's assuming office, he wasted no time setting up similar clandestine lines directly to Brezhnev and the Politburo. The channel Kissinger opened was through the wily old Moscow intriguer Anatoly Dobrynin, who had survived in the Soviet embassy in Washington throughout the turbulent Khrushchev years. Dobrynin became ambassador to the United States in 1962, and would serve through the terms of six U.S. presidents. But his relationship with Kissinger, who went around newly appointed Secretary of State William P. Rogers to establish personal links to Moscow, was unique.

In a private, one-on-one meeting, Kissinger let Dobrynin know very early on that the only access to the new president was through him. The meeting was held in Kissinger's White House office. Even though Kissinger was secretly offering the fullest cooperation with the Chinese in turning over U.S. intelligence on Soviet military operations in Asia, he assured Dobrynin that the Nixon administration was "not going to interfere in the present-day Soviet-Chinese conflict in any way."

Dobrynin reported to Brezhnev that Kissinger was a "smart and erudite person" who did not hesitate to let the Soviets know he would be the contact point for future relations. The normal channels through the State Department were to be used only for the most mundane matters.

Dobrynin told his superiors in Moscow: "During our conversation he, for example, without any excessive humility, announced that in all of Washington only two people can answer precisely at any given moment about the position of the USA on this or that question: these are President Nixon and he, Kissinger."

Thus, from the beginning of the Nixon administration, back-channel diplomacy became the principal method of handling the dangerous affairs of the Cold War—out of sight of the media, Congress, and the world. The wreck of the K-129 was likely a pawn in this grand, clandestine, geopolitical game.

21

SINCE THE END OF THE COLD WAR, at least three former Soviet admirals who were involved with the K-129 investigation shortly after its disappearance have described details of the damage to the submarine that could only have been obtained from viewing the USS *Halibut's* photographs.

The Soviet officers who claim to have seen the pictures have repeated the story that someone slipped an unmarked envelope of photographs and other material under the entrance to the Soviet embassy in Washington. The photos, just a few of the thousands taken by the crew of the *Halibut*, clearly depicted the damage that sank K-129.

While political expediency would not let these former Soviet naval officers admit their submarine might have destroyed itself during a launch attempt, some of these men must have suspected that possibility. Both Soviets and Americans had conducted hundreds of test firings, and there had been dozens of accidents on submarines and aircraft carrying nuclear weapons. In no case had a nuclear warhead trigger exploded prematurely in a launch tube or missile silo, destroying the thermal core. The conclusion drawn in the DIA's probability analysis that the submarine had attempted to launch in the vicinity of the American base was probably as shocking to the Communist hierarchy as it had been to the U.S. intelligence analysts.

Since Soviet line officers from the Pacific Fleet who were involved in the investigation at the fleet command level had access to the photographs, surely leaders in the Kremlin were fully apprised of the material. There is no doubt that Soviet military intelligence had somehow received detailed information, probably film and photographs of the K-129 wreck, and parts of the U.S. Navy and Defense Intelligence Agency assessments.

At the end of the Cold War, American intelligence agents attending a meeting in Moscow were "spooked" by the intimate knowledge a former Soviet intelligence agent revealed to them about the Americans' files on the K-129 incident.

Still, the implications for national security of the leaked material at the political level were considerably more significant than at the military intelligence level.

It matters little whether the U.S. intel packet delivered to the Soviets came from a spy or from an approved back-channel source in the Nixon administration. The dramatic impact on key figures in Moscow was the same. The origin of the photographs seen by the Soviet naval men could only have been Washington, D.C. The *Halibut* photographs and accompanying analysis were classified top-secret, and had been available to only a few key intelligence operatives in the U.S. government at that time. The Soviets could not have produced the photographs themselves for two main reasons: They did not even know the location of their lost submarine, and they did not have the technology to dive deep into the ocean and gather this type of information.

It is logical to assume that this leaked or stolen information quickly found its way to a perplexed general secretary Leonid Brezhnev.

One of Kissinger's most audacious personal relationships was in the Soviet embassy in Washington. He frequently met Soviet Ambassador Dobrynin for private conversations and off-the-record negotiations, without the U.S. State Department being aware of the meetings. Former Soviet admirals freely acknowledge that Kissinger, through his contacts with Dobrynin, was the source of "sensational information" about the K-129. A published account of the Washington-to-Moscow conduit alleged that the information was shared in 1974 or 1975, but just how early the official exchanges began has never been established.

A likely purpose of sharing the K-129 information with the Soviets was geopolitical blackmail. Nixon and his insiders used similar tactics to achieve desired results at this critical period in the Cold War. As unorthodox as the shadowy diplomacy seems, its ultimate outcome may well have been to spare the world a devastating exchange of nuclear strikes.

In Moscow, Brezhnev was almost certainly kept in the dark about the true nature of the K-129's final actions until he was briefed on the American intelligence finding. Kremlin reaction on learning of an attempted rogue attack on America by one of its submarines can only be imagined. The Soviet navy still did not know where its submarine had sunk. Early in the investigation, and before the U.S. intelligence package arrived in Moscow, the admiralty held firmly to the theory that K-129 had been rammed by the USS *Swordfish*, almost a thousand miles from where the sub actually went down.

At that time, the USSR was barely holding on to its vast collection of satellite states in Eastern Europe and neo-colonies in Africa and Asia. The Soviets, going broke providing costly aid to Third World Communist governments, relied heavily on propaganda to maintain the loyalty of Third World states in its sphere of influence.

The Soviets had not forgotten the damaging impact of photographic intelligence presented to the United Nations during the Cuban Missile Crisis. Now, confronted with a package of highly technical evidence of another warlike assault on the United States only a half-dozen years later, the cost would be very high.

Even if he pleaded that the K-129 was a rogue, Brezhnev could take little comfort. His leadership had been under constant internal challenge from the beginning of his rise to the top of the USSR. He could not afford for the Politburo, let alone leaders of the client states, to learn of his regime's tenuous control over the Soviet nuclear arsenal. If Brezhnev was too weak to secure his own nuclear missiles, he was too incompetent to lead the Soviet Union against the technically superior U.S. forces led by the aggressive new administration in Washington.

Brezhnev was already embroiled in an internal fight for control within the Kremlin. This power struggle between Brezhnev and the ideologically Stalinist cabal came to a head shortly after the information about the K-129 incident became available in Moscow.

Something strange took place in the highest circles of the Kremlin in late 1969. The power struggle within the Politburo and the Secretariat of the Communist Party saw an emboldened Brezhnev openly confront his rivals. The confrontation came to be known by Sovietologists as the "Moscow Mini Crisis," and remains an unsolved mystery to this day.

The hard-liners, led by the shadowy party ideologue Suslov and his protégé KGB Director Andropov, were challenged by Brezhnev and the top generals and admirals. A review of recent reports on the Kremlin power struggle suggests that the timing may very well have coincided with the arrival of the secret K-129 packet from Washington. Certainly, such information would have led to urgent internal investigations into who in the Soviet Union might have had the means and motive to attempt an unauthorized and potentially devastating sneak attack against an American target.

Suspicion was apparently quickly directed at Suslov and the KGB. Suslov had earlier been Brezhnev's mentor, as he had been to other successful leaders since the Stalin era. But the two men were suddenly bitter enemies.

Suslov led a group in denouncing Brezhnev over his proposed policies to change the Soviet economy, and went so far as to file a list of charges and demands with the party secretariat. To everyone's surprise, Brezhnev did not cower before Suslov's challenge to his leadership. Showing amazing fortitude for a bureaucrat who had always been considered weak, Brezhnev took an unannounced trip to Belarus, to meet secretly with his generals. The Red Army was engaged in massive annual Warsaw Pact maneuvers. He met with the powerful minister of defense, Andrei. A. Grechko, and a number of other generals and admirals. Although Brezhnev had appointed General Grechko to head the military establishment in 1967, Grechko was still considered to be above politics and 100 percent committed to the Red Army.

Whatever evidence Brezhnev put before the normally apolitical Red Army marshals, it was convincing enough to push them in the unprecedented direction of involvement in Kremlin politics. The Soviet generals and admirals had a very good reason to stay out of politics. They remembered only too well the bloody purges of the military leadership by Stalin in the late 1930s, which had decimated the top ranks of the army and navy, just before the outbreak of World War II.

Brezhnev could have produced no more powerful incentive for the Soviet military leaders to break with long-standing protocol than evidence that renegade plotters in the KGB had usurped command of a Soviet nuclear submarine in an attempt to start a nuclear war. It is reasonable to surmise that Brezhnev may well have used the K-129 incident to convince the generals to back him.

General Grechko, along with other admirals, generals, and marshals, gave Brezhnev assurances that the Red Army (and Navy) would be with him in the power struggle against the hard-liners led by Suslov. A confident Brezhnev returned to Moscow in December 1969 and initiated a power play, declaring himself the "great Leninist and leading fighter for peace."

An internal struggle ensued over the next several months, with posters of Brezhnev gradually replacing those of other contenders for supreme leadership. April 1970, which was a little more than two years after the sinking of K-129, turned out to be a particularly unhealthy month for those who had opposed Brezhnev. It ended with *Pravda's* announcing a spate of illnesses among the top leaders. They were conspicuously missing from the reviewing stand above Lenin's Tomb where they would be expected to line up for the big May Day parade of Soviet military might.

Pravda reported that Suslov, suffering from recurring tubercular attacks, had retired to his *dacha* for a long rest. The newspaper noted that Nikolay Podgorny, first party secretary, was at home with a "feverish cold." Alexsey Nikolayevich Kosygin, chairman of the council of ministers, was reported to be simply ill in the hospital. Alexsandr Shelepin, head of the council of trade unions, had an emergency gall bladder operation. These men, and lesser functionaries who had sided against Brezhnev and the army, soon retired from active roles in government. A badly chastened Andropov, who had been Suslov's golden boy, dropped from political activities for a time, but retained his title as chairman of the KGB. He ultimately redeemed himself with the party. He went on to become general secretary of the Communist Party just days after Brezhnev's death, and ruled the USSR for a little more than a year until his own death in 1983.

Others outside the Soviet military had joined Brezhnev in countering the Stalinists. In his play for power, Suslov had launched a campaign to rehabilitate Stalin, which created great consternation in many circles of Moscow. Central Committee members, writers, musicians, journalists, and actors also signed petitions of support for Brezhnev and against bringing back the Stalin era.

But it was the military, which came out of its cloistered nonpolitical encampment, that actually gave Brezhnev the power to face down the pro-Stalinists Suslov, Andropov, and the KGB.

As feared as it was, the KGB was no match for the mighty Red Army. Something had made the military men angry enough to insinuate themselves into a Communist Party feud for the first time. The K-129 incident is a likely candidate for the catalyst that drove the generals out of their stoic neutrality.

Drastic, and heretofore unexplained, changes in naval procedures also support the theory that Brezhnev and the Soviet military were alarmed by intelligence that K-129's sinking might have been the result of a rogue attempt to launch a nuclear missile.

A significant new procedure was adopted early in 1970, requiring the launch codes for all ballistic missile submarines to be held by General Staff headquarters. This change in long-standing procedures thereby denied any rogue or mutinous crew the ability to arm and aim its missiles without direct orders, accompanied by arming codes, from a central command.

The submarine missile launch codes were also removed from the operational fleet and returned to supreme Soviet navy headquarters. Before this change, the captain kept most of the necessary targeting and launch codes, and awaited only a confirmation code from fleet headquarters to be delivered with the final order to attack. That additional code, when added to the captain's code, unlocked the fail-safe system. Under the new procedures, submarine commanders were no longer entrusted with the firing codes before they sailed on missions; no codes were kept in the ships' safe in the captain's quarters. All instructions necessary to arm the mechanisms and set the target courses would henceforth be radioed to submarine commanders only after a red alert condition was declared.

Shortly after the launch procedures were changed, the Soviet military took another step to safeguard deployment of nuclear weapons. The KGB was stripped of its key role as custodian of nuclear warheads. Control of nuclear devices was given to the Soviet army, navy, and air force units that deployed these weapons. Up until the end of 1969, the KGB had physical possession of all nuclear warheads for land, sea, and air delivery. Military commanders had to requisition nuclear weaponry from the KGB. When the military took charge of distribution of the Soviet Union's nuclear weapons, the KGB was relegated to guard duty at the arsenals.

These sudden changes in long-standing launch procedures and the removal of KGB authority over the nuclear stockpiles did not take place in a vacuum. Something significant must have forced the action. The possibility that the world might be told the Soviet military had lost control of one of its nuclear-armed submarines could certainly have prompted such dramatic remedies.

Compromises were reached in the Kremlin and, for the first time, the losers in the struggle were not purged. But their powers were strictly curtailed. Suslov was relegated to a second-tier post. Representatives from each camp were placed in positions to checkmate the other. For all practical purposes, the government was paralyzed.

Without further ado, Suslov withdrew his attacks against Brezhnev in the Communist Party plenum. The all-powerful KGB, also uncharacteristically, took its loss of prestige and control meekly. Some extremely damning piece of evidence would have been required for Brezhnev's sudden success in smashing the opposition within the party and the Politburo. A copy of the U.S. intelligence assessment of a rogue submarine attack could well have been the instrument that ended the so-called Moscow Mini Crisis, and shifted power to the Soviet military and a more moderate group of leaders in the Kremlin.

President Nixon did not rely solely on the intimidating evidence from the K-129 incident to bully, blackmail, and coerce changes from the Soviet and Chinese Communists. In late 1969, he launched what has recently been revealed in declassified documents as the Nixon "madman strategy."

This astounding tactic was apparently a deliberate attempt by the Nixon administration to make adversaries believe they were dealing with an irrational American president with his finger on the doomsday button. The only logical reason for such strange behavior in dealing with deadly weapons in a tense world would have been a psychological warfare plan aimed at frightening the Russians into making concessions in the Vietnam War and the long-stalled arms control negotiations. One of Nixon's first acts under the madman strategy was to place all military forces of the United States on full nuclear alert in October 1969.

Initiation of this madman strategy may have been an early reaction to Nixon's learning about the K-129 incident, because the first sign of an aggressive new policy came when Nixon ordered a massive increase in surveillance of all Soviet ships, including submarines, in the Atlantic and Pacific. Navy submarine hunters increased aerial cover of Soviet naval maneuvers, and American submarines and surface antisubmarine warfare ships more doggedly tailed Soviet vessels. Naval intelligence activities were stepped up to a near-wartime level.

Next, Nixon ordered dangerously provocative strategic aircraft maneuvers and sudden, periodic blackouts of all Allied military communications. Soviet spies may well have interpreted these strange maneuvers as preparations for an attack. It was a dangerous cat-and-mouse game.

The war in Vietnam was still raging, and Nixon took his aggressive policy into that theater of operations, even though the United States did not directly face the Soviets there. He ordered seemingly irrational patterns of military action in Vietnam, which included abruptly increased bombing raids into Cambodia and Laos, followed by unexplained pauses in the bombings. He ordered several purposeless sea raids on North

Vietnamese territory. It was a bag of dirty tricks designed to convince an already jittery enemy that they faced a maniac in the new American president.

The American people were kept as much in the dark about this saber-rattling strategy as they were about the conclusions drawn regarding the Soviet submarine's attempted attack on Hawaii. The government's probability analysis on the K-129 had to be kept from the public, because revealing such a doomsday scenario would have dire consequences for both the nation's economy and its security. Even a hint at how close America came to a catastrophic nuclear attack on one of its cities would have panicked the public and sent the nation into a new frenzy of bomb-shelter building. The Cuban Missile Crisis had had a similar effect a few years earlier. The incident off Hawaii brought the public to within seconds of a nuclear attack. While the Cuban crisis was played out in the media, the attack on Pearl Harbor and Honolulu would have come without warning.

The incident involving the Soviet submarine was most likely used successfully during the early days of the Nixon administration as both carrot and stick to begin changing the recalcitrant conduct of America's two most powerful enemies. Had the K-129 story ended there, the relic submarine would already have had a significant impact on the outcome of the Cold War.

But Nixon and his advisors had further use for the wreck lying three miles down in the Pacific, northwest of Hawaii.

In January 1969, Dr. John Craven had taken an unpaid leave of absence from his position as chief scientist at the Navy's Special Projects Office to teach at the Massachusetts Institute of Technology. The following December he received a call from the Navy, asking him to serve on the DIA Scientific Advisory Board. Upon returning to the agency as a consultant, he learned that, under the new administration, much of the submarine intelligence program had been taken over by the Central Intelligence Agency. Both the Navy and the DIA were unhappy about the arrangement.

It was in this rancorous atmosphere that Dr. Craven and others in the Navy's underseas intelligence community learned of one of the strangest projects in the history of American intelligence.

At the height of Kissinger's back-channel diplomacy with the Soviets and Chinese, and when Nixon was aggressively employing his madman antics, an even stranger scheme emerged from the White House. The Central Intelligence Agency was tasked with recovering the entire K-129 wreck from the bottom of the ocean.

The clandestine Forty Committee authorized a fantastic operation to recover the Soviet submarine on October 20, 1969. Committees such as this one had been formed to supervise covert operations for every president since Dwight Eisenhower. Under Nixon, the committee answered directly to Kissinger in his role as national security advisor. The Forty Committee included high-level assistants from Department of State, Department of Defense, CIA, DIA, and NSC.

In this case, the Forty Committee approved an operation for the CIA to physically recover the wrecked

K-129. The operation, which came to be known as Project Jennifer, required the construction of a special-purpose spy ship called the *Glomar Explorer*.

To accomplish the huge project Nixon removed the Navy from the K-129 loop, except on a need-to-know basis. He turned the project over to a special working group in the Central Intelligence Agency. What had been, until then, primarily a military intelligence project led by the DIA became a clandestine political operation run by the CIA and the White House. As with many CIA covert operations during that period of the Cold War, bitter interservice rivalries led to leaks of information. But, overall, the operation was kept closely guarded within a small group of insiders.

Once the project was approved, Nixon's men called on a civilian who was no stranger to the United States government's weird world of espionage to front the mission. The eccentric billionaire Howard Hughes, using the cover of one of his oil companies, was commissioned by the CIA to build and operate a fantastical boat for an almost science-fiction-type covert operation.

22

THE PROJECT TO RAISE THE SOVIET SUBMARINE from the bottom of the Pacific Ocean quickly became the "CIA's most expensive and ambitious operation of all time." Over the lifetime of the operation, it would go through several phases and have a number of code names, but the name that stuck was Project Jennifer.

Rapidly improving relations between the United States, the Soviet Union, and the People's Republic of China would seem to have overtaken the need for such a dramatic and large-scale covert operation. By the time the CIA clandestine mission to retrieve K-129 was fully underway, Kissinger's back-channel diplomacy had cracked open the door to Beijing and Moscow.

The K-129 incident may have provided some of the impetus for these world-changing geopolitical events, but the larger strategy of triangulation and brinkmanship was the real engine driving the Nixon administration's breathtaking foreign policy successes.

On another front, the Vietnam War, Nixon also seemed to be making progress, after deliberate escalation in 1969. Nixon had ordered a wild dash by American troops into Cambodia in May 1969, opening a new war front in the face of public outrage in the United States. The eight-week Cambodian incursion succeeded in destroying the supply bases along the southern leg of the Ho Chi Minh Trail, which drastically curtailed the fighting for the next two years. The relative lull in combat was long enough to set in motion the beginning of an orderly withdrawal of troops from Vietnam.

The first major Nixon foreign policy breakthrough came, not in Soviet-American relations or in the Vietnam War, but with the People's Republic of China. Kissinger, whose title was still national security advisor to the president, made an unannounced visit to China in July 1971. The topics covered in that first meeting in China are still classified. However, because of the timing of the meeting, there is reason to suspect that Kissinger or his aides capitalized on the earlier leaks of intelligence about the K-129.

The delegation also wanted the Chinese leadership to know that the Nixon administration was concerned about the prospect of a full-scale Sino-Soviet war breaking out. Chinese and Soviet armies were involved in frequent skirmishes all along their common border. More ominously, following a large battle on the Ussuri River in which several hundred soldiers and militiamen from both sides were killed, the Soviets had threatened to use nuclear force against China.

Kissinger used the border conflict between the Communist states as leverage. The transcript from a meeting between Chairman Mao and Kissinger flatly stated that the Americans favored China. Kissinger told the Chinese tyrant that the entire world would suffer if the Soviets successfully invaded China. "It would dislocate the security of all other countries and will lead to our own isolation," Kissinger told Mao. He said the United States did not want to see China defeated, because it would elevate the Soviet Union to the most powerful nation on earth, ruling a territory astride Europe and Asia. At the very time Kissinger was expressing concern over the destruction of the Communist states from a Sino-Soviet war, one of his working groups was planning just that fate for both. The Forty Committee, which Kissinger chaired, was actively issuing mandates to the CIA to "create and exploit troublesome problems for International Communism, impair relations between the USSR and Communist China and between them and their satellites, complicate control within the USSR, Communist China and their satellites, and retard the growth of the military and economic potential of the Soviet bloc."

The strategy of intrigue seemed to have produced a big payoff for Nixon's foreign policy goals. Without explanation, the Cold War suddenly began to thaw, despite the fact that both the Soviet Union and Communist China were then under the leadership of hard-liners.

The role of the K-129 incident as a wedge in these early talks has never been publicly revealed. But it is reasonable to assume that Kissinger benefited from the interpretation that the Soviet plot, rogue or not, intended to blame the attack on China's Golf I submarine. The U.S. intelligence material turned over to the Chinese would not have emphasized a conclusion that K-129 was possibly a rogue submarine rather than an authorized, albeit secret, Soviet mission. A suspicious intriguer such as Mao, who also held so much personal animosity toward the Soviet leadership, would have been impressed by details of such a sinister plot.

Many of the groundbreaking conversations between Chinese officials and Kissinger's delegation remain classified. However, a large number of the official transcripts of Kissinger's visits with Chou En-lai and Mao were declassified in the 1990s after the end of the Cold War. No official document has yet been declassified that indicates Kissinger delivered the message of Soviet perfidy about the rogue submarine to the Chinese.

Secret meetings between Americans and Chinese leaders continued throughout 1971. By early 1972, a breakthrough was achieved in a relationship that had seen America and China in a virtual state of undeclared war since 1949, and a real war on the Korean Peninsula in the early 1950s. U.S.-China rapprochement was concluded in early 1972, and a victorious President Nixon went to China.

Despite the continuation of openly hostile rhetoric between the Americans and the Soviets, there was also an inexplicable cooling-off period in the Cold War at about the same time. Something had scared the bellicose Soviets back to the bargaining table. After being stalled for years, the United States and the Soviet Union suddenly came to terms on a strategic arms limitation treaty. Once again, timing coincided with frenzied American efforts to exploit the K-129 wreck. And once again, nothing about a subject of such vital inter-

est to the Soviets is mentioned in any of the newly declassified transcripts of secret meetings between
Kissinger and the Russians. However, it should be remembered that major international negotiations between the United States, the Soviet Union, and Red
China were rapidly coming to successful conclusion
during this brief period in the Cold War.

SALT I was signed by Nixon and Brezhnev in
Moscow on May 26, 1972. Shortly afterward, a mutu-
ally acceptable antiballistic missile accord was reached,
which offered an imaginary degree of protection for
some American and Russian cities. Later, the U.S. Congress ordered an end to the Johnson administration's
Sentinel ABM deployments.

A flurry of other agreements quickly followed these
early geopolitical breakthroughs. Nixon and Brezhnev
inked more treaties in 1972 than all the presidents of
the two belligerent states had signed in the previous
fifty-year history of Soviet-American relations.

Despite his remarkable international successes, Nixon
doggedly pursued the fantastic scheme to raise the
sunken Soviet submarine, and for an unreasonably high
price, at a time when U.S. military budgets were astro-
nomical. What could possibly have compelled the
Nixon administration to pursue a project that, if discovered, could have derailed Soviet-American détente, and
the Salt I and ABM treaties? Why was the physical recovery of an old-type Soviet submarine so important?

After the project was finally revealed, there was
much speculation in the media and government circles

about why the CIA and Nixon undertook Project Jennifer in the first place. Guesses ranged from the standard canard that the intelligence to be gained was essential for national security, to the trite explanation that Nixon designed the project as a "pork barrel" payback to his campaign contributors. Neither of these explanations seems supportable, considering the extraordinary high cost and high risk involved.

The most expensive CIA operation in history, Project Jennifer became one of the single highest priorities in the Nixon years. Like every other detail of the project, the official price tag was, and remains, top-secret. Funds were drawn by the CIA from the Navy's covert deep-sea intelligence budget, and additional funding was hidden throughout the "black ops" budgets of the spy agency. Estimated costs range widely, from a high of $550 million reported in *Ships of the World: An Historical Encyclopedia,* to the much lower and less precise estimate "in excess of $200 million," cited in a Federation of American Scientists intelligence report. Even at the low end of these estimates, the cost of the project was enormous for that period, especially since the American taxpayers were already groaning under the burdens of the six-year-long Vietnam War. The most commonly quoted cost estimate appearing in the national media for Project Jennifer was $500 million. That was almost enough money to build four nuclear-powered submarines at the 1970 cost of approximately $130 million per boat.

It is known that the single costliest piece of hardware for the project was the special supership constructed to serve as the platform for raising the K-129.

"The ship took five years to build . . . on time and under budget [$70 million]," reported author Mark Riebling in WEDGE: *The Secret War Between the FBI and CIA*.

Nixon and the CIA apparently believed the clandestine project was worth the cost and risks, because they doggedly pursued it, in the face of considerable disagreement. Knowledgeable intelligence experts from that era argued that any military secrets the older-style submarine might yield could be gained by other means, more cheaply and much more quickly.

The USS *Halibut* had already exploited the wreck for many of the military and technical secrets, at the very least exhaustively filming much of the boat and probably extracting some items as well. Despite the age of the submarine, its missile and communications systems were still of interest to the U.S. Navy. Some of the secrets the Navy wanted to harvest from the submarine were the Serb ballistic missiles and guidance systems, the nuclear-tipped torpedoes, code machines and codebooks, the internal guidance and navigational systems, the radio equipment, samples of the submarine's plate welds, mechanical parts, official trip logs, and personal letters of the crew. Most valuable on this shopping list were the nuclear missiles and the code machines and codebooks. This list of military secrets, however, did not seem to justify a $500-million program to raise the entire submarine.

The U.S. Navy, through its underseas intelligence-gathering program, already had the ability, or was in the process of developing the technology, to recover much of this trove from the seabed. For some time the Navy had been scouring the bottom of the seas, locating and recovering Soviet rocket parts, including heavy sections of missile reentry vehicles. First-generation robots were already in use by the USS *Halibut* and surface ships such as the *Mizar*. Cable-controlled underwater recovery vehicles (CURV) that could grapple or snare were lowered to the sea floor to bring large objects into the bays of mother ships.

Some items may have been lifted from the K-129 wreck using this technology. Dr. Craven, the Navy scientist in charge of the Deep Submergence Systems Project, testified before the United States Senate that the *Halibut* had already used "investigative equipments" for "optimum recovery" from the wreck before the CIA entered the picture. In 1966, the navy's *Mizar* employed a robot to pick up a hydrogen bomb from the bottom of the Mediterranean Sea. The bomb had fallen into deep water after the midair collision of a B-52 and a refueling tanker off the coast of Palomares, Spain.

Even if existing equipment was not yet available to extract and raise one of K-129's Serb missiles, special deep-diving robots to do such a chore could certainly have been built for less money, in less time, than the special recovery ship that was central to Project Jennifer's scheme to raise the whole submarine.

There is a well-established record that the U.S. Navy did not believe the recovery mission was worth the enormous cost, and certainly not if the Navy's budgets for underseas intelligence programs were to be raided to pay for the CIA project.

The Navy brass were not the only naysayers. Kissinger expressed doubts about the risk-benefit ratio of such a scheme. The danger of upsetting precariously balanced agreements by public disclosure of an American attempt to steal the Soviets' submarine hardly seemed worth further risks.

The Soviets would have seen an American effort to seize their wrecked submarine as an act of aggression during a time of peace. If the Soviets learned of the attempt, the possibility of a confrontation in international waters loomed large. Kissinger feared the project would derail détente in its delicate stage of infancy, and hamper other secret negotiations to end the Vietnam War. The carefully crafted SALT I and ABM treaties could have also been jeopardized.

Finally, the charge that Nixon may have undertaken the expensive project simply to reward political patrons with huge, under-the-table contracts paid for with black operations money can be easily refuted. The speculation that Project Jennifer was a giant boondoggle with the purpose of repaying West Coast campaign contributors does not seem likely when the contractors for various parts of the project are examined. The largest single expenditure—$70 million for the construction of the ship—was paid to an East Coast shipbuilding consortium. The subcontracts for the various complicated machinery, parts, and equipment for the boat were scattered among American and European companies.

There appeared to be little opportunity for patronage in the project. Nixon would more likely have gained favor with his supporters in the military defense industry by allowing the worthless Sentinel ABM shield project started by his predecessor to be fully deployed. There was almost twice as much budget for that massive missile defense project as there was in Project Jennifer.

So if there was no military intelligence value to the project that could not have been gained cheaper and faster by picking the wreck apart with existing technology, and the most important foreign affairs official in the Nixon team did not support it for geopolitical reasons, what esoteric purpose would raising the K-129 serve? Apparently the president himself, along with a handful of advisors, was obsessed with continuing Project Jennifer. Unless Nixon wanted the whole Soviet submarine physically brought to the surface, dismantled, and reassembled in some hidden place in the United States like a bizarre, giant trophy of war, there seemed to be no explanation for the expensive, high-risk venture.

Despite having achieved détente with the Soviets and rapprochement with the Chinese, nobody in the Nixon administration counted these two Communist giants as new friends of the Americans.

If the DIA's conclusions about a Soviet-attempted attack, based solely on photographs and scraps of tangible evidence, had proven useful in blackmailing the Soviets and inducing the Chinese to change their behavior, then the physical possession of the actual submarine would have been of even greater value in future dealings. The skillful dissemination of evidence of the K-129's attempted nuclear attack might have already been instrumental in Nixon's successful negotiations of the SALT I and ABM treaties with the Soviets, and in rapprochement with China. The Nixon strategists may have reasonably concluded there was yet more bargaining power to be gained by having the entire wreck in American custody.

Détente did nothing to lessen competition among the superpowers. In the early 1970s, the battle for the hearts and souls of mankind, particularly in the non-aligned nation-states, was more intense than ever. Brezhnev stepped up Soviet troublemaking after the accords had been reached by supporting Marxist revolutionary governments in Angola, Mozambique, Somalia, Ethiopia, Grenada, Nicaragua, and South Yemen. The Soviet and Chinese competition for leadership in the Third World intensified in Africa, Asia, and Latin America. The United States was no less competitive in efforts to win these states to the Western camp.

Hundreds of billions of dollars in aid for programs that amounted to little more than public relations were being expended by the governments of the Eastern and Western blocs. In comparison to the price for humanitarian and military aid to woo the uncommitted states, the relatively low cost of a scheme such as Project Jennifer, which could potentially humiliate a competitor, must have seemed reasonable. Hard evidence that Brezhnev and the Soviet military had lost control of nuclear armaments would have threatened the Soviets' coveted position as the peaceful proletariat protector of the Third World.

The most probable answer to the motivation for Project Jennifer is that some of Nixon's key men knew the Soviets could later discount the claim of K-129's rogue intent by charging that the *Halibut* evidence was forged. The photographs, electronic intelligence, and probability analysis either were circumstantial or could have been fabricated. At the time, many people in the world, no less in the United States, believed America had actually staged the Apollo moon landings in Hollywood movie studios or in the deserts of the Southwest.

A reassembled, 324-foot missile submarine would offer unassailable proof—a true smoking gun—with concrete evidence to be gleaned from the launch controls and missile guidance system. Data programmed into the computers could be physically retrieved to identify the target as Pearl Harbor. The remains of the exploded missile warhead and damage to missile tubes, conning tower, and hull would prove to anyone from the United Nations or any doubting foreign delegation that a Soviet submarine had destroyed itself in an attempted sneak attack. With tangible evidence to touch and see, no one could say the American case was purely circumstantial.

A number of key civilians in the Nixon administration were well aware of the U.S. embarrassment and propaganda value Khrushchev had squeezed from the display of the downed American U-2 spy plane a decade earlier. The display of a Soviet missile submarine that had attempted a sneak attack, rogue or not, would have had an even greater propaganda impact on world opinion.

For Nixon and a handful of others in the White House and the CIA, the half-billion-dollar Project Jennifer was indeed worth the cost and risk.

The project continued apace, hidden in the deepest secrecy of any endeavor since the Manhattan Project, which created the first atom bomb during World War II.

23

WHEN MOST PEOPLE think of Cold War spy paraphernalia, they imagine tiny gadgets such as lapel-pin cameras, fountain-pen guns, poison umbrella darts, and two-way wrist radios. But when the CIA was given the mission to raise the sunken Soviet submarine K-129 from three miles deep in the Pacific Ocean, it ordered an oceangoing ship that weighed sixty-three thousand tons and was as long as a modern battleship. Like something in a sci-fi movie, the huge vessel had an arm that could reach the bottom of the ocean, with a giant, grasping claw to grab the wreckage and bring it to the surface.

The fantastic vessel at the center of the recovery operation had spiderlike legs above and below sea surface. Its tallest point was a twenty-three-story (263-foot) derrick in the center of the deck. Unseen legs reached one hundred feet below the surface, with stern and bow thrusters to keep the craft stationary in all but the wildest seas.

Mission heart of the ship was a 199-foot-long by 75-foot-wide moon pool in the middle of the hull, with huge doors that opened the belly of the ship to the ocean. The moon pool was specifically designed for this mission. It was wide enough to accommodate two sections of the submarine's 27-foot-wide hull at one time.

The 324-foot Soviet submarine had broken into sections when it hit the ocean floor. Since the designers of the recovery vessel had access to the photographs of the wreck taken by the *Halibut,* they knew exactly what the salvagers would be dealing with in terms of lengths, widths, and weights. Workmen were given the space to disassemble a section of the submarine in the moon pool and remove the pieces to adjoining storage bays in the hold of the ship, while the recovery team was piecing pipe together to lower the giant claw back down for another piece of the wreck.

The recovery operations centered in the ship's moon pool — more or less out of sight — by dropping steel pipe from the derrick with the giant claw at the end, joint by joint, three miles down to the bottom of the sea. The steel talons of the claw were designed to close around the object to be retrieved and slowly hoist it to the surface. The claw was controlled from a CIA van which had been assembled onshore and loaded onto *Glomar Explorer* by crane. Technicians observed the operation on television monitors from inside the van. The supporting system and claw assembly, which was nicknamed Clementine, weighed more than six million pounds — three thousand tons. After being lowered over the broken sections of K-129 on the three-mile steel "string" of pipe, the claw could gently close over the hull and securely grasp it for its journey back into the moon pool.

The ship, built and sailed for that one mission, became famous or infamous, depending on one's nationalistic point of view, as the *Hughes Glomar Explorer*.

Despite the physical and financial size of the project, few people in Washington were aware of the Jennifer Project when it was launched in the early 1970s. The whole story of this operation is not known even today, three decades later. Many versions have been disseminated over the years since the venture was discovered by snooping news reporters in 1974.

The *Hughes Glomar Explorer*, a 618-foot, oceangoing behemoth, was named for the man who fronted the venture for the CIA—eccentric billionaire Howard Hughes. He had a decades-long relationship with the U.S. military and the intelligence establishment.

Hughes Tool Company of Houston was chosen to manage the CIA project and subcontract all other phases of construction and management. The primary subcontractor was Global Marine, Inc., a world leader in building and operating ships mounted with marine drilling rigs. "Glomar" was the combination of the two words in the company title. The company operated another ship, remarkably similar to the *Glomar Explorer* but about two-thirds the length. That ship, the *Glomar Challenger*, had been operating all around the globe for years, in deep-sea drilling projects sponsored by a consortium of oceanographic institutions. Its primary mission was to take earth-crust samples beneath the sea for the Joint Oceanographic Institutions for Deep Earth Sampling (JOIDES).

A positioning system had been developed to enable a ship to hold a steady position on the surface, even in moderately rough seas, while a drill-pipe stem was lowered to the ocean floor to take corings. To maintain this

stability, the ship's computers received constant positioning data from sensors planted on the bottom of the
sea. The sensors sent signals to the computer, which activated bow and stern thrusters, or propellers, that held
the ship steady against the constantly moving current.
This technology was copied in the larger sister ship,
Glomar Explorer.

On the ocean surface, the *Glomar Explorer* looked
very much like a longer version of the *Glomar Challenger.* Any observer, especially one forced to remain
some distance from the working boat, would see what
appeared to be a huge floating oil derrick amidship of
the boat. Everything else surrounding the towering der-
ricks on both ships was a confusing jumble of specialized equipment designed to support the drilling or
grappling operations.

With a reputation as one of the world's leading deep-
sea oil exploration and drilling companies, Global Marine was a logical choice to conceal the CIA's ambitions,
since it would appear that the new ship's purpose was to
extract minerals from the seabed. Howard Hughes's companies were also in the offshore oil business, with operations all over the world. But in the case of the *Glomar
Explorer,* the drilling technology had been adapted to retrieve booty much heavier than oil from the ocean floor.

To some in the know, the mission and the cost of
Project Jennifer did not make sense. The Navy scientists who had earlier gathered most of the information
of military value with the USS *Halibut*'s dive in 1968
saw no reason to investigate further the K-129 site.

Their arguments against the project carried little
weight because, from the beginning, someone in the

Nixon administration was determined to recover the sunken Soviet submarine. It was Nixon himself who ordered the CIA into the operation. And it was Nixon who demanded every possible means be used, with no expense spared, to raise the entire submarine. Even the top man in the CIA had initially been skeptical of the strange mission. CIA Director Richard Helms told the briefing officer, "You must be crazy," when first presented with the plan.

Contracts were let in early 1970 to design and build the ocean salvage vessel. The gigantic project proceeded in all haste under a mandate from the Central Intelligence Agency to "protect sources and methods."

After the CIA took control of the project, the Navy was gradually muscled aside, until finally only a few top admirals and civilian Department of Navy officials were still in the loop. But the project probably never would have gone beyond the talking stage were it not for one political appointee in the DOD who more or less handcarried it through the red tape for his friend, the president. That man was Deputy Secretary of Defense David Packard, cofounder of the pioneering computer company Hewlett-Packard. Packard was one of Nixon's first civilian appointees, and served in the subcabinet post for three years. One of his first assignments was approving Project Jennifer, which included Navy funding for a large part of the cost to build the *Glomar Explorer*.

Years later, even after all the controversy, Packard told author William J. Broad, "The Cold War probably would have turned out as it did without that endeavor. But you never know."

The CIA operation was on legal thin ice, even under

American law—not to mention blatant violation of international maritime law. It was authorized by the National Security Council's 10-2 rule of 1948, which permitted clandestine operations outside the purview of Congress. That rule allowed funding for "special operations, always provided they were secret, and sufficiently diminutive in size as to be plausibly denied by the government."

The 10-2 authority existed long before Project Jennifer and was ideal for the Nixon administration's geopolitical ambitions in the early 1970s. However, under no circumstances could Project Jennifer, with cost estimates as high as a half-billion dollars, have been considered "diminutive in size."

Arguably, the whole black operation was illegal from the outset. The cost and details of the operation were always kept secret from Congress.

A final contract was signed between Hughes Tool Company and the U.S. government. A special Howard Hughes company called Summa Corporation was created to manage the project. Global Marine created a subsidiary, Global Marine Development, Inc., especially for the operation.

Secret subcontracts were let to a German bearings company and a number of top U.S. companies, including Lockheed Missiles & Space Company, Mechanics Research, Inc., Sun Shipbuilding & Dry Dock Co., the National Steel and Shipbuilding Co., Western Gear, Minneapolis Honeywell, Houston Systems Manufacturing, General Electric, and Cosmodyne Corporation. Global Marine was in charge of the design and engineering of the *Glomar Explorer*.

These companies all had experience working within the military-industrial complex of the Cold War, and several had direct experience with the CIA's strange requests. The contractors and subcontractors were not told how their contributions fit into the bigger picture, or even how their products were to be used. It remained a need-to-know operation all the way to the White House.

The construction contract to build the *Glomar Explorer* was awarded to Sun Shipbuilding & Dry Dock, Chester, Pennsylvania, in April 1971.

To complete the project, one other significant piece of very large, very conspicuous equipment was required. The six-million-pound claw was so heavy and unwieldy that it could not be hoisted onto the ship after being specially tooled and assembled. So an enormous, submersible barge called Hughes Mining Barge (HMB-1) was built to house the assembly of the claw. While *Glomar Explorer* was under construction on the East Coast, the barge was being built at the Todd Shipyard in San Diego, under the direction of Lockheed Missiles & Space Company. The barge, which weighed forty-seven hundred tons, was 180 feet long and had a 70-foot-high arched, retractable roof. It was designed to carry the claw to the host ship. Once the two vessels met, HMB-1 submerged and maneuvered under the ship. The *Glomar's* moon pool doors opened to the hovering barge and the HMB-1's roof retracted. A pipe-stem shaft was lowered into the barge and the claw connected. The claw was lifted by the derrick into the moon pool of the ship, where it would await its mission.

The ship, the barge, the claw, and all the hundreds

of special pieces of equipment needed for the operation were designed, engineered, and fabricated in 1971 and early 1972, while Nixon's clandestine negotiations with the Soviets and the Chinese were moving ahead at a fast pace toward the major peace accords that would be signed in the spring of 1972.

The *Glomar Explorer* and the floating hangar HMB-1 were completed at the shipyards on the East and West coasts late in 1972. Sea trials for the vessels were conducted in February and March of the following year. In October 1973, the *Glomar Explorer* arrived at its new home port in Long Beach, California, where it was to be outfitted with all the special equipment needed for the mission to raise the Soviet submarine.

By then, the Watergate hearings, which had begun months before, were consuming the nation's attention. The political whodunit playing out in the nation's capital diverted investigative reporters from follow-up on the sightings of the odd ship and barge moving around ports on the California coast, and temporarily prevented probes into Project Jennifer.

Nevertheless, some newsmen began to hear rumors about the *Glomar Explorer* and its mission to recover a sunken Soviet submarine.

A smoke screen of secrecy had already been laid down by the CIA to protect the covert operation taking shape on the Pacific coast of the United States. One of the biggest cover-ups and disinformation campaigns in the espionage history of America had been launched in 1970, even as contracts for Project Jennifer were being let. As a result of this major cover-up operation planned by the CIA and the Nixon administration, the truth about the K-129 sinking was to remain tightly wrapped in that cloak of secrecy for more than a decade after the end of the Cold War. None of the documents have ever been declassified.

The motives for raising the obsolete submarine at the risk of creating an international furor were never explained because the questions were never asked at the time. The Watergate scandal became an unwitting contributor to the cover-up of the K-129 incident.

At first, the secrecy surrounding the sinking of the Soviet submarine was strictly in response to the practical need for maintaining national security at the height of the Cold War. The Americans did not want the Soviets to know how advanced their satellite and deep-ocean surveillance capabilities had become. And the U.S. Navy did not want to reveal that spy subs such as the *Halibut* even existed.

To safeguard that intelligence, the Navy planted the story that K-129 had been investigated by the surface ship *Mizar*, which had all the technology used by the *Halibut*. That cover story held firm from 1968 until the end of the Cold War in 1991.

The Nixon assignment to the CIA to raise the submarine set into motion an even greater campaign of disinformation. As with the project itself, nobody has explained why such a major, long-term cover-up was required.

Nixon's purpose for spending $500 million for the recovery of the K-129 notwithstanding, the Jennifer Project was, from the very beginning, a calculated exercise in deliberate duplicity, even within the U.S. government. Once the CIA took over, the project was wrapped in a fabricated story as elaborate as the fantastic equipment being built to raise the submarine.

A ship of the size and unusual superstructure of *Glomar Explorer* could not be built at any shipyard in America without attracting attention. For that reason, the billionaire Howard Hughes's name and reputation became an integral part of the operation. Everyone knew the Hughes Tool Company and other Hughes enterprises had served as fronts for covert government projects since the beginning of the Cold War. His companies were also legitimate leaders in the field of offshore oil exploration and development. And Hughes was known for his eccentric gambles long before the CIA drafted him for its cover story. Who would think this venture any stranger than the rest?

Howard Hughes's company took over the management of the cover story and issued elaborate press releases. Spokesmen held press conferences about the vessel being built at the Chester, Pennsylvania, shipyards near Philadelphia, and Hughes's Summa Corporation, which controlled the project, announced it was going into deep-ocean mining on a grand scale.

The corporation's ostensible purpose was to begin the underseas mining of so-called "black pearls," ore-rich nodules, primarily manganese, found throughout the world's deepest oceans. It apparently never occurred to anyone that there was no shortage of manganese and other ores available for mining on the earth's surface, at far less cost than a deep-sea operation.

The deep-sea mining cover story set off a frantic scramble to open the world's oceans to exploitation and caused a tidal wave of events that roiled the seas well into the 1990s. The bogus CIA story indirectly led to the ultimate passage of the United Nations' Law of the Seas Treaty. Nations of the world frantically declared two-hundred-mile exclusive zones to protect their waters from being exploited by private mining corporations. Shortly after Howard Hughes's company announced it was going to use the covert CIA boat for a giant mining venture, a dozen energy and mineral companies, including a number in the Fortune 500, went into the ocean-mining business.

Investigative journalist, author, and documentary producer David Helvarg said the *Glomar Explorer* had another significant, unintended consequence.

"If the opening of America's western frontier can be traced back to the Lewis and Clark Expedition of 1804–1806, the declaration of America's Blue Frontier can be traced to a 1972 Central Intelligence Agency cover story," Helvarg opined in the opening sentence of his authoritative environmental book, *Blue Frontier*.

The CIA quietly sat back and let arguments rage over who could claim the rights to the world's ocean-floor minerals. At the time, however, the unasked, real question concerned the legality of salvaging another country's sunken ship in international waters, without the owner nation's knowledge or permission. Since America planned to do just that, the ocean-mining story was simply a massive distraction.

While the cover story was being spun throughout the media world to hide the real purpose of *Glomar Explorer*, the CIA was taking great pains to protect other operational aspects of Project Jennifer. The Agency established headquarters for the operation in a seedy office building in the San Fernando Valley near the Los Angeles International Airport. The Summa Corporation also had offices in the building, but they were separate from the CIA's operations center on the sixth floor. The CIA set up a series of safe houses in apartments near the main office, and other blinds were established in nearby commercial buildings. There were seventy-five people working in the project headquarters, only about one-quarter of whom knew the true purpose of the operation. The rest of the employees thought they were recruiting seamen to handle the ship, oilfield drillers to string the pipes, crane operators to run the derrick engines, and other personnel required for a unique, deep-ocean, commercial mining venture.

The career CIA agents and a small group of contractors who knew what they were really doing wore disguises. They were issued fake ID cards and given elaborately colorful biographies. A host of spies became mining engineers; intelligence analysts became oceanographers. Everyone in the know was given a legend.

After *Glomar Explorer* arrived at the nearby port of Long Beach, no recognizable government official was allowed to visit the ship. Seamen were recruited from West Coast port facilities, carefully screened, and required to sign oaths of secrecy before being told about the purpose of the operation. Oil field equipment riggers, roustabouts, and roughnecks were recruited by agents scouring the Gulf Coast towns that served as ports for commercial offshore drilling operations.

Offshore oil drillers are a breed unto themselves, known as the toughest, most close-knit and closemouthed men in the dangerous business of finding and bringing in oil wells. The men hired for this project were paid considerably more than they normally earned in that already high-paying dangerous trade. These oil workers, too, were carefully picked, had their backgrounds screened, and were then sworn to secrecy.

One of the roughnecks hired for the project answered the questions posed by a quizzical newsman years later:

"They told us they [the secrecy oaths] were the same kind of documents Daniel Ellsberg [former Defense Department employee who was prosecuted for leaking the Pentagon Papers] had signed." The implication was that to talk about any aspect of the project would subject the participant to criminal prosecution.

When the operating crew of about two hundred men was finally assembled, they were put through a crash training course at a contractor's facility in Redwood City, California. Some of this group would be washed out before the mission began. To their surprise, a complete mockup of a Soviet Golf submarine was located in a hangar there. They were trained to dismantle the ship and look for the special equipment, parts, and pieces to be retrieved from the wreck. They were taught how to handle radioactive material and work with contaminated scrap. They even learned a smattering of Russian, to be able to identify Cyrillic writing on various pieces they might discover from the wreck.

The CIA's cover story about the deep-sea mining operation was so complete that agents secured tons of manganese nodules, similar to the so-called black pearls the *Glomar* was supposedly going to mine. The mineral-laden nuggets had been dredged up off the coast of Mexico to use as samples of the ore to be sought. These gnarled, potato-size nodules were given to interviewees for the Project Jennifer jobs to show off to friends and relatives.

In total, Project Jennifer required more than seven thousand men and women at various stages of the project, working for government agencies and contractors, and actually serving aboard the ship. All were either sworn to secrecy or allowed to learn only the smallest part of the operation, as their particular assignment required. Multiply the people working directly and indirectly on Project Jennifer by the friends and relatives in their immediate circles, and the number of people who knew small or large secrets about K-129 soars. Before the project was completed, tens of thousands of Americans were involved, or knew someone involved, in the big CIA project. Even then, very few knew the truth about it.

Considering the massive size of the strange ship and barge, the huge expenditure of taxpayer money, the thousands of people involved, and the scrutiny of the Nixon administration by the news media and Congress during that period, it seems nothing short of amazing that the cover story held together as long as it did. Even thirty years later, there have been no truthful, firsthand accounts published in the media or aired in documentaries regarding the extraordinary operation.

24

THE U.S. NAVY WAS SHUT OUT of day-to-day participation in the Jennifer Project by the Central Intelligence Agency. But the spies had to call on the sailors again to find the wreckage. Before *Glomar Explorer* could be dispatched to the area of the Pacific where K-129 lay buried three miles deep, the location had to be pinpointed. The job could be done only with another clandestine dive by one of the Navy's special spy submarines. The USS *Seawolf* (SSN 575) was dispatched to plot the wreckage field, and set out electronic devices to guide the surface ship to the exact location. *Seawolf* was assigned to the Navy's Submarine Development Group One (SUBDEVGRU ONE), a secretive organization created in 1967 to conduct deep-ocean espionage against the Soviet Union.

Relocating and marking the wreckage of the Soviet submarine was the *Seawolf*'s first mission as a special operations boat, following its conversion from a nuclear-powered attack submarine at Mare Island Naval Shipyard.

By this time in 1974, the Soviet missile carrier K-129 had been on the ocean floor for more than six years.

Ironically, the USS *Halibut*, which had originally located K-129 in the summer after it sank on March 7, 1968, was not available for the follow-up assignment, because it was prowling the waters around the doomed Soviet submarine's original home port on another covert mission. In late June 1974, when Project Jennifer was finally ready to execute the long-delayed recovery operation, the *Halibut* was tapping the underwater communications cables between Rybachiy Naval Base at Petropavlovsk and Soviet Pacific Fleet headquarters at Vladivostok. This was the very cable that K-129's deputy commander, Captain Second Rank Alexander Zhuravin, had used in 1968 to notify his wife Irina that his submarine had returned from another patrol.

The Navy was indispensable to this phase of the project because, at the time, it possessed the only sophisticated equipment in the world capable of the particular type of deep-sea exploration needed for the mission. In the 1960s, the Navy's Underwater Systems Center had developed the means to guide blind submarines to locations where objects of interest—such as underseas communications cables or Soviet missile parts—lay on the bottom of the sea.

When finding such lost or hidden objects, submarines from SUBDEVGRU ONE planted signaling devices called transponders on the ocean floor to provide precise directions for subsequent trips. Specialized vessels could then return to the sites and lower cameras or retrieval tools on towed robots, or even human divers, to exploit the objects. In very deep water, the transponders provided steady signals so the mother ship was able to maintain a fixed position while working for long periods.

A transponder placed on the ocean floor was activated by a signal from the search vessel using another device called a transducer. The transponder could only be triggered by a coded signal on a selected frequency; any other ship that might be searching for the object would be unable to intercept or eavesdrop on the signal. In this case, transponders were planted by *Seawolf* in each of the areas where large sections of K-129 lay. When the *Glomar Explorer* neared the site, transducers on that ship sent signals that activated these transponders so the search vessel could home in on the site.

The target was difficult to find, even though the *Halibut* had made detailed charts of the location after finding the wreckage in the summer of 1968. The debris field was located in a hundred-mile-wide, irregular plain littered with coral and lava mounds. It was located about seventy miles in a diagonal, northerly direction from the Necker and Nihoa islets and subterranean atolls of the Hawaiian Leeward Islands. There, the ocean floor was anything but smooth.

On Independence Day 1974, the sixty-three-thousand-ton *Glomar Explorer* was guided smoothly by the electronics to the site above the wreckage. Weather for the recovery was perfect. The special CIA ship was immediately able to begin an operation that James Clay Moltz, research professor at the Monterey Institute of International Studies, has described as the "granddaddy" of all deep-sea recovery attempts.

The large black-and-white ship with a distinctive three-story-high derrick could not be missed by any spying Soviet trawler or spy submarine. The CIA hoped its well-circulated cover story that *Glomar Explorer* was on a quest for manganese ore nodules would divert attention from the ship's real mission. Even if a snooping Soviet trawler did approach the ship closely enough to watch its activities, very little could be seen. Most of the tasks were performed behind the high walls of the sixty-five-foot-deep moon pool, out of sight of prying eyes.

The *Glomar Explorer*, with an eclectic working crew of about two hundred—including drillers, mechanical engineers, mechanics, welders, roustabouts, sailors, scientists, electronics technicians, cooks, and spies—was ready for business as soon as it arrived on the site.

The recovery operation was only slightly different from a deep-sea drilling operation. Instead of a drill at the end of the string of pipe, the *Glomar Explorer* had a giant grasping claw. This did not lessen the need to keep the ship stationary.

Fortunately, during its entire time over the wreck site, the *Glomar Explorer* encountered ideally calm seas. Planners had loaded the ship with the latest meteorological forecasting gear, to make sure there were no sudden surprises from the weather. A surge in seas or heavy wave action caused by a sudden squall could have caused considerable damage at certain stages of the operation. However, once the pipe was strung beneath the ship with the claw attached, the long stem reaching into the depths actually helped to stabilize the ship, serving the function of a heavy, extended keel.

Offshore oil drillers are adept at stringing long lines of pipe dangling from platforms above open water. The techniques used on *Glomar Explorer* were basically the same as those used in the oil industry. Cannon-barrel-quality steel was used in the pipe and each section measured sixty feet in length. The pipe for the string measured from twelve to seventeen inches in outside diameter, with the thicker pipe added last, to provide extra strength closest to the ship, where the weight was the greatest.

The giant claw with its huge supporting frame was connected to the first length of pipe to be lowered. When the first few sections of pipe had been connected to the claw and hung below the derrick, the ensemble was held firmly by a giant brake mounted at the base of the derrick. The moon pool doors were then opened to the ocean. Slowly, the claw was lowered into the water to begin its three-mile journey into the depths.

One by one, each section of pipe was connected, with each new piece of pipe gradually lowering the whole rig, one sixty-foot section at a time. The next piece of pipe was hoisted from storage by a crane, pulled into place up the derrick and connected to the preceding piece of pipe. Over time, the weight grew, and workers had to constantly cool and lubricate the braking device.

Eventually the entire, three-mile-long string holding the claw was lowered directly above the first section of the submarine to be recovered. The operators aboard ship maneuvered the frame with the claw into place with the jaws open. The final mating of the claw and the submarine hull was accomplished using hydraulic thrusters on the claw frame. The operators had a perfect view of the operation via television cameras, also mounted on the frame.

Direct television lines and the hydraulic cables controlling the claw and frame were carried to the site inside the pipe string. Workers had inserted these cables into the hollow pipes from large spools mounted under the derrick on the ship as each pipe section was fitted.

Once positioned exactly above a piece of the submarine's broken hull, the talons were slowly dropped the last few feet over the prey and gently closed around the wreckage.

To bring the prize to the surface, the pipe-stringing procedure was reversed. The crew on the *Glomar Explorer* removed one section of pipe at a time, as powerful diesel engines huffed and puffed, straining to raise a section of the submarine held firmly in the claw at the end of the pipe string.

When the claw holding a section of the submarine arrived beneath the ship, the operation paused while divers inspected the pieces of wreckage to make sure everything would fit easily into the moon pool. Finally, the derrick hoisted the last section of pipe. The claw with its burden was pulled inside the ship, and the moon pool doors closed. Then the claw was opened, releasing the section of submarine to rest on the floor while water was pumped out of the moon pool.

Workmen swarmed over the wreck like furious ants scavenging an insect carcass. The wreckage was connected by steel cable to cranes mounted at each end of the moon pool. The tangles of steel hull, wires, and pipes that had been compartments of the submarine were moved to work bays, to be dismantled by welders and mechanics under the watchful eye of intelligence experts.

The *Glomar Explorer* had to be moved a short distance to a new site to reach the next section of the broken submarine. Once the ship was repositioned, the whole operation began again. Since the submarine had most likely broken upon impact with the seabed rather than on the surface before it sank, the major pieces were not strewn over a large area.

Clyde W. Burleson, author of *The Jennifer Project*, interviewed dozens of crew members who worked on the recovery. Eyewitnesses told Burleson that the K-129 was raised in four or more sections, with crews working back-to-back, twelve-hour shifts. The crews were able to add pipe around the clock, at an average rate of 340 feet per hour, to reach the debris field, approximately sixteen thousand feet below the surface.

Glomar Explorer was on site under good operating conditions for approximately five weeks, from July 4 to August 12. Each trip to the bottom took forty-five to forty-eight hours; the return trips took approximately the same amount of time. Even with delays for maintenance, repairs, relocation of the ship to different sites, and crew rest periods between each recovery, there was enough time on this mission to have made five to seven round trips.

Despite an elaborate cover-up and the eventual claim that Project Jennifer had been a failure, most of K-129 and the remains of the crew were, in fact, raised from the bottom of the Pacific and brought into the *Glomar Explorer*. Once the retrieval of the submarine was accomplished, the debris was diagnosed in one of the largest autopsies in history. Experts in every related field of science and technology had been assembled by the CIA to begin analysis of the treasure while the recovery ship was still at sea.

For intelligence purposes, it was most important to

recover the center of the submarine. This included the control room beneath the conning tower, the whole conning tower with adjoining missile launch tubes, and the two ballistic missiles and one nuclear warhead that had not been destroyed by the initial blast. The missile in tube one had been completely demolished. The warhead was blown off the missile in the second tube, adjacent to the area of the explosion. The pressure hull, the upper deck, and the sail adjoining missile tube one were damaged from the exploding missile, but except for the ten-foot-wide gash, this section had remained intact. If this vital section could be recovered, the intelligence experts thought they might retrieve irrefutable proof that K-129 had been destroyed in an attempt to launch a nuclear missile.

The command center located immediately beneath the forward section of the conning tower contained the codes, charts, and written records of the mission. The CIA circulated a rumor that scientists at NASA's Lewis Center had developed technology using lasers and vacuum chambers to treat paper damaged by salt water. According to the planted story, the CIA claimed it could restore and peruse any papers, logs, charts, books, diaries, and notes recovered from the K-129 wreck, even those that had soaked for more than six years on the bottom of the ocean.

Other evidence to be gained by physically reclaiming the control center of the sunken submarine might have proved useful. Guidance and launch data programmed on cassettes in computer consoles could provide clues about the submarine's intended target on March 7, 1968.

Logically, the overseers of an operation as extensive as this one would have gone for the most valuable evidence first. The center of the submarine, including the conning tower and the missile tubes, had to be the first target for recovery.

The CIA later claimed that only the forward-most section of the submarine was recovered. They acknowledged they did recover two nuclear-tipped torpedoes from the undamaged first compartment. There has been no mention of the disposition of any regular torpedoes that might have been in the compartment. If this section had been recovered in undamaged condition, the nuclear torpedoes would not have leaked radioactive material from the warheads into that compartment. Torpedoes carrying nuclear warheads were built to withstand depth pressures up to twenty thousand feet. They would not explode or rupture unless they were damaged when the submarine smashed into the ocean floor.

Several eyewitnesses, however, later told reporters of high levels of radiation present in the wreckage brought into the *Glomar Explorer*. The only other sources of radioactive material on K-129, which was a diesel-electric-powered submarine without a nuclear reactor aboard, were the three missile warheads located in the center of the submarine. Two of these warheads were ripped apart in the initial explosion, scattering fissile material throughout the conning tower and probably the operations center. Photographs from the USS *Halibut* had confirmed this damage. The third Serb missile with its warhead remained undamaged in launch tube three.

The radioactive wreckage encountered by the *Glomar* crew dismantling the section of the submarine had to be from these warheads. The eyewitness stories about the radioactivity in the wreckage were strong evidence that much of the central section of the submarine was raised into the moon pool of the recovery ship.

After the initial section was raised, a high-level CIA official called a meeting of the work crews and warned that the submarine was "hot." He gave them an option to continue to work or not. For those who opted to stay on the job despite the possibility of exposure to radiation, "special uniforms" were provided, including a "full-length cotton jumper and a shiny outer uniform that seemed to have a metallic content." The workmen's sleeves and ankles were taped, and they wore oxygen masks, hoods, and built-in microphones while they dismantled the parts. The crewmen reported that they had to scrub for hours after each work session, and all their clothing had to be tossed overboard.

Another description of the dangerous working conditions on *Glomar Explorer* was reported in *A Matter of Risk* by Roy Varner and Wayne Collier, published in 1978. Coauthor Collier was a federal undercover agent with intimate details of the operation. He had been the chief personnel recruiter for the project.

"Sensors brought into the area, however, registered a high level of radioactivity emanating from inside the metal mass," the eyewitness accounts in *A Matter of Risk* revealed. "Those who were finishing the job of wedging timbers underneath the Target Object quickly backed off when told it was hot."

25

WHILE THE CREW ABOARD the *Glomar Explorer* was intently focused on its work, the CIA had to deal with another problem—Soviet spy ships. The Soviets took notice of the *Glomar Explorer* activities, but they showed no strong interest in disrupting the operation, as the Americans had feared before the mission began. There were reports that the Soviets knew about the mission long before the recovery ship sailed. On several occasions, Soviet spy trawlers dropped by the work site, stayed a few hours, then sailed away.

The CIA most likely took extra measures to ensure the operation was not disrupted once it was underway. There is evidence that the CIA dispatched a decoy ship to the site where the Soviets thought their boat had sunk, hundreds of miles north of the actual location. Even though the Nixon administration had probably already shared tantalizing bits of information about their lost boat with the Soviets, the true location of the wreck site was never revealed and, in fact, has remained one of the most jealously guarded secrets of the K-129 incident.

The *Glomar Explorer*'s sister ship, the smaller *Glomar*

Challenger, was so similar in appearance that a spy boat standing off at a distance would be hard-pressed to distinguish between the silhouettes of the two ships. The most prominent feature of both ships was the odd derrick towering above the decks. In hull structure, the two ships were similar. Their profiles were both festooned with cranes, jumbles of pipes, and equipment that only knowledgeable observers could have identified. The main difference was their overall size. The *Glomar Explorer* was approximately fifty feet wider and two hundred feet (or a third) longer than the *Glomar Challenger*. At 618 and 399 feet long, respectively, both were large. Similarly painted, both ships would make highly visible images on a distant horizon.

If the *Glomar Challenger* showed up at a location several hundred miles north of the actual recovery site and within the zone searched earlier by the Soviets, a snooping spy would almost certainly believe he had found the right ship. The Soviet would confidently watch the *Challenger*'s crew raise and lower pipe into the ocean in an operation that mimicked the work going on aboard the *Glomar Explorer*.

Protecting the location had always been vital to the K-129 recovery. The CIA's most widely reported site for the sunken boat was 40° N latitude by 180° W longitude. It was a deliberately misleading location, far from the real site. That location would have placed the wreckage of the Soviet submarine approximately 1,700 miles from Pearl Harbor and well north of any U.S. landfall. More important, the false location would send any Soviet surveillance aircraft or ships far from the site where *Glomar Explorer* was operating. A number of other reports about the wreck site were leaked, placing the location 750 miles northwest of Pearl Harbor. Another rumored site was just over 830 miles northwest of Hawaii. The last two locations would have been consistent with areas normally patrolled by Soviet missile subs. If the CIA then dispatched the *Glomar Challenger* to one of those more distant locations, any Soviet spy ship or dual-purpose fishing trawler would be well away from the real action.

The whereabouts of the *Challenger* during midsummer 1974 remains a mystery, even though most of that research ship's schedules for other projects before and after this period are readily available in published scientific records.

Its location in the spring of that year is known. The *Challenger* was conducting oceanographic research about one hundred miles off Cape Horn in April 1974, when it was boarded and temporarily detained by an Argentine navy gunboat. The Argentine captain suspected the ship was involved in illegal oil exploration. The ship was quickly released when it was proven that its purpose was ocean-floor core sampling between the capes of Africa and South America. *Challenger* was involved in the well-documented Deep Ocean Drilling Project from 1968 to 1983, and the legs of its journeys have been fully logged. Yet no activity is reported for this ship in early to late summer 1974.

Recently released information from Soviet naval intelligence does include some of the comings and goings of the *Glomar Challenger*, and indicates the Red Navy was quite suspicious about its activities. This Soviet account makes a strong case that the *Glomar Challenger* was, in fact, used by the CIA as a decoy to lure the Soviets away from the site where the *Glomar Explorer* was working that summer.

The first step in a plan to make sure the Soviets would be looking for the wrong ship in the wrong place was a clandestine operation that occurred in Washington, D.C., shortly before the recovery mission began.

An anonymous note was dropped off at the entrance door to the Soviet embassy. The note read, simply: "Certain special services are taking steps to raise the Soviet submarine which sank in the Pacific." It was signed, "A Well-wisher."

A hard-working, but frustrated, young Soviet naval intelligence officer in the Pacific Fleet was not privy to the note until the *Glomar Explorer*'s mission was over. Though ignored by his superiors, he had actually been on to the operation from his own intelligence sources from the beginning.

The intelligence officer was Captain Anatoliy Shtyrov, who would rise to the rank of admiral before his career in the Soviet navy ended. He had already been trying to follow the strange maneuverings of the *Glomar Challenger* in the North Pacific. Shtyrov's account of his attempts to follow Global Marine company's drilling activities in the early months of 1974 revealed that Soviet intelligence agents were closely monitoring the site where they believed K-129 had sunk. Shtyrov later recorded his experiences tracking Global Marine ships. He admitted being confused about which ship was which.

Someone had made an effort to attract the Soviets' attention to the area around 40° N latitude and the

180th meridian, the site seventeen hundred miles northwest of Honolulu and over a thousand miles north of the actual location of the K-129 salvage operation.

Making several attempts to learn what was going on, the Soviet officer sent spy ships, recruited a passing Soviet merchant ship, and dispatched a Tu-95 Bear reconnaissance plane to the site. Cloud cover prevented the Soviet plane from visual observation of the American recovery ship, but the pilot confirmed radar contact at that location. All planes and ships sent by the intelligence officer reported American activity at the scene. Shtyrov concluded that a vessel named *Glomar Explorer*, which he could not find in published directories of ships, was attempting to raise the lost submarine. His dispatch to Moscow read, in part:

"To the Chief of Naval Intelligence. Analysis of the operations conducted by the U.S. ship *Glomar Explorer* at the K-point 40° N 180° W provides grounds to suppose that some agencies in the USA are about to complete preparations, and may soon recover the Soviet submarine K-129, lost in 1968, from the Pacific Ocean."

The intelligence officer urgently requested that the radio-electronics surveillance ship *Primorye*, which was spying on American missile tests at Kwajalein Atoll in the South Pacific, be rushed to the site. For some inexplicable reason, Captain Shtyrov was promptly reprimanded with a terse message: "Do not pop up with your stupid ideas; pay more attention to a better quality of performance of planned operations."

Shtyrov had received reports from several Soviet ships sailing in that area. A Soviet patrol boat, the *Pe-*

leng, operating out of Kamchatka; a small recon ship named *Chazhma*; and a Soviet freighter diverted from its commercial route had all reported a mystery ship busily raising and lowering pipe in the deep, open seas. All three ships reported that a vessel with the name *Glomar Explorer* painted on its stern was conducting what appeared to be drilling operations. A ship's name is easily changed with a bucket of paint and a brush. It certainly would not have been the first time such a trick had been used to hide a ship's identity.

These spying ships encountered nothing unusual at the scene. They each observed the busy Americans for several days, then sailed away with notations in their logs that all appeared normal. No interchange between the crews of the American and Soviet ships at that location was mentioned.

That was not the case for Soviet fishing trawlers plying their trade in the Hawaiian Leeward Island fisheries. At least two fishing boats, on separate days, came upon a strange ship operating approximately 350 miles northwest of Honolulu, Hawaii. No report about the odd operation has ever been published by the crew of either Soviet fishing boat. But there are American accounts of the confrontations.

Divergent tales provide strong evidence that two similar ships were operating in the Pacific at the time. Several crewmen from the real *Glomar Explorer* laughingly confirmed incidents involving Soviet trawlers that approached their ship during the recovery operation in late July 1974.

When the first trawler came close enough to the American ship for the crew to see the Soviet seamen pointing cameras at them, they raised their hands in unison and shot them the international high sign or "bird." Later, another group of workers sunning themselves on the large helicopter pad on the back deck of *Glomar Explorer* reportedly dropped their trousers to "moon" a snooping Soviet fishing trawler.

Neither of these Russian trawlers had been dispatched by Captain Shtyrov to look for a strange American ship operating that far south. These were probably just regular fishing boats with curious crews that happened onto the scene of the real recovery operation.

Years later, Shtyrov stated unequivocally and somewhat angrily that the Americans who were manning the ship that his spy boats had observed "did not lower their pants and did not show bare butts to the Soviet sailors."

While Soviet spy boats did not hamper the operation, another strange twist in the saga was about to occur, which could have derailed the project, even as it was nearing completion. The originator of the fantastic Jennifer Project, Richard M. Nixon, was facing impeachment and early eviction from the White House.

During the first weeks of the recovery operation, the president had personally taken a keen interest in operations at the site of the K-129 wreck. Both the White House and CIA headquarters received daily reports via encrypted radio transmissions. The *Glomar Explorer*, which had been on station since July 4, was only three days away from completing its mission when President Nixon suddenly announced he would resign, rather than face an impeachment trial in Congress.

On August 9, 1974, Nixon departed the White House after telling his staff goodbye and protesting that he had done nothing wrong. Within two hours, Gerald R. Ford was hurriedly administered the oath of office. He then assured the people that the "long national nightmare" was over.

Within hours of taking office, President Ford was confronted by the CIA with details on the status of Project Jennifer.

Ford had been given a minimum briefing on Project Jennifer shortly after assuming the appointment as vice president to replace Spiro Agnew. As the new president, he had to decide if the recovery operations should continue, in the face of almost certain outrage by the Soviets if the mission were exposed.

Project Jennifer was so sensitive that it was not discussed in the written President's Daily Brief. The president received only verbal updates, and no records of these conversations were kept. Ford wrote in his memoirs that a grim-faced group of his highest advisors approached him about the project early in the morning of his second day in the Oval Office. Secretary of State Henry Kissinger, National Security Advisor Brent Scowcroft, Secretary of Defense James Schlesinger, and CIA Director William Colby—who had all assumed their positions after the project had been hatched four years earlier—came into his office to request his immediate decision. President Ford had to reaffirm the secret project and authorize its completion. This may well have been his first official act as thirty-eighth president of the United States.

"I did not feel the *Glomar* action was a gamble. I was

convinced we had to take the risk," President Ford wrote in his memoirs.

Within a few days of the new president's taking office, the *Glomar Explorer* concluded its mission, and Project Jennifer was ready to sail into the next, even stranger phase of the already weird K-129 episode.

26

PRESIDENT NIXON'S UNTIMELY DEPARTURE from office, just as the *Glomar Explorer* completed recovery of all or most of K-129, left the CIA at sea with more than two thousand tons of scrap metal. While incoming president Gerald Ford was briefed about the project immediately, he certainly did not have time to design a grand scheme for a way to use the extraordinary new intelligence the material might yield. In the confusion of the presidential transition, no one seemed to know what to do with the wreckage of the Soviet submarine. To make matters worse, it was highly radioactive.

On August 12, 1974, the crew pulled the giant claw called Clementine into the moon pool for the last time and proceeded toward Maui in the center of the Hawaiian Islands, about four hundred miles from the recovery site. The *Glomar Explorer* seemed to amble around the Pacific for days longer than the trip to the nearby islands would normally have taken, and then sailed around the islands aimlessly for a few more days. Crewmen said later that a large amount of worthless material, such as mattresses from crew bunks, insulation, and other trash from the wreckage was placed in weighted barrels and dumped at sea. There was a burial at sea with full military honors for some of the Soviet crew's bodies and body parts recovered from the inner hull of the submarine.

The CIA filmed the ceremony so they could later show the Soviets that the six bodies they claimed to have recovered had been accorded a respectful burial. The film provided another strange piece of evidence, as well. The bodies shown were so well preserved by the great depth and cold that the sailors' facial features were visible through the thin material used as shrouds. This proved that the cold, oxygen-sparse environment at the sixteen-thousand-foot depth preserved organic material such as flesh—and paper.

The ship docked on August 30, eighteen days after leaving the wreck site. Upon arriving at Maui, some of the scientists and CIA agents debarked with the most valuable secrets retrieved from the submarine. Other Agency and contract technicians remained on board with the bulk of the submarine, including the boat's frame and hull plates, parts of nuclear weapons, computers, navigation gear, and electronic and mechanical hardware.

Their work completed, the drillers and derrick riggers who had been aboard to string the pipe and retrieve the wrecked sections of the submarine were dropped off and disappeared into waiting charter planes. These skilled technicians, along with mechanics and welders with unique credentials, had been selectively hired and intensively trained on mock-ups of K-129 in a hidden Lockheed facility at Redwood City.

But they were not asked to keep in touch for future missions aboard the *Glomar Explorer*.

The CIA never mentioned that they would be needed again, so they flew off to exotic locations scattered around the world—places such as Indonesia, Arabia, Venezuela, and U.S. sites in the Gulf of Mexico—where the offshore oil industry exploits the beds of lakes, swamps, and seas. All these men were sent home with fat paychecks and a reminder that they were bound to silence by confidentiality contracts. Their work was done, the mission was accomplished, and some, being the independent types they were, would talk.

It now remained for the few CIA technicians and the ship's basic crew to bring the ship and its trophy back to the mainland. Still, there seemed to be no direction given to complete that task in a timely way. The *Glomar Explorer* left Hawaii at the end of August and did not arrive back on the West Coast until late September. The trip from Hawaii to California should have taken no more than ten days of continuous sailing, but it had taken almost a month.

There has never been an accounting of the month it took the *Glomar Explorer* to reach its next sighting at the ship's temporary home port of Long Beach, California. In the dark of night, at a secluded pier in the harbor, a sizable convoy of nondescript trucks, as many as twenty-five, lined up to unload crate after crate from the *Glomar*. One observer said enough crates were unloaded to have packaged a complete submarine.

No bill of lading from the recovery operation has ever been published, and exactly what the *Glomar Ex-*

plorer salvaged from the Soviet submarine has been hotly debated for three decades. But a reasonably accurate catalogue of recovered items with intelligence value would not be difficult to prepare.

Starting from the front of the submarine and working toward the stern, the first section would have yielded active and passive sonar arrays, and one or two nuclear-tipped torpedoes, known to have been carried by the Golf II Soviet submarines. It is not likely the CIA would have kept any of the regular torpedoes because the U.S. Navy had plenty of these, previously recovered by American submarines from Soviet tests. Keeping a score of rusting, live torpedoes on board the recovery ship would not have been a very good idea.

From compartment two, which housed the officers' quarters, captain's safe, and sonar room, the most valuable cache was the officers' personal papers, including the diary of the young missile officer previously mentioned, and some of the sonar control equipment.

Odd as it may seem, compartment three, which housed the control center and the action center above with its periscopes, would have yielded very little military hardware of interest, because all the instruments and control panels for this type of submarine were already well known to U.S. Navy intelligence. The items of major interest in this center section would have been the missile control consoles and navigation instrumentation. It is questionable whether the launch control cassettes and computerized programming data for the missile system survived either the fiery blasts that sunk the submarine or six years in the briny deep. However, if cassettes containing launch codes or missile guidance instructions were recovered in readable condition, they might well have provided the "smoking gun" to prove that Pearl Harbor had been the intended target of the aborted missile launch.

Since, after the initial blast, the flaming rocket fuel would probably have engulfed the command center located adjacent to the missile tubes, there is a good possibility that everything else exposed in the room—charts and maps, delicate instruments, and human bodies—was consumed in the first seconds following the explosion of the missile fuel in number-one tube.

The next compartment—four—contained some of the most valuable items the mission was designed to seize. The Defense Intelligence Agency, the Navy, and the Central Intelligence Agency all had special interests in what could be found in this section. Of course, the three missile tubes originally contained R-21 Serb (SS-N-5) ballistic missiles, each carrying a one-megaton nuclear warhead. Each tube also contained the D-4 underwater-launch system. Photographs from USS *Halibut* had earlier revealed that at least one missile was still intact after the submarine hit the bottom of the ocean. So the recovery effort almost certainly yielded at least one Soviet ballistic missile.

The missiles and launch systems were, however, rapidly becoming obsolete as the Soviets deployed newer and larger missiles on nuclear-powered submarines. The new missiles carried larger payloads and achieved far greater range than the older ones deployed on the Golf II–type submarine.

The one complete missile was located in launch tube number three, nearest the center of the submarine. If that missile remained intact, the great pressure at a depth of more than three miles would still have crushed the outer casing. Even then, the missile and warhead would have yielded some valuable intelligence about sources of fissile material, electronics, and guidance systems. Recovery of a fail-safe device on the missile might have provided a clue to the cause of the missile malfunction in tube one.

There was yet a greater prize, unique to the K-129, to be found in compartment four. This was the result of the special modification ordered by Captain Vladimir Kobzar back in 1966, while the boat was undergoing upgrades. During that retrofit, the captain had arranged to have the cipher room—which held the codebooks, encryption gear, and microburst transmitter secrets—moved from its normal location in compartment two to compartment four. Thus, there was highly valuable code and communications equipment located in this section of K-129, which would not normally have been in compartment four of a Golf II submarine.

Rumors have long circulated that the K-129's encryption equipment and codes were recovered with the wrecked boat. Even though the CIA has acknowledged recovering compartment two of the submarine, the Agency has vehemently denied that any vital military secrets were salvaged.

Recently there was confirmation by a highly authoritative source in U.S. Navy circles that these sensitive codes and electronics were, indeed, recovered in the *Glomar Explorer* operation. Dr. Gary E. Weir, historian of science and technology at the U.S. Naval Historical

Center, and Walter J. Boyne, former director of the National Air and Space Museum of the Smithsonian Institution, revealed in their 2003 book *Rising Tide* that these valuable intelligence items had been recovered during Project Jennifer. From a military point of view, this recovery was probably the most valuable intelligence taken from the K-129. Weir and Boyne point out that it was more than a year after the 1974 *Glomar Explorer* mission was successfully completed before the Soviets found out that their naval codes had been compromised.

The CIA mission "retrieved the Globus-encrypted communication system, as well as Akula system cryptographic equipment that could send and receive high-speed encrypted radio transmissions," according to Weir and Boyne. These systems gave the Americans access to the heretofore unreadable microburst transmissions of Soviet submarines. Until that time, the microbursts had only been used by Navy surveillance specialists to locate the deadly Soviet missile submarines. But for more than a year, the Americans were able to decode and read the transmissions of Soviet warships.

The Globus system, a tomelike book, was lead-covered to ensure it could be thrown overboard and rapidly swallowed into the depths of the sea if the Soviet vessel was in danger of being boarded or lost. The Soviets never considered that someday the Americans would go to the bottom of the sea and snatch up their secret—not just the lead-jacketed book, but the entire submarine itself.

An inventory of the remainder of K-129 would not likely find any additional items of military value for the spies who ran Project Jennifer. Aft of compartment four were the compartments containing the diesel and electric motors that drove the submarine — machinery of World War II vintage holding little or no interest for the Americans. The only purpose for raising these sections — compartments five through eight — would have been if the CIA had been tasked with capturing the entire submarine as a macabre trophy of war, or for some geopolitical or propaganda purpose. If K-129 broke into four or more pieces, as eyewitnesses have attested, the *Glomar Explorer* spent enough time on the site to have recovered all sections, with everything that was aboard K-129 on March 7, 1968.

After the ship was unloaded at Long Beach, the *Glomar Explorer* left port and was later seen at a sheltered cove of Catalina Island, off the California coast. It was there that the ship again met up with the strange HMB-1 barge. As with the operation to load the giant claw up through the moon pool from the barge, the unloading operation also required the mating of the two specialty vessels. At this clandestine meeting, the barge was submerged beneath the ship's moon pool for the claw to be lowered and disconnected. HMB-1 left the scene with the claw enclosed in its hangarlike roof.

Its role in Project Jennifer successfully completed, *Glomar Explorer* sailed away to other fantastic, albeit not so covert, adventures. The *Glomar Explorer* is still at work today, conducting commercial, deep-drilling operations in the Gulf of Mexico.

The HMB-1 had many more missions to accomplish for the CIA and Navy intelligence. The barge soon returned to its mysterious port in the marshes and backwaters of San Francisco Bay at the facilities of Lockheed Marine Division in Redwood, California.

From Long Beach Harbor the dismantled submarine had also been transported to a secured building on this large tract of land. The site was hidden on a narrow canal by the swampy wilderness of Bair Island, fifteen miles south of San Francisco. This area in South San Francisco Bay was home to nautical versions of Lockheed's skunk works, the secret aviation projects that developed some of the world's most futuristic combat and spy aircraft. Lockheed and other defense contractors had facilities all around the south bay and its navigable inlets, many of the facilities dating back to World War II.

The crated Soviet submarine was probably taken to one of the most secret of all these facilities, located east of U.S. Highway 101, on a dredged canal fed by Redwood Creek. A dockside building, where the welding and dismantling work crews of the *Glomar* had been trained on a life-size model of the boat, was now used to house the recovered submarine. The highly radioactive parts had to be handled in a special facility equipped to screen leakage from radiation.

The site is today a modern industrial park, but at the time, the hidden buildings were located on unnamed roads between such landmarks as Deepwater Slough and Smith Slough. Lockheed's spy buildings at 100 and 200 Cardinal Way were demolished after the Cold War. However, before the site and buildings were decontaminated and cleared, they were used for another mysterious HMB-1 project. The barge, docked next to these buildings, served as the assembly facility and mother ship for the Navy's stealthy *Sea Shadow*, an experimental, radar-evading vessel.

A Lockheed worker who was witness to some of the follow-up operations in Project Jennifer said that when the parts of the submarine arrived at Redwood City, security went from "tight to air tight" at the building where the submarine was at least partially reassembled. "The Russian submarine" was stored in this sealed warehouse and the guards had orders to "shoot to kill," the former Lockheed contract worker said.

At the same time, the giant claw, which was still aboard the HMB-1, was dismantled, cut apart with electric torches, and completed destroyed. The eyewitness also said that occasionally workmen involved with the project were told not to come to work until after noon, and guards later said "important-looking suits" had visited the building on those mornings.

Whether the entire Golf submarine—all 324 feet of it—was reassembled inside the warehouse is not known. During this phase of the operation, the warehouse floor looked much like a modern-day hangar used in a National Transportation Board probe. NTB investigators put together the pieces of crashed airliners on hangar floors to determine the cause of a crash. The purpose of reassembling the submarine was the same—to determine exactly what caused the explosion that sank the boat.

The whereabouts of the recovered submarine parts are unknown. There are any number of large, highly secured buildings scattered around the bay at Navy facilities on Mare Island, Alameda, and at the abandoned, but still secured, Hunters Point Navy Shipyard, ten miles up the bay from the old Lockheed site. If K-129 was no longer needed for any intelligence or political value, it may also have simply been buried with the many other secrets of the Cold War. The nine-hundred-acre Hunters Point Shipyard is the site of a sixty-three-acre landfill, which is highly toxic from radiation waste dumped there over the years. The dumpsite could easily accommodate and disguise the irradiated hull plates and interior sections of a dismembered Soviet submarine, along with its accumulation of other radioactive parts from naval nuclear reactors of that era. In 1989, the Environmental Protection Agency declared a section of the shipyard to be one of the most contaminated sites in America, and added it to the Superfund clean-up list.

A public brouhaha was soon to follow the unpublicized arrival of the salvaged K-129 on American shores. The CIA's peculiar conduct over the next several months was further testimony to the importance the government placed on keeping the entire clandestine operation from the world.

The truth that Project Jennifer was a success became deeply buried in the CIA's own strange version of the recovery. The original cover story about the *Glomar Explorer* being an ore-mining ship began unraveling three months after the recovery was completed and the Soviet submarine returned to the San Francisco Bay area.

After the mission succeeded and valuable encrypted codebooks and encryption equipment were recovered, the CIA did not want the Soviets to learn that the U.S.

Navy could read their most sensitive naval communications. This secret held for more than a year, before the Soviets apparently learned American intelligence could capture their microburst transmissions.

But after all the compelling reasons for secrecy were no longer necessary or valid, even years after the end of the Cold War, the CIA continued to orchestrate one of the biggest clandestine campaigns in the history of the United States. The campaign to hide the facts about K-129, the *Glomar Explorer*, and Project Jennifer took on a life of its own. Long after the operations to raise the sunken sub were completed, keeping the secrets became a major CIA project.

27

BEFORE THE MAGNIFICENT RECOVERY SHIP *Glomar Explorer* was temporarily put into America's National Defense Reserve Fleet in Suisun Bay, an arm of San Francisco Bay, the CIA began spinning a yarn that painted its own operation as an incompetent boondoggle of near Keystone Kops proportions.

During the Cold War years, the Agency had been adept at creating legends to hide the identities of its deep-cover operatives and foreign espionage agents. In the case of Project Jennifer, it created a major legend to completely subvert the truth. The big lie at the heart of the legend was that only the front thirty-eight feet of K-129 had been retrieved. Since little of value was located in that section of a Soviet Golf submarine, the mission could be considered a $500 million failure.

The disinformation campaign posited that nothing of intelligence value, except two nuclear-tipped torpedoes, was retrieved.

According to that story, the mission was aborted when the giant claw became disabled during the first dive and no more recovery attempts could be made. Supposedly, while raising the *whole* submarine, the giant claw had cracked under the four-thousand-ton weight of the water-filled wreck. About halfway to the surface, most of the K-129 was dumped back into the deep.

The CIA even embellished the story of failure with a hair-raising episode that would thrill the tabloid journalists. They claimed that, just as the Soviet sub was being raised, one of the nuclear missiles slid out of its launch tube and headed to the bottom. The projectile gained speed as it went down. The implication was that the missile could have exploded beneath the ship and set off a nuclear blast that would have blown *Glomar Explorer* and the whole brave crew to kingdom come.

This melodramatic tale was aired in several television documentaries. In one show, a cartoonlike submarine is depicted being hoisted from the ocean floor by a giant claw. Suddenly, teeth in the huge device break and the submarine begins to fall apart, spilling a one-megaton ballistic missile. The missile races to the bottom, nose first, to the sound of throbbing music. A scene focuses on the face of a worker on the *Glomar Explorer*, implying this man and the crew are about to be destroyed in a nuclear blast when the wayward missile reaches the bottom, three miles down. Then, nothing happens. Since the depicted scene never did occur, that was the most accurate part of the presentation.

The CIA knew full well that simple impact would not have set off the nuclear warhead. During the Cold War, there were several instances when nuclear bombs either fell accidentally from aircraft without exploding or survived the impacts of bomber crashes. In the case of the K-129, the missile never slipped from the launch tube in the first place.

In all probability there was only one missile left, that in tube number three. The tube itself would have suffered implosion as the submarine sank, squeezing around the missile and preventing it from falling out.

The CIA claimed that no nuclear warheads, no ballistic missile, no codes or radio transmitters, no missile guidance system, and no navigational systems—nothing of value—could be recovered in the operation. To reinforce the new legend, even this disinformation was stamped top-secret. This clever cover story was to become a major success by the standards used to measure the successes of Cold War spydom—perfect disinformation.

The CIA learned that a number of journalists were beginning to nose about the huge project, and hurriedly developed the disinformation campaign in the event of a major leak. Agency officials may have reasoned that if there had to be a leak, the damage could be mitigated by obscuring the truth with nonsense. But neither of these explanations would seem to justify the enormity of the cover-up to come.

A change in direction from the legitimate need to keep intelligence operations secret for reasons of national security to a clumsy cover-up that generated conspiracy theories, international ill will, and a suspicion that the Americans were hiding a high-seas crime, was swift and certain. By then, several thousand military personnel and civilians had been involved, so leaks were bound to happen. The CIA decided that nothing truthful about K-129—the location of the sinking, or the recovery operation—could ever be revealed. Rumors had to be quashed with lies, to obscure every aspect of the incident.

First and foremost, the location of the sinking and subsequent recovery had to be forever obfuscated. Stories about the recovery have placed it as far away from Pearl Harbor as the other side of the earth in the Atlantic Ocean, and 1,700 miles northwest of the Hawaiian Islands in the open Pacific. The official version is that the wreck occurred 750 to 800 miles northwest of Pearl Harbor in the open North Pacific, while the real location was likely little more than 350 miles away, just north of the Hawaiian Leeward Islands.

During the recovery operation, the actual position of the sunken submarine would have been known only by ranking members of the *Glomar* crew and the CIA managers. The oil drillers, mechanics, and welders would have known only that they were far out in the open ocean, with no landfall in sight. The Leeward Islands were still far south, beyond the horizon and out of view of the workmen on the *Glomar*. The effort to permanently confuse the rank and file in the crew about their location would also explain the seemingly aimless meandering of their ship after it left the recovery site, and the unusual number of days it took the ship to reach the Hawaiian Islands.

The legitimacy of falsifying locations became dubious as time passed, and the CIA's sole purpose for perpetuating the lie seemed to be to safeguard its own cover story. The CIA had to make sure that no future dives on the wreck site could be accomplished by American or foreign oceanographers. Only a select few people in the Navy, the CIA, and the *Glomar Explorer* senior crew ever had any need to know exactly where the wreck site was located. Any future attempts to search for what the official story claimed was more than two-thirds of the submarine would be futile, because the cover stories all pointed to locations hundreds of miles from the actual site. No future diving expeditions were likely to set out into the vast ocean without even a clue where to start looking. It was key to the permanent cover story that no one ever locate and inspect the wreck site, because to do so would blow the cover and prove that the Soviet rogue submarine had been almost completely retrieved and carried away. Any future divers would likely have found only small areas of scattered debris left behind after the main sections were recovered.

A second layer to the cover story was created to further discourage anyone from looking for the remains of the wreck, even if they did learn the real location. Intelligence officials seeded another elaborate yarn. This story claimed that when K-129 slipped from the broken jaws of the *Glomar Explorer*, it fell back to the bottom of the sea with such impact that it simply dissolved like "Alka-Seltzer in water," and nothing could be seen of the submarine's hulk.

Of course, that story is patently ridiculous on the face of it. Anyone who has seen documentary film of the *Titanic*, the giant liner that sank on April 14, 1912, knows that steel ships do not disintegrate when they crash to the bottom of the ocean. The *Titanic* had a much more traumatic collision with an iceberg than K-129 suffered from an explosion in a launch tube. Both ships hurtled vertically downward more than two and a half miles before impact with the ocean floor. Furthermore, the *Titanic* had sat in corrosive salt water for more than a half-century longer than the K-129.

Coincidentally, there is a thriving scrap-iron business in European coastal waters, centered completely on the salvage of surplus World War I and World War II submarines. These war-surplus U-boats were deliberately scuttled in deep water of the Baltic and North seas to get rid of them after the two world wars. Yet, decades later, they remain in such good condition that the pristine steel in their hulls is highly prized in the European steel industry.

It is probable that if any major part of K-129 had actually fallen back into the sea or was purposely jettisoned by the *Glomar Explorer* crew, it would be clearly visible to a deep-diving submersible today. Of course, there is nothing to see, because most of the submarine was retrieved.

The CIA claimed it recovered six bodies from the wreckage. But there has been evidence reported by ex-Soviet admirals that all or part of at least sixty bodies were recovered, most of them crammed into the first two compartments of the submarine. According to the CIA's account, only the bodies of six Soviet sailors were found in the small section the Agency claims it recovered.

This part of the tale is also implausible, because with the raising of all or most of the sections of the submarine, many more bodies would certainly have been recovered.

The first major news leaks about the operation came even before the *Glomar* sailed. In June 1974, the CIA had managed to kill stories that appeared in early editions of the *Los Angeles Times* and the *New York Times*. These stories were about a break-in at Hughes Summa Corporation headquarters in California. Along with a large amount of cash, some artwork, and other documents, a memorandum describing the true mission of the *Glomar Explorer* had been taken. The burglary was reported in first editions of both papers. The sudden interest of the Federal Bureau of Investigation in what seemed to be a routine local burglary alerted a few reporters that something big was happening. Sources told the reporters about the missing memorandum, which suggested a CIA tie-in to *Glomar Explorer*. The articles even mentioned that the U.S. Navy might be trying to retrieve a lost Soviet submarine. That story was scotched after the CIA made personal calls to the top editors of both newspapers.

The CIA then successfully convinced these reporters who had tripped onto Project Jennifer that they would get better and exclusive stories later. Shortly after the recovery was completed, these newsmen were told that the *Glomar Explorer* had to go back and get the rest of the submarine in a second trip. The big lie about the operation was planted. That trip could not be conducted until a window of good weather conditions returned to the North Pacific, probably in the late spring of 1975, according to the CIA spokesman. There is evidence that, even as the reporters were agreeing to hold their inquiries into the huge project, the giant claw necessary to grab the wreckage was already being dismantled at the Lockheed facility in Redwood City, California.

The first reporter to get a solid tip that Project Jennifer was indeed a much bigger deal than first believed was Seymour Hersh, a Pulitzer Prize–winning investigative reporter for the *New York Times*. Hersh heard that the CIA operation had already recovered the Soviet submarine. He now knew for sure that *Glomar Explorer* was a CIA ship and not, as the world had been so loudly told, a Howard Hughes ore-mining vessel.

On December 18, 1974, Hersh called CIA Director William Colby for confirmation. Colby, who had been appointed CIA director in 1973 by President Nixon, persuaded the reporter that release of the story would severely damage national security. The CIA director again pleaded that the mission was not completed and that premature disclosure would prevent the Agency from returning to recover the rest of the submarine and its valuable intelligence data. Hersh and the *New York Times*, believing the high-level lie, and for the sake of national security, agreed not to publish. But he extracted a promise that the *New York Times* would be the first to get the story when the time was right.

Hersh was already one of the most famous investigative reporters in America, or infamous in some circles inside the Beltway, for breaking politically embarrassing articles based solely on "leaks." Most of the top newspaper reporters assigned to the nation's capital were especially aggressive in developing confidential sources in the various agencies of government, having been recently trounced by the *Washington Post* on the Watergate story.

The diligent, post-Watergate groundwork by investigative reporters in developing the authoritative sources or leaks in the Pentagon and the Agency was about to pay off in this case—though possibly not with the results the reporters and their newspapers had expected. The top news outlets in the United States may well have become the unwitting purveyors of the Central Intelligence Agency's most masterfully executed bait-and-switch scheme of the Cold War.

On the one hand, the CIA appeared to be trying hard to keep the *Glomar* mission a secret from the American press. On the other, there was an inexplicable effort to keep the Soviets apprised of what was going on with the *Glomar Explorer*'s recovery effort. In 1974, through official channels in Kissinger's State Department, Soviet Ambassador Dobrynin was given a formal account of the operation. Kissinger gave Dobrynin the names of three of the sailors whose bodies had been recovered and buried at sea, along with their documents and personal belongings.

Once again, Kissinger seemed to have found some diplomatic value in the wreck of the K-129.

28

IN HINDSIGHT, THE QUESTION might be: "When is a leak not a leak?" And the answer: "When it's a plant."

In that regard, a denial that the CIA schemed to plant false information in the American press was published later in Director Colby's autobiography. The indignant disclaimer sounds strangely like a gloat.

Director Colby wrote: "There have been a number of published postmortems on the *Glomar*, and the more prevalent of these were a measure of the disrepute to which the CIA had sunk at the time. For they tended to impute a deviously manipulative motive to my handling of the events. For example, there were those who were convinced that the *Glomar* project was completely successful and that then, in order to keep this a secret, I deliberately went around to all those newsmen to plant on them a false story that it wasn't, fully aware that if I told enough people, the story was bound to leak eventually."

In the love-hate, cat-and-mouse game between the news media and the intelligence community, that scenario and others like it are played out all the time. Colby's denial is probably the most accurate account of what really did happen with the media in the Project Jennifer case.

By early 1975, Seymour Hersh of the *New York Times* and Daniel Schorr, who was with CBS, were getting substantial amounts of information from somewhere inside the intelligence community. Once again, a number of editors agreed not to run the story after Colby convinced them that to do so would jeopardize further intelligence gains from a second probe of the wreck site by the *Glomar Explorer*. But by then the story was too big and too widely known to be contained.

Congressmen began picking up on the impending media storm. But even in the face of severe congressional criticism, the CIA doggedly maintained that the mission had succeeded in raising only a small portion of the boat. The CIA was certain to be blamed for a half-billion-dollar failure and, for some unknown reason, it was willing to take the heat.

Finally, the cover was blown off Project Jennifer when radio and television commentator and exposé columnist Jack Anderson broke the story in full detail on March 18, 1975, seven years and a few days after K-129 blew up and sank off Hawaii. Colby had made a last-ditch effort to dissuade Anderson from going public with it. When Anderson refused to hold the story any longer, the CIA director called all the other news editors and released them from their commitments.

About his encounter with Colby, Anderson wrote: "I told him [Colby], 'Look I have a record of killing stories that genuinely affect the security of the country. But are you trying to tell me that the Soviets don't know what's in their own submarine?'"

Anderson later criticized the media for agreeing with the CIA to hold the story for so long after it was clear the Soviets already knew about *Glomar Explorer*'s mission. The news media had learned that some information about the recovery effort had already been shared with the Soviets, even as the CIA tried to keep details from the American public.

"I was disappointed to see the reemergence of the pre-Watergate practice of cozy intimacy between press and government," Anderson wrote. "It was a dubious ethic that allowed a camaraderie of secrets to be shared by the press peerage, but kept from the public."

Anderson's source had told him that only a part of the submarine had been recovered, but that seventy bodies were found in the forward section.

After the Anderson broadcast, a flood of front-page articles appeared in major newspapers across the country. All the majors seemed to have their own inside sources, but the leaked versions remained fairly consistent with the official CIA story. On March 19, the *New York Times* filled most of its front page with articles and photographs of the *Glomar Explorer*, the HMB-1 barge, and a Golf-type Soviet submarine. The *Washington Post*, likewise, carried its coverage on the front page for the next several days.

Moscow, which could have been expected to respond with a firestorm of angry protests and threats, now that the world had learned of their lost submarine and America's recovery effort, was strangely quiet. Not only was there no response from the Kremlin or the Soviet military, but there was zero coverage about it for home consumption in *Pravda* and *Izvestia*.

In the days before worldwide satellite TV broadcasts, it was an easy matter to keep such controversial information from the Soviet citizenry. The families of K-129 heard nothing about the Americans' retrieval and honorable burial of some of their lost sailors' remains.

An ironic incident involving Colby's own autobiography, published three years later, in 1978, further suggests that a clever game with the truth was being played out at the time the story was leaked or planted.

It now appears Director Colby's autobiography, *Honorable Men*, was used to reinforce the impression that the CIA was trying to keep the *Glomar Explorer*'s operation a secret and, at the same time, plant a story that the operation had largely failed. A description of the K-129 recovery was excised from the original American edition of Colby's book by the CIA censor. A comparison of this English-language edition with the French edition, in which the passage was (mistakenly) not deleted, reveals that the information the CIA cut contained nothing more than what the Agency itself had already planted. But the CIA feigned outrage at the director's leak.

The section of the book that the CIA excised from the American edition, but which later appeared in the French edition, entitled *William Colby: 30 Ans de C.I.A.* (*William Colby: 30 Years in the CIA*), reads in translation:

> A deep-sea exploratory ship, built under cover of Howard Hughes's Summa Corporation, the *Glomar*, had been taken on sea trials in the spring of 1974. Represented to the world as a

daring experiment by Howard Hughes in the possibility of mining manganese nodules from the depths of the ocean, it started sailing in the summer. In fact, its mission was to recover a Soviet submarine stranded some 16,500 feet deep at the bottom of the Pacific. The security of the project and its cover were a dazzling success. So much so that a Soviet ship, which had come to the area on a reconnaissance mission at the very moment when the *Glomar* was attempting to bring up the submarine, sailed away after a few days without its crew having noticed anything suspicious.

The refloating itself was less satisfactory. At a depth of 10,000 feet, the *Glomar* underwent some damage. The Soviet submarine itself was broken into two pieces and only the fore part, about one-third of the ship, was eventually brought back to the surface, while the aft fell to the bottom of the sea with its nuclear missiles, its guiding apparatus, its transmission equipment, its codes, in other words with all the things the CIA had hoped to recover through this unprecedented operation.

The charade continued, and in September 1981, the Reagan administration Justice Department filed a lawsuit against former director Colby.

"The Reagan administration means to serve notice that it will not tolerate security leaks or breaches of contracts between the federal government and its workers," the *Washington Post* reported on September 20, 1981.

"Colby's alleged breach of security occurred when galley proofs reached a French publisher before the CIA could demand that certain passages be deleted."

Although Colby was publicly chastised and fined thirty thousand dollars for the leak, the CIA had obviously pulled the ruse to reinforce the misinformation they wanted to plant on the Soviets and the American public in the first place. What was removed from the American edition was exactly the information that Colby had so eagerly planted on columnists, reporters, editors, and broadcast news directors in 1975, in actions obviously calculated and sanctioned by the Agency.

The larger unanswered question regarding the secrecy surrounding the K-129 is why intelligence officials still tried so hard to keep information from the public, long after some details were aired in the American press. The Russians obviously knew that at least part of their submarine and some of its secrets had been recovered. One reasonable explanation is that the well-publicized cover story was intentionally false, or at least incomplete. Perhaps some damning detail had not yet been discovered by the press and the government did not want the full story revealed.

All of the intrigue surrounding the incident will probably never be officially revealed, like so many other secrets of the Cold War. But investigative reporters and authors, and a few insiders brave enough to risk punishment for violating confidentiality contracts with the CIA, began to uncover and publicize pieces of the real story.

The first book published about the recovery was a well-documented description of the *Hughes Glomar*

Explorer. Clyde W. Burleson, admittedly with the help of insiders in the CIA, wrote *The Jennifer Project.* Although the material in the book was detailed, and the operation apparently well described, there was no information leaked to that author or any of the others to follow regarding K-129's sinister mission or true location of the sinking. When *Jennifer Project* was published in 1977, the CIA and Navy intelligence also withheld any mention of the USS *Halibut's* role in finding K-129. Instead, the source for the information planted the story that the sub had been found and thoroughly investigated by the deep-sea research vessel *Mizar.*

It was not until after the end of the Cold War that larger pieces of the story began to appear in print. Even then, the true intention of the rogue submarine's crew was never hinted at by Navy or intelligence spokespersons who were providing bits and pieces of new information to reporters and authors.

At the height of the espionage operation surrounding K-129, very few officials were privy to the whole truth about the incident. Each piece of the top-secret operation was compartmentalized and revealed to persons working on carefully assigned parts of the whole, on a need-to-know basis only. Few participants who were, at the time, senior officials with knowledge of the whole story are still alive.

To this date, top-level officials from the Nixon administration who were apprised of all phases and secrets of the K-129 incident, the *Glomar,* and the uses of the resulting intelligence findings, have remained silent about the real purpose of Project Jennifer. Henry Kissinger, Alexander Haig, and DOD and CIA heads

James R. Schlesinger and William Colby never hinted at the whole story in their writings. Richard Helms headed the CIA from 1966 to 1973, a period covering the K-129 incident and the initiation of Project Jennifer. In his memoir, *A Look over My Shoulder*, he freely discussed the assassinations planned by the CIA during his term, but did not reveal the secrets he carried about Nixon and the K-129 episode. Helms died in 2002, taking those secrets to the grave.

Certainly, no one has publicly admitted that the fruits of the clandestine operation were used to blackmail the Soviets into détente or to bribe Mao into opening up China to the West. Nevertheless, the K-129 incident and the strange Project Jennifer have been alluded to frequently as having some mysterious role in turning the tide of the Cold War.

A few retired Department of Navy officials and Navy officers have published some information or been interviewed and quoted on the technology and missions of many of America's spy submarines during the Cold War. These admirals and Navy intelligence officers, however, were largely shut out of the larger story of K-129 after the CIA took control of the operation.

The story of the espionage role and deep-sea surveillance capabilities of U.S. naval forces, particularly submarines, was revealed for the first time in 1998. The best-selling, nonfiction book *Blind Man's Bluff: The Untold Story of American Submarine Espionage*, by Sherry Sontag, Christopher Drew, and Annette Lawrence Drew, revealed the thrilling and important role of U.S. naval underseas spy activities in winning the Cold War. That book covered some aspects of the

K-129 sinking and parts of the recovery effort. For example, the world learned that K-129 was located by a spy sub, USS *Halibut*, and not by the surface research ship *Mizar*, as the Navy had claimed. Information leaked to the authors by intelligence sources, however, carefully maintained the cover stories about this mysterious episode in history.

Other revelations about the extensive amount of intelligence lifted from the wrecked Soviet submarine were made in William J. Broad's book, *The Universe Below: Discovering the Secrets of the Deep Sea*, published in 1997. Dr. John Piña Craven filled in additional pieces of the bigger puzzle in his autobiography, *The Silent War: The Cold War Battle Beneath the Sea*, published in 2001. While Dr. Craven provided new insight into the K-129 incident, he and most of the other Navy men, civilian Defense Department personnel, and espionage agents are all sworn to a lifetime of confidentiality concerning their work in the Cold War. Any secrets about the story of the K-129 incident they may carry with them can never be told.

The mystery surrounding the sunken sub has given rise to a number of other books on various aspects of the K-129 incident and Project Jennifer. The CIA's elaborate effort to keep the details secret may have increased interest in the story, although much that has been written by authors, journalists, and historians relies, at least in part, on the Agency's version of what happened.

Perhaps even more chilling than the CIA's attempt to hide the truth from the public is evidence that the Agency may have denied many of the facts to the nation's top decision-maker. There is a small, but revealing, notation in a declassified "Memorandum for the Record" (sometimes known as a cover-your-ass or CYA memo) that George H. W. Bush, then CIA director, who was to become the forty-first president of the United States, wrote to himself.

Time magazine, in its December 6, 1976, issue, reported that all of the K-129 had been retrieved with a "technical mother lode" of intelligence material. The Bush memorandum noted that President Ford had been briefed about the *Time* story on the extent of the *Glomar Explorer*'s retrieval from the K-129 wreck site. He wrote:

"Glomar Explorer: I stated to the President that we had leveled, and that the *Time* magazine story which was out yesterday was totally false."

A startling conclusion could be drawn from that terse notation. The CIA may have denied even the president of the United States a full accounting of the clandestine Project Jennifer. Or, a different conclusion could be drawn. This may be the first documented case of the Agency providing a president with another kind of cover that came to be known as "credible deniability."

Project Jennifer was so wrapped in secrecy, disinformation, official propaganda, and downright lies that even today, years after the sinking of K-129, dozens of widely different versions of the story persist.

29

MANY OF THE MOST SENSITIVE FILES on major events of the Cold War era—the Cuban Missile Crisis, the Kennedy assassination, the toppling of regimes, and many highly secret operations—have long since been declassified by the U.S. government and made available to the public and historians.

Why then, more than three decades after the sinking and recovery of the wrecked Soviet submarine, and a decade after the Cold War ended, do the Central Intelligence Agency and other branches of the United States government so tenaciously cling to the secrets of the K-129 incident? What truth is so terrible that it cannot be told? Only a handful of men in the highest levels of American and Russian governments were ever privy to the complete story of events that left even the admirals and generals "out of the loop."

The incident occurred in an era when mutual assured destruction (MAD) was the prime defense policy that prevented the use of weapons capable of wiping the human race from the planet—when presidents and premiers played madman war games as strategy. Billions were spent on defense in the Free World, and the

Soviet Union spent itself into ruin, trying to keep up. Public knowledge that these games with nuclear weapons had spun wildly out of control, and that all the treasuries of the superpowers could not have prevented the rogue attack, would certainly have destabilized society. Leaders would not have wanted the dark secret revealed, either in the Soviet Union or in America.

It would be unthinkable to admit that the reckless proliferation of weapons of mass destruction had brought the world so close to the edge, that mankind was only a ten count and a fail-safe device away from a rogue nuclear attack on a major city. How could the safeguards have been so flawed that a handful of fanatical men and an old-model submarine came so close to determining the fate of billions of people?

For almost fifty years, American and Russian leaders practiced this kind of brinkmanship with nuclear weapons, bringing their people close to atomic Armageddon.

The fact that this "mad" proliferation policy came close to creating doomsday in the lone rogue scenario can provide an explanation for why the CIA and the Federal Security Service (FSB), successor to the KGB in Russia, have doggedly kept information about the K-129 hidden in confusion and secrecy for so long. Both governments apparently determined that the near-catastrophe of the K-129 incident was a secret the people could never be told.

Investigative journalists and public watchdog groups in the United States apparently suspected that something of that magnitude was suggested by the extreme confidentiality the U.S. government placed on the files of the *Glomar Explorer* operation. In an attempt to pry loose public disclosure about Project Jennifer, two major, precedent-setting lawsuits were filed in U.S. District Court in Washington, D.C., under the 1966 Freedom of Information Act (FOIA).

Journalist Harriet Ann Phillippi, who was the Washington correspondent for *Rolling Stone* magazine, sued the CIA in U.S. District Court in Washington after the Agency refused her FOIA request of March 21, 1975, for information about the project. Felice D. Cohen and Morton H. Halperin, representing the Military Audit Project, a defense expenditures watchdog organization, sued the CIA over its denial of a similar request for documents in a FOIA action filed on April 3, 1975. In both cases the district court issued summary judgments in late 1975, upholding the CIA's refusal to provide documents about Project Jennifer and the *Glomar Explorer*. The plaintiffs then took their cases to the United States Court of Appeals for the District of Columbia Circuit, setting off six years of legal battles that were waged in the federal courts throughout the terms of three CIA directors. The core issues of freedom of information versus government secrecy were not finally resolved by the federal appellate court until 1981. The legal precedents established by the so-called Glomar cases provide much of the cover that intelligence agencies and other government bodies use today to hide information from the public.

The government's defense of CIA secrecy in the matter—what the intelligence community sought to hide—turned out to be highly revelatory in and of itself.

The Agency argued that the project had to be kept secret because any "official acknowledgement of involvement by U.S. Government agencies would disclose the nature and purpose of the program and could . . . severely damage the foreign relations and the national defense of the United States."

While the CIA had authorized the release of fewer than two thousand pages of heavily redacted classified information about Project Jennifer, it held "about 128,000 documents" related to the operation, according to the lawsuit.

The CIA noted in its response that "the government has not officially confirmed the purpose of the Glomar Explorer Project."

The government argued that, despite the unofficial leaks, the FOIA request should be denied because the CIA "still has something to hide; the reported purpose of the *Glomar Explorer*'s mission may well be notorious, but, the government implicitly suggests, its actual purpose may well still be a secret, or, at least, unresolved doubt may still remain in the minds of the United States' potential and actual adversaries as to the true purpose of the mission."

The FOIA case was brought by journalist Phillippi in an effort to "reveal the purpose of the *Glomar Explorer* venture" and its results. But the FOIA request went further, and challenged the CIA's campaign of disinformation and distortion of facts. The suit additionally demanded release of records of the 1975 conversations surrounding the cover-up between former CIA Director William Colby and the news media.

"In response to the appellant's March 1975 request

for records, the CIA refused even to confirm or deny the very existence of such records," Phillippi's appeal noted.

The appeals court acknowledged that complaint to be true. However, the court found that, even though some information had leaked and the intelligence agency might have planted false stories, there was justification for withholding additional information. "If the CIA were not allowed to engineer controlled leaks of information, it would not be able to protect its possible fallback cover," a confirming appellate judge stated.

The appeals court found it understandable that the CIA might need to "buttress the credibility of a widely disseminated fallback cover story." Thus, the law condoned the government's legal authority, not only to refuse access to certain types of information, but to fabricate stories to mislead the news media.

"Once the story was out, reporters and editors began to speculate as to why the CIA had undertaken the apparently hopeless mission," the court review noted.

The appeal cited a *Time* magazine conclusion in its March 31, 1975, issue: "There are several theories. . . . The last theory . . . suggesting that raising a Soviet submarine was not [the project's] mission at all, but the supreme cover for a secret mission as yet safely secure."

In ruling against both FOIA applicants, the appeals court found that the CIA's case for secrecy should be upheld. The decision stated, "It is far from clear that either the purpose of the *Glomar Explorer* mission or the technology used to accomplish that mission are in fact known. We have been given two stories [by the government] which purport to explain the *Glomar Explorer*'s mission: first, we were told the *Glomar Explorer* was designed to mine manganese nodules from the ocean floor, and then, we were told that it was designed to lift a Russian submarine. Both stories, though very different, were plausible. The truth may lie in yet a third direction."

The ruling concluded: "In sum, neither we nor the appellants can be sure we know what intelligence capabilities and purposes were embodied in the *Glomar Explorer*."

In upholding the federal district courts' earlier rulings that refused the journalist and the watchdog group access to CIA records, the appeals court established a sweeping new precedent that gave government intelligence agencies an important exemption to the Freedom of Information Act. That exemption came to be known as the "Glomar response" or "Glomarization."

The precedent-setting ruling that established the Glomar response provides that a government agency does not even have to acknowledge it has specific information requested under federal freedom of information laws, let alone defend its classified status against a FOIA request.

This Glomar exception has since become a favorite tool of the American intelligence community and other government agencies to circumvent the Freedom of Information Act. The U.S. Solicitor General's Office frequently reminds all government agencies of their immunity from responding to media questions on sensitive matters. A 1998 memo from that office reads: "As you may know, a Glomar response is an agency's express refusal even to confirm or deny the existence of any records responsive to a FOIA request."

Since the Glomar response became law, the CIA has taken full advantage of this legal cover, and not even the smallest detail about the K-129 incident—no matter how apparently insignificant—has been declassified. Requests for information made by citizens, veterans' organizations, authors, reporters, and historians can be routinely denied using the Glomar response to the Freedom of Information Act, without further explanation. The agency invoking the exception does not even have to acknowledge the existence of the files in question.

The world knew the Cold War was truly over when, in October 1992, America's top spy was sent to Moscow to pay a state visit to his former nemesis, the KGB. CIA Director Robert M. Gates arrived in Moscow in October 1992. Significantly, the gift the American spy chief selected to take to the former Soviets was an item from the decades-old K-129 incident.

"As a gesture of intent, a symbol of a new era, I carried with me the Soviet naval flag that had draped the coffins of the half-dozen Soviet sailors whose remains the *Glomar Explorer* had recovered when it raised part of a Soviet ballistic missile submarine from deep in the Pacific Ocean in the mid-1970s," Gates wrote in his autobiography, *From the Shadows*. "I also was taking to Yeltsin a videotape of their burial at sea, complete with prayers for the dead and the Soviet national anthem—a dignified and respectful service even at the height of the Cold War."

Director Gates not only delivered the mementos of

that controversial episode, but also was the first head of an American spy agency to tour the former fortress of the KGB's First Chief Directorate. It was truly a thaw in cold relations, since this was the foreign intelligence arm that had been locked in mortal competition with the CIA and other American intelligence agencies since the end of World War II.

But even this goodwill gesture rang rather hollow, since the peace offering paid only lip service to the lingering mystery of the K-129. Tellingly, Gates stuck to the CIA cover story that only six bodies had been recovered from the wreckage, even though eyewitnesses had already told the public that several dozen more bodies were retrieved. During the visit, Gates also met with his counterpart, Yevgeny Primakov, the head of the Russian intelligence service, and pledged cooperation in resolving the outstanding issues that stood in the way of a full reconciliation between the two former adversaries.

An opening in relations seemed swiftly to follow this historic meeting, but the K-129 was to remain a point of contention between the former Soviets and the Americans.

30

SHORTLY AFTER THE EXCHANGE between the spy agency chiefs, presidents Boris Yeltsin and George H. W. Bush went a step further toward resolving some of the major remaining conflicts from the long, undeclared Cold War.

The two presidents announced the formation of the U.S.-Russia Joint Commission on POW/MIAs (USRJC). The commission, to be staffed by high-level military men and diplomats, would provide the forum for both nations to determine the fate of their missing servicemen from World War II, the Korean War, the Vietnam War, and the Cold War. The K-129 incident and Project Jennifer were to become among the most contentious matters before the commissioners. The debate over the lost submarine did not reach the point of rancorous exchanges until the American delegation failed, over and over again, to answer the Russians' questions and provide requested information.

Whether the American delegation, cochaired by Ambassador Malcolm Toon, knowingly stonewalled the Russians, or was simply unable to provide the information because the CIA would not supply it, is not known. But the Russians, headed by Colonel-General Dmitrii A. Volkogonov, were never satisfied with the United States' explanations about the K-129.

The Russians began seeking information about their lost submarine and the fate of its crew of ninety-eight from the first plenary session of the commission, held in 1992. In August 1993, at the sixth plenum, held in Moscow, the United States was finally ready with a response.

Ambassador Toon addressed the Russians sitting across the conference table in the Hall of Government Meetings in the Kremlin.

"We have important information on the Golf-class submarine lost in 1968 in the Pacific," Ambassador Toon began. He reminded the Russians of rumors that had persisted for years claiming their submarine had sunk as the result of a collision with an American submarine.

"At my request, U.S. naval intelligence searched the logs of all U.S. subs that were active in 1968. As a result, our director of naval intelligence has concluded that no U.S. sub was within 300 nautical miles of your sub when it sank."

Technically, that answer was correct.

The ambassador's revelation of this heretofore secret information about the precise location of K-129 should have been a bombshell for the ex-Soviet military men. By stating there were no American submarines within *300 miles* of the doomed K-129, the Americans revealed startling information that the CIA had struggled for years to keep secret. The ambassador did not say 750 miles, or 1,700 miles, which, under various cover stories, had been floated as the distance of the wreck site from Pearl Harbor. He instead acknowledged that no American submarine was within 300 miles of the sunken ship. Ambassador Toon had, in effect, revealed more accurately the true location of the rogue submarine.

The reason the U.S. intelligence could be so precise as to location, and truthful, too, was that the American submarines were indeed more than 300 miles away. There were dozens of U.S. submarines at Pearl Harbor, approximately 350 miles to the southeast of the site where K-129 exploded and sank in its abortive missile launch.

No one appeared to catch this slip of the tongue by an American diplomat who probably did not himself realize the significance of the information he had shared. One of the most revealing pieces of intelligence to come from the K-129 incident had just been casually laid on the table by the U.S. representative.

And there was more to come.

Next, Ambassador Toon stated, "Recently, general, [addressing commission cochairman Volkogonov directly] we learned that the sub's bell had been recovered. Both I and my colleague Strobe Talbott [also a U.S. representative on the commission] asked CIA Director James Woolsey to allow us to present this bell to you. I'd planned to present it to Primakov . . . I thought, in the meantime, it would be interesting for you to have a look at the bell."

A staff member brought the bell to the head table.

The Russian general grunted acknowledgment of the gift, but seemed unimpressed. "I'm sure we'll find a place for it in a museum. It's an important memorial and I'm deeply gratified. We'll tell the relatives."

Volkogonov, of course, was an army general, and did not recognize the astounding significance represented by this piece of hardware from the K-129. An ex-Soviet submarine admiral, or even a lowly seaman, would have seen the implication of this revelation immediately. This piece of evidence put the lie to years and years of CIA disinformation, cover stories, denied FOIA requests, and protestations of a failed mission. In a single casual moment, the years of clandestine web spinning and building stories within stories was swept away—and no one realized it.

K-129's brass bell sat on a polished table in the heart of the Kremlin, revealing more than all the leaks to American newsmen, intel from moles in the Pentagon, and background briefings by government officials had uncovered in the three decades since the submarine disappeared.

The bell, now missing its clapper, had originally been permanently fixed by a bolt to a steel bar welded firmly behind the bridge of the Golf submarine. It was located in the center of the conning tower, just forward of the area housing the missile tubes. The fact that the Americans possessed the bell was telling evidence that *Glomar Explorer* had indeed raised considerably more of the boat than was earlier acknowledged by the CIA or admitted to in these talks with the Russians.

Glomar Explorer was designed to retrieve large sections of the submarine. It is technically impossible for the claw to have retrieved only the small part of the conning tower in which the bell was firmly attached to the boat's frame. It is unlikely that special efforts would have been selectively expended to locate and retrieve the bell. Most probably, the bell was found when the center section of the submarine was being cut up, after it was raised into the moon pool of the *Glomar.*

Thus, the bell was virtual proof that far more than the front thirty-eight feet of the submarine was recovered, as the CIA had steadfastly maintained. The bell was located inside a section more than 150 feet aft of the boat's bow. If the bell was recovered, then the attack center in the conning tower and the control center were probably recovered as well. Since that compartment, along with the adjoining compartment housing the three missile tubes, was the strongest and most reinforced section of a Golf, it is likely that the entire center of the submarine was raised. The presence of the bell strongly suggests that all the vital parts of K-129 were recovered, and that most of the secrets of that deadly final mission were in the hands of American intelligence agencies.

After this session, when the Russians returned home with the bell, former Soviet submarine admirals would have recognized the astounding evidence they had been handed. Whether this was an intentional admission by someone in the CIA or an oversight of breathtaking scope is unknown. But when the Soviets came back to the next plenary sessions, their demands for information about their lost boat became more angry and more blunt.

In the Eighth Plenary Session, held at the Pentagon in Washington in February 1994, Ambassador Toon noted, "certain unpleasantness had crept" into the commission's relations.

"We are continuing our research for further information on the Soviet Golf-class submarine," Toon assured General Volkogonov, noting that formal requests had been made of the U.S. Joint Chiefs of Staff.

"We will look again and work harder," promised Denis Clift, U.S. cochairman for the Cold War Working Group of the USRJC.

The former Soviet military men were incensed.

"After press reports that documents were raised from the submarine, we cannot accept an answer that nothing was found. It concerns 300 families of 98 crews members," a Russian colonel on the working group angrily replied. "Since we do not know the circumstances, the pension (for the families) is only 30 percent of the serviceman's salary. This is purely a humanitarian effort; it does not matter why the submarine sank."

The meeting ended angrily, with the U.S. delegation promising to "investigate more fully the circumstances of the loss of the submarine, and the possibility of the return of documents and personal effects recovered."

This demand for personal documents belonging to the lost crew and recovered by the *Glomar Explorer* may have also produced an unexpected piece of evidence. At one of the subsequent plenary sessions, a photograph or negative of a man dressed in a Soviet navy uniform was given to the Russians. The photograph was reportedly of a person whose body was found at the wreck. Russian naval investigators combed the old Soviet navy rosters and circulated the picture among veterans who had served at Rybachiy Naval Base at that time. They ran the picture in veterans' publications and Russian newspapers, requesting that anyone who knew the man assist in identifying him. No one came forward.

This man was obviously not a Soviet submariner, because records on these elite seamen were meticulously maintained. Then why was he on the doomed ship? Had the lower-echelon investigators accidentally stumbled onto the photograph of one of the KGB operatives?

The Tenth Plenary Session of the USRJC opened again on a rancorous note with Ambassador Toon stating, "In the past, you have raised with me the Golf-class submarine case both privately and in plenary sessions, expressing your concern that not all information pertinent to the loss has been made available to your side. Just before my departure on this trip, I met with our most authoritative officials and experts at the highest levels of my government on the subject. I can offer the following:

"I can state that the U.S. had nothing to do with the loss of the submarine. Further, we do not know why the submarine was lost.

"I have been asked, if this is the case, how did the U.S. locate the submarine on the bottom of the Pacific. The answer, first, is that Soviet search and rescue efforts tipped U.S. armed forces off to the fact that something had happened in the Pacific. This then allowed us to review data from our sensors in the Pacific after the fact. That review of data led us to identify the location of the submarine.

"We do not have the submarine's log. We have turned over to the Russian side all humanitarian items and information relating to this loss. There is nothing further I can add. The U.S. side has completed its contribution to this aspect of the work of our Joint Commission."

In the Eleventh Plenary Session, held in Washington, D.C., in December 1994, the Russians were even angrier, and demanded the U.S. delegation turn over the logs from the USS *Swordfish*, which they still maintained had sunk K-129 in a collision. An American commission member again stated, "We have done everything possible to research this incident and have provided you everything we had on the incident."

The ever more bitter exchanges continued in subsequent plenary sessions of the POW/MIA commission for five more years, and came to a head in the Sixteenth Plenum of the USRJC, held in Moscow, in November 1999.

Russian Federal Security Service's Colonel Vladimir Vinogradov opened the Russian side of the meeting with an angry challenge to the Americans. High-level military and civilian leaders from both countries were present when the intelligence officer loudly complained that the Americans' previous responses to inquiries about the K-129 incident were inadequate.

"I do not understand the Commission's difficulty on this matter," said an obviously perplexed Colonel Vinogradov. "Our inquiry has taken on the psychology of a criminal that had been caught and claims that guilt must now be proved."

Denis Clift again argued that all the information the Navy or CIA had on the incident had already been given to the Russians.

"The U.S. has provided Russia with a full explanation

of the incident. It would be difficult to say more," said Clift, who was at the time with an organization known as the Joint Military Intelligence College. "Last year the CIA reviewed its files again to be absolutely sure there was no more information."

Clift said the CIA's letter had been turned over to the joint commission's previous session, and that former CIA directors Gates and Woolsey met with President Yeltsin to brief him on the incident. Clift added that the K-129's bell had been returned to the Russians.

Vinogradov replied that the Russian experts were still doubtful about the information they had received on the K-129 incident.

Despite the logical need for military secrecy concerning the K-129 affair ending with the Cold War in 1991, there is obviously a continued sensitivity about the release of any information to the rank and file in either Russia or the United States. No additional information about the K-129 incident has been provided to the Russians in the U.S.-Russia Joint Commission on POW/MIAs.

Several months after the stormy POW/MIA session in Moscow, another submarine tragedy ripped open old wounds over the K-129 incident, and this time the anger of former Soviet submariners swept into the open. The newest Russian nuclear cruise missile submarine, the *Kursk*, sank in the Barents Sea near Murmansk on August 12, 2000, carrying 118 sailors and officers to their death. The immediate response from former Soviet submarine officers was that the cause had to be a collision with a NATO spy submarine.

"Russia's initial suspicion of a sinister American role

in the sinking of *Kursk* is rooted in distrust of U.S. motives—distrusts so firmly held that Russian officials still press for answers in the sinking of a Soviet sub in 1968," read a lead story in the *Washington Post*.

News outlets all over Russia revisited the all-but-forgotten K-129 sinking, with far more information being given after the *Kursk* disaster than at any time since the 1968 incident. In fact, when K-129 sank, there was no information released to the public that a submarine was even missing. Russian authorities soon found the *Kursk* sinking was caused by an onboard explosion in the forward torpedo room and had nothing to do with the Americans. Still, a hue and cry arose throughout the former Soviet Union for an explanation about the K-129.

This sudden spotlight on a mystery that the former Soviet admirals had kept secret for so many years made a number of officials in Moscow nervous. Faced with new evidence that the Soviet submarine sank much closer to American territory than the location in the far North Pacific, an official scrambled to explain why K-129 seemed to be so far off its designated course.

The former ranking Soviet admiral in the Pacific Fleet offered an explanation that made the reason for dispatching K-129 on this mission even more sinister. He suddenly came up with a claim that the missile submarine had been sent on a spying mission to Pearl Harbor. That explanation is highly unlikely, since only the attack submarines of the Soviet navy were used for reconnoitering. Ballistic missile submarines were far too valuable in the strategic scheme to be risked on spy missions. In 1968, the Pacific Fleet had 85 long-range and 171 medium-range attack submarines assigned in the Pacific Ocean. So there were ample resources for underseas spy missions without calling on a missile submarine such as K-129.

The Russian Federation, which also wanted to scotch the rampant rumors, finally issued an "official" cause of the sinking of K-129. The new official version was that K-129 was destroyed when the submarine accidentally exceeded its maximum diving depth and was crushed by the deep-sea pressure.

The new openness that existed temporarily in the Russian Federation under President Boris Yeltsin led to the belated recognition for the families of the sub-mariners lost aboard the K-129. The government posthumously awarded ninety-eight crew members Medals of Courage and acknowledged that their deaths had been due to circumstances beyond their control. This belated recognition of the lost crew was certainly appropriate for most of the men of K-129. Some of the officers and men probably were true unsung heroes and went to their deaths trying to stop an unspeakable act of terror. The recognition allowed the surviving widows to draw full pension benefits for their husbands' service.

At least eleven named on the roster of the honored were rogues, and the names themselves were probably aliases carefully prepared by someone high in the KGB. They did not deserve medals, but to withhold the honor would have been to admit something was terribly wrong on that mission.

Nevertheless, a stone memorial to the lost crew was also commissioned and erected near the K-129's home port on the Kamchatka Peninsula.

Another memorial was placed in a cemetery in Moscow for at least one of the lost sailors, who was likely among the real heroes of that doomed mission. Irina Zhuravina, the widow of K-129's first officer, Alexander Zhuravin, had a tombstone erected over an empty grave with the photograph of her lost submariner etched into the stone. The state's honors had been painfully long in coming. Their son, Mikhail, who had become an engineer in a Soviet nuclear plant, died of cancer in 1992, without ever knowing that the new Russia had honored his father's naval service. The son is buried beside his father's empty grave.

"We were told nothing for months, and then warned, 'Do not place your personal interests above the interests of the state,'" the widow, who is now in her seventies, laments. "You could not talk about it. The secrecy was so strong, we could not even think about it. An admiral of the fleet once told me that I needed to forget about it and not stir up the past. Neither the old Soviet government nor the new Russian Federation government has ever told us anything about what happened, or what they learned from the Americans," she said. "But we will keep on asking, anyway."

When the *Kursk* sank, several of the surviving widows of the K-129 traveled to Vidyayevo, the doomed boat's home port in far northern Russia, to offer solace to the young wives of the newly lost submariners.

The Russian families of K-129 are not the only ones left in government-sanctioned darkness by the layered mystery. A well-orchestrated campaign by professional secret makers and keepers in both the former Soviet Union and the United States has done an expert job of keeping everyone, both high and low, in ignorance about this most strange Cold War incident.

The official silence and deliberate obfuscations about the sinking of K-129, along with the eerily similar mysterious sinking of the USS *Scorpion* less than two months later in the Atlantic, originate at the highest levels of government.

Retired Navy captain Peter Huchthausen, who has written several books on the submarines of that era, was confronted with this stone wall of deliberate silence shortly after the end of the Cold War. Captain Huchthausen told *Seattle Post-Intelligencer* military reporter Ed Offley of a strange encounter he had in the former Soviet Union after asking about the lost submarines.

"Captain, you are very young and inexperienced, but you will learn that there are some things both sides have agreed not to address, and one is that event [the *Scorpion*] and our K-129 loss, for similar reasons," a Soviet admiral told Huchthausen, who was then serving as U.S. naval attaché in Moscow.

The saga of K-129 contains one of the greatest mysteries in maritime history. It is no accident the secrets have been kept.

EPILOGUE

THE INCIDENTS OF EARLY 1968, and the subsequent détente with the Soviets and rapprochement with Red China, did not end the Cold War. But the horrific reality of what had almost happened at Pearl Harbor in 1968 profoundly affected the outcome, and may have prevented that long Cold War from turning any hotter.

The Soviet empire did not fall for another twenty-three years, largely because the discovery of sixty oil fields and soaring oil prices that resulted from the Arab oil embargo of 1973 gave the Communist system a temporary reprieve. The economic collapse, which was forecast to begin in the 1970s, and may have been a major impetus for the plot behind the K-129 affair, did ultimately occur. In 1991, the Iron Curtain came down, and with it the ruthless totalitarian Communism that had held the Soviet Socialist Republics in captivity for more than half the twentieth century. George Herbert Walker Bush was presiding over the U.S. government when the end finally came. President Bush declared that this was the beginning of a "new world order," a time of peace and prosperity all over the globe. Huge peace dividends were expected; and, indeed, disarmament on a massive scale seemed possible for a time.

A year after the end of the Cold War, Russia stopped its massive submarine-building program and began to dismantle much of the nuclear fleet, which had numbered more than five hundred boats at the peak of the crisis. The United States also began to dismantle and mothball some of its submarine force.

Unfortunately, both the Americans and the Russians were naively arrogant enough to think that if they called a halt to hostilities against each other, all the world's hostilities would cease. Some political philosophers even pronounced this the "end of history," and predicted the world would now concentrate on making permanent peace through global capitalist democracy. That was in 1991.

One decade later, on September 11, 2001, the world was brutally reminded there could be no peace after all, only different and more deadly enemies to challenge world order. It has become increasingly clear that the proliferation of chemical, biological, and nuclear technology currently poses an even greater threat to humanity than it did at the peak of the Cold War.

The still-secret incident of K-129's near nuclear strike on an American city becomes a cautionary tale. It resonates in today's global war on terrorism, as rogue states rush to acquire weapons of mass destruction.

Now, instead of two major powers with weapons capable of killing civilian populations on a massive scale, there are thirteen countries known to have biological, chemical, or nuclear weapons. Terrorist states are eagerly developing these types of weapons, and stateless terrorists are avidly seeking to acquire them. Russian Federation intelligence officials recently reported that al-Qaeda has been seeking to buy loose nuclear weapons on the black market since the mid-1990s.

One of the causes for alarm over this new threat is that terrorists or even rogue states are not constrained by the notion of mutual assured destruction, as were the great powers of the Cold War. The MAD strategy as a deterrence against starting nuclear warfare in the Cold War era has been replaced today by a policy of preemptive strikes against fanatics whose primary strategy is mass murder for the sake of creating chaos and terrorizing whole populations. The stated aim of al-Qaeda is the use of unconventional means to destroy Westerners and their modern civilization. There is more than ample proof now that the goal of the anti-West terrorists is to acquire weapons of mass destruction and any means necessary to deliver them on population centers of America, Europe, the Middle East, and southern Asia.

Not only are WMD proliferating, but around the world unstable and/or terrorist-friendly nations are acquiring submarines to stealthily deliver the deadly weapons. A half-dozen European and Asian nations are now making and selling sophisticated submarines to the highest bidder—no questions asked.

The Canadian National Defense Association Network warned that in the post–Cold War world "submarines could be a factor in drug running, illegal immigration, or disagreements over rights of passage." The 1997 report said Canadian maritime forces must be prepared to protect its ports and support peace operations overseas.

The three largest powers have reduced their strategic forces considerably since the end of the Cold War. The United States currently maintains an active fleet of about 75 nuclear submarines, the Russian Federation has 65 nuclear submarines, and the People's Republic of China has 64 nuclear submarines. Today the navies of lesser military powers maintain a combined 255 submarines. Many of those are advanced diesel-electric models similar to the K-129. Most of these diesel-electric boats have been upgraded to make them comparable to modern-day nuclear submarines when running on their battery-powered motors.

Chillingly, one of the largest submarine fleets in the world is now operated by a totalitarian rogue state, the People's Republic of Korea. North Korea alone maintains a fleet of 50 attack submarines, although only half of them are believed to be operational, and another 36 midget subs. While this fleet would be no match for the modern submarines of the three major military powers—the United States, Russia, and China—the North Korean submarines are nevertheless stealthy, and capable of delivering deadly packages to any place on earth.

The Defense Intelligence Agency recently raised the estimate of North Korea's nuclear arsenal from two weapons to eight, and forecast a potential production capacity of six additional weapons a year by 2007. Experts are concerned that because of its economic plight, North Korea might sell a nuclear weapon to a terrorist organization. North Korea could also sell one of its surplus submarines along with a nuclear weapon.

Other countries identified at various times as sponsoring terrorism maintain submarine forces, including Iran, with three regular attack submarines and three midget subs, and Libya, with two attack subs.

In addition, the CIA recently announced it had identified eleven commercial blue-water surface ships that are owned or under the control of the al-Qaeda terrorist organization. One of the greatest new fears is that terrorists will deliver chemical, radiological, or biological weapons to the harbor of a major American or European city in the cargo hold of a tramp freighter.

As ludicrous as it sounds, even narco-terrorists have tried to acquire submarines. Colombian government troops who raided a suspicious warehouse in Facatativa, Colombia, in the year 2000 discovered a home-made submarine being built by Russian mobsters for a South American drug cartel. The hundred-foot, nearly completed submarine would have been capable of carrying at least 150 tons of cocaine to the Unites States, submerged out of sight of the U.S. Coast Guard.

China's aggressive development of a submarine-based nuclear missile program is proceeding in the opposite direction from the American and Russian programs. China today maintains a fragile balance of power between the progressive civilian leaders and the hard-liners in control of the PRC's powerful army and navy. There are fewer safeguards to prevent a disgruntled Chinese submarine commander or group of plotters from repeating the K-129 rogue scenario.

In the event of another coup d'état such as the one that brought the now-friendly military regime to power in Pakistan, there is no international protocol to keep a radicalized Islamist military, or even a terrorist group, from getting their hands on a Pakistani submarine, complete with a nuclear weapon.

Robert Baer, a twenty-two-year veteran of the CIA with extensive experience as a field officer in the Middle East, recently warned of the devastation a rogue submarine attack on the Sea Island Oil Terminal off Saudi Arabia could have on the Western economy. Baer said that a commando or submarine attack on the offshore loading terminal could take almost five million barrels per day of vital oil supplies off the world market for months. He said the loss of that much oil would raise the price to $150 a barrel, at least triple the mid-2004 price. Such an event would result in economic and social calamities. Baer noted that an attack on this most vulnerable link in the world's oil supply would be simple to accomplish. He warned that any enemy of the West with a submarine "available in the global arms bazaar" could devastate the great Western powers.

In April 2004, al-Qaeda terrorists attempted to cut off the flow of nearly one million barrels of Iraqi oil in a thwarted seaborne attack against offshore loading facilities near Basra.

It would not take a sophisticated missile system to deliver a nuclear, chemical, or biological bomb to the harbor of any city in the world. A large, bundled WMD device could easily be dropped by a submerged boat that had silently crossed an ocean and sneaked into the unprotected ports of America, Europe, or friendly countries of Asia. In the United States, key ports and harbors are wide open, with only naval reserve units in charge of mobile inshore undersea warfare (MIUW) available for defense.

Recently discovered mission logs of a Soviet Foxtrot submarine, which is now on exhibit in Seattle, revealed that the boat had successfully evaded U.S. defenses during the Cold War and sailed undetected into Puget Sound. And that penetration of homeland waters by an enemy submarine was accomplished in a time of much more extensive U.S. antisubmarine warfare operations.

The threat that stateless terrorists or rogue governments will acquire nuclear weapons or other WMD has caused a major rethinking of U.S. defense policy. The National Security Strategy promulgated in September 2002 warned, "The gravest danger our Nation faces lies at the crossroad of radicalism and technology. Our enemies have openly declared that they are seeking weapons of mass destruction, and evidence indicates that they are doing so with determination. The United States will not allow these efforts to succeed. America will act against such emerging threats before they are fully formed."

Only a fail-safe device prevented a nuclear attack on Pearl Harbor on March 7, 1968, which would have been far more catastrophic in loss of American lives than either the December 7, 1941, sneak attack that precipitated U.S. entry into World War II or the September 11, 2001, attacks that launched the global war on terrorism.

In the K-129 incident, a group of ruthless men, probably no larger than the al-Qaeda cell that more recently attacked America came very close to successfully putting a nuclear weapon on a U.S. city. While the enemy's ideology is different today—fanatical religious Islamism, as opposed to fanatical secular Communism—the motivation to destroy or severely cripple democratic society is no less fervent.

There are no fail-safe systems to prevent the kind of asymmetrical warfare now being waged against the West by stateless terrorists. A combination of vigilance, imagination, and new policies on many fronts will be required on a scale not yet implemented by our government. And to date, the potential of an attack from the sea—as real as ever—has been largely ignored. Only by knowing and facing the truth can the American people make the right choices in their individual lives and elect the right leaders to steer the Free World through the troubled waters ahead.

AUTHOR'S
POSTSCRIPT

Since the publication of *Red Star Rogue* in autumn 2005, I have been contacted by a number of naval and clandestine service veterans who have shared personal accounts of their experiences surrounding the mystery of the Soviet ballistic missile submarine K-129. While a few continue to parrot the "official" cover stories from Project Jennifer, many, many more of those contacting me "off the record" have brought forth compelling new bits of information that support the revelations first made in this book. Among the most intriguing new evidence is an eyewitness account by a handful of veterans concerning a specific secret mission involving the wreck of a Russian submarine.

According to participants in that mission, a U.S. Navy bathyscaph, *Trieste II* (DSV-1), made six dives on the wreck of a Soviet ballistic missile sub between November 1971 and August 1972. One of these dives earned the crew of the bathyscaph and its two support ships a meritorious unit citation for the recovery of an object of extreme value from the ocean floor adjacent to the wreckage—probably the warhead from the sub's number two missile silo. Importantly, these clandestine dives were conducted in Hawaii's Northwest Leeward Islands, near the location that *Red Star Rogue* posited was the most likely spot where the Russian submarine met its ultimate fate.

No secret in the saga of K-129 has been more controversial or more closely guarded than the location where the doomed boat sank. Both the American and Soviet official versions of what happened to the sub were underpinned by carefully leaked misinformation about the location. The Soviets and some U.S. sources identified a site in the middle of the open ocean at 40° north latitude and nearly 1,700 miles northwest of Honolulu. Most U.S. sources referred to a location 750 to 800-plus miles northwest of Pearl Harbor, at about 30° north latitude.

An approximate location much nearer to the strategic Pearl Harbor naval bastion was revealed for the first time in *Red Star Rogue*, placing the wreck 350 to 400 miles northwest of Honolulu. The book includes a hypothetical ship's log of the last voyage of K-129, constructed from confirmable facts, including the boat's starting point, known radio transmissions, normal operational speeds and depths, and known distances traveled.

Ironically, since the publication of *Red Star Rogue*, excerpts from another ship's log have surfaced that provide significant new insights into this mystery. Shortly after the book was published, the excerpted log was brought to my attention by crew members from the support vessels that accompanied *Trieste II* on its dives. The identification of these crewmen must still be withheld due to the general lifetime confidentiality that the

U.S. Navy tries to impose on such missions. I want to quickly note that none of the *Trieste II* hydronauts—the officers who piloted and crewed the deep-diving vehicle to the bottom of the sea—would agree to an interview because of specific confidentiality agreements they signed at the time of their service. Other crewmen knowledgeable about the contents of the log and these excerpts were under no such personal restrictions; and several crewmen who participated in this mission did agree to interviews. A recap of the mission involving the dives on K-129 follows.

In late fall 1971, a San Diego–based U.S. Navy deep submergence exploration and recovery outfit known as an Integral Operating Unit (IOU) was deployed to the Central Pacific Ocean on a classified mission. The unit consisted of a *Trieste II* (DSV-1) deep submergence vessel with an operational depth of at least 20,000 feet; its mother ship, the huge floating, dry dock *White Sands* (ARD-20); and a powerful, oceangoing tug, the USS *Apache* (ATF-67). The crew members were not permitted to discuss their destination or mission with their families, even though the unit had recently completed a well-publicized series of deep-ocean dives to explore the wreck of the USS *Scorpion*, 400 miles southwest of the Azores in the Atlantic.

The small research flotilla arrived at a site just north of the Northwestern Hawaiian Leeward Islands, where those barrier islets, atolls, and submerged seamounts roil the oceans in a zone marked on sea charts as "Areas to Be Avoided," because of the multiple hazards of wild currents, shallows, and reefs. A few miles north of the islets of the Gardner Pinnacles, the French Frigate

Shoals, and Necker and Nihoa Islands, the shallows drop precipitously to gloomy depths in excess of 16,000 feet.

The *Trieste II*, with its three-man hydronaut crew, separated from its mother ship, *White Sands*, and was towed to an expanse of ocean where the spy submarine USS *Halibut*, more than two years earlier, had thoroughly explored and photographed the wreck of the Soviet submarine K-129. On November 4, 1971, the 78-foot-long, 15-foot-wide *Trieste* silently dove into the blackness of the Pacific to a depth of 16,400 feet. The first of what was to be at least six dives on the mysterious wreck was a surveying mission that took ten hours and twenty-five minutes.

This initial dive proved that the rugged, deep-sea submersible could easily locate the wreck and operate at these extreme depths. The subsequent working dives were delayed until the following spring, due to rapidly deteriorating weather conditions in the wintry Pacific. The dives were resumed by the crews of the *Trieste II*, *White Sands*, and *Apache* on April 25, 1972, with subsequent dives on July 15, July 18, August 2, and August 7 of that year. The dives were concentrated north of the area between Gardner Pinnacles and Necker Island, at approximately 25° north latitude. This location is very close to the site revealed by *Red Star Rogue* as the place the K-129 most likely came to rest after being destroyed in the abortive effort to launch a ballistic missile.

On one of the early dives in 1972, an important piece of Soviet military hardware was recovered. From the eyewitness descriptions of crew members, it is likely that a nuclear warhead was recovered and brought to the deck of the *White Sands*. This warhead was probably from missile tube number two. Earlier reports by persons who had seen the *Halibut* photographs described the warhead on the missile in tube two as missing from an otherwise damaged but intact missile lodged in that tube. It seems fair to assume that the item recovered was a nuclear warhead because of the strange account of how the recovered item was handled.

One of the large food freezers had been emptied to serve as a special storage receptacle on the aft deck of the *White Sands*. When *Trieste II* returned from that dive, a large object was secured in the boat's retrieval claw, a scallop-shaped device nicknamed a "kluge." The item, which was concealed from the crew members' view by a tarpaulin, was hoisted into the commandeered cooler and sealed inside. Whatever the object recovered by the DSV was, it is reasonable to assume that it was radioactive, since it had to be placed inside the airtight, leak-proof, and insulated freezer. The chest and its contents remained under armed guard for the duration of the mission.

The sixth dive was concluded in early August 1972, and the three vessels returned to a base in San Diego in September.

Importantly, the eyewitnesses with access to the official log report that a single, handwritten entry in the official log of the *Trieste II* apparently escaped the best sweepers of the Central Intelligence Agency. A simple notation reading, "Russian sub" appears in the comments column of the official log.

That this secret mission was highly successful is also

without doubt. The crew members of the *Trieste II,
White Sands,* and *Apache* were awarded a Meritorious
Unit Commendation for "courage, innovation, perseverance, and unfailing devotion to duty" during a period covering the dates excerpted in this log. The
citation, while not specific, did mention that the three
vessels: ". . . recovered a research instrument from the
ocean floor at a greater depth than previously recorded.
This singularly significant achievement is the deepest
navigation, search and recovery operation in the world
and provided the United States Navy a capacity to conduct deep-ocean search, location and object recovery
operations in eighty percent of the sea areas of the
earth."

Not mentioned in the citation was the fact that *Trieste* and the support units were quite capable of completing the salvaging of vital secrets begun by the
Halibut from the Soviet submarine in the summer of
1968. These dives by the *Trieste* unit were conducted by
the Navy some two years prior to the CIA's dispatching
the *Glomar Explorer* in July 1974, offering additional
evidence that the Nixon operation to raise the entire
Soviet submarine was most probably geopolitical, and
not just a quest for military secrets of the Soviet Union.

Kenneth Sewell
February 22, 2006

NOTES

FOREWORD

PAGE

xiv   *It had only been a few years*: The author served aboard the USS *Parche* (SSN-683), assigned to Submarine Development Group One. Although the *Parche* was listed by the Navy as an ocean research vessel, in 1987 the book *Blind Man's Bluff* disclosed that it participated in some of the most daring and critical covert missions of the Cold War.

PROLOGUE

PAGE

1   *This was not simply*: From transcript of "Cold War Chat," conducted March 14, 1999, with retired KGB major general Oleg Kalugin and former CIA senior analyst Melvin Goodman. Online chat was moderated by CNN Interactive senior editor John Hashimoto (accessed March 2003): http://www.cnn.com/SPECIALS/cold.war/guides/debate/chats/spies/

CHAPTER 1

PAGE

7   *In the dark hours of March 7*: The exact date of the sinking of a Soviet Golf II submarine in the North Pacific has been elusive, with various authoritative accounts from sources in both Russia and the United States ranging

from March 7 to March 11, 1968. The author will more closely fix the time and date from new analysis of existing material, in later chapters of this book.

7   *The coat was much too large:* Open letter, written in 2000, by Soviet Rear Admiral Rudolf A. Golosov (Retired) in response to accounts of the K-129 incident that had appeared in several Russian publications during the previous year. Golosov was commander of the K-129's squadron at the time of the incident. In Russian: Online Kamchatka Database Project. Translations by author's Russian researcher, Eugene Soukharnikov, January 24, 2003: http://library.iks.ru:8081/law?doc&nd=6&nh=1.

8   *Each carried a one-megaton:* Pavel Podvig, ed., *Russian Strategic Nuclear Forces* (Cambridge, Mass.: MIT Press, 2001), p. 288.

9   *That harsh command:* Excerpts from interviews with former Soviet submarine commanders and intelligence officers conducted by Paul Neumann, a naval historian and engineer in Vancouver, B.C., were provided to the author, February 2004. Included in this material was information that the bodies of at least sixty Soviet submariners were recovered from K-129's two forward compartments, an area where no more than a handful of men would normally be berthed or working.

11   *Their course was:* Author's calculations of the real location of the K-129 at the time of an attempted launch of a ballistic missile are based on new information from several sources, which will be fully developed in later chapters of this book. In previous documents and publications, this location has been widely disputed, with estimates ranging from six hundred miles to seventeen hundred miles northwest of the Hawaiian Islands.

CHAPTER 2

PAGE

20   *The Soviets had struggled:* Gary E. Weir and Walter J. Boyne, *Rising Tide: The Untold Story of the Russian*

Submarines that Fought the Cold War (New York: Basic Books, 2003), p. 30.

23   *The Soviet navy also had:* "Russia: Pacific Fleet," prepared by Dr. James Clay Moltz, assistant director, Center for Nonproliferation Studies at the Monterey Institute of International Studies, May 1, 2000; via NTI (Nuclear Threat Initiative), (accessed July 28, 2003): http://www.nti.org/db/nisprofs/russia/naval/nucflt/pacflt/pacflovr.htm

25   *The Chinese wasted no time:* David Miller, *Directory of Submarines of the World* (London: Salamander Books, 2002), p. 421.

26   *"[Soviet] relations with China":* Central Intelligence Agency, Top Secret National Intelligence Estimate (NIE) #190422, "Soviet Strategic Attack Forces," September 9, 1969; declassified by CIA Historic Review Program, p. 6.

27   *Even as this new nuclear:* U.S. Navy report to the Committee on Armed Services, 90th Congress, 2d Session, *The Changing Strategic Naval Balance—U.S.S.R. vs. U.S.A.* (Washington, D.C.: U.S. Government Printing Office, 1968; declassified 1999), p. 14.

28   *The U.S. Navy's report:* Ibid., p. 42.

28   *A National Intelligence Estimate:* CIA, NIE No. 190422, "Soviet Strategic Attack Forces," p. 30.

29   *The Kamchatka Flotilla based:* Podvig, *Russian Strategic Nuclear Forces,* p. 290.

29   *The Kamchatka Flotilla also included:* Ibid., pp. 293, 297.

30   *It was almost certainly:* Eric Morris, *The Russian Navy: Myth and Reality* (New York: Stein and Day Publishers, 1977), pp. 118–19.

CHAPTER 3

PAGE

33   *K-129 looked rawboned:* Podvig, *Russian Strategic Nuclear Forces,* p. 258.

33   *The volcanic peaks:* "Ballistic Missile Submarine

Units," Global Security.org (accessed December 22, 2003): http://www.globalsecurity.org/wmd/world/russia/plarb.htm

35   *In appearance:* Robert Hutchinson, *Jane's Submarines: War Beneath the Waves, From 1776 to the Present Day* (New York: HarperCollins, 2001), p. 104.

35   *It had a problem-free:* Joseph Allbeury, "Specifications" in *Russian Cobra: Foxtrot-class Submarine* (Sydney, Australia: Jasper Communications, 2002), unpaginated booklet.

36   *A similar system:* Hutchinson, *Jane's Submarines,* p. 104.

36   *Golf submarines served:* "Project 629 Golf, Weapons of Mass Destruction," updated September 26, 1998, Federation of American Scientists: http://www.fas.org/nuke/guide/russia/slbm/629.htm

38   *Every submarine built:* William E. Burrows, "Imaging Space Reconnaissance Operations during the Cold War: Cause, Effect and Legacy," 1996, *The Cold War Forum,* Bodø Regional University, Norway: http://webster.hibo.no/asf/Cold_War/report1/williame.html

39   *Even though they proved:* Peter Huchthausen, Captain USN (Retired), *K-19: The Widowmaker* (Washington, D.C.: National Geographic, 2002), p. 176.

39   *The Golf was built:* Podvig, *Russian Strategic Nuclear Forces,* p. 288.

43   *The new sea-launched:* Ibid., p. 318.

45   *During the overhaul:* Admiral Anatoliy Shtyrov, an intelligence officer with the Soviet Pacific Fleet who investigated the K-129 incident; from interview and correspondence conducted by Paul Neumann. Excerpts of transcripts provided to author.

46   *Coincidentally, in September:* "Type 031 (Golf Class) Missile Submarine," *Chinese Defence Today:* http://www.sinodefence.com/navy/sub/golf.asp

46   *China had been testing:* "Peoples Republic of China Nuclear Weapons Employment Policy and Strategy,"

Defense Intelligence Agency (DIA), March 1972, via Federation of American Scientists (FAS):
http://www.fas.org/irp/ dia/product/prc_72/index.html

46   *In addition, a dozen*: Dr. Srikanth Kondapalli, "China's Naval Equipment Acquisition," *Strategic Analysis: A Monthly Journal of the IDSA* 23, no. 9 (1999).

47   *That meant it was*: Podvig, *Russian Strategic Nuclear Forces*, p. 315.

47   *K-129 was one of six*: "Weapons of Mass Destruction (WMD) Around the World, 629 Golf," September 26, 2000, Federation of American Scientists (accessed May 28, 2003):
http://www.fas.org/nuke/guide/russia/slbm/629.htm

CHAPTER 4

PAGE
49   *The submarine officer*: Dmitry Mikheyev, "The New Soviet Man: Myth and Reality," *World and I*, vol. 3 (February 1988), p. 655.

51   *Captain Kobzar was one of the most*: Admiral Shtyrov, correspondence with Neumann (see Chapter 3).

52   *"Submariners are a special brotherhood"*: "Memorable Quotes," *Submarine Sailor dot.com*:
http://www.submarinesailor.com/quote.asp

54   *The rapid career advancement*: Huchthausen, *K-19: The Widowmaker*, p. 52.

55   *Submarine commanders bore*: Weir and Boyne, *Rising Tide*, p. 74.

59   *One former Soviet*: Captain Third Rank (Retired) Igor E. Kolosov, former officer who served on Soviet attack submarines, interviewed by author, Los Angeles, July 2003.

59   *At the end of January*: Rear Admiral Nikolai Mormul, *Accidents Under Water*, 2d ed. (Murmansk, Russia: Elteko, 2001), p. 126.

60   *A special security officer*: Huchthausen, *K-19: The Widowmaker*, p. 52.

CHAPTER 5

PAGE

70   *Coincidentally, the U.S. Navy:* Sherry Sontag, Christopher Drew, with Annette Lawrence Drew, *Blind Man's Bluff: The Untold Story of American Submarine Espionage* (New York: HarperCollins, 1998), pp. 225–26.

78   *The order to embark:* Soviet submarine commander, retired in Russia; interviewed from Moscow and St. Petersburg by author via telephone and e-mail during 2003, on condition his identity not be published.

79   *Headquarters gave:* Admiral Shtyrov, correspondence with Neumann.

80   *In peacetime, Soviet:* Interviews with retired Soviet admirals of Pacific Fleet, by Neumann (see Chapter 1).

81   *K-129 was not the only option:* Central Intelligence Agency, National Intelligence Estimate—Secret, May 16, 1968, "Table IV: Estimated Numbers and Deployment of Soviet General Purpose Ships and Submarine by Type, by Fleets." Declassified August 12, 2003.

82   *Captain Zhuravin, without telling:* Conversations and interviews with Irina Zhuravina, widow of first officer of K-129, conducted by Svetlana Stepanova (pseud.), Russian journalist and interviewer for the author, Moscow, October and November 2003. Interview transcripts translated by Kalash Moulayanov.

84   *As members of the navy's elite:* Sami Soininen, "A Soviet Submariner Recalls His Days at Sea," *Helsingin Sanomat,* October 29, 2002, p. 1.

85   *These last-minute assignments:* Article on ceremony honoring lost crewmen of K-129, *Independent Military Review* (Moscow), September 17, 1999. Translated by author's Russia-based researcher, Eugene Soukharnikov (accessed September 26, 2003):
http://submarine.id.ru/memory/K129.htm

87   *Their aloofness:* Soviet submarine commander, retired in Russia, interviewed by author.

89   *Admiral Golosov handed*: Golosov, open letter (see Chapter 1).

CHAPTER 6

PAGE

92   *Captain Zhuravin gave orders*: Allbeury, "Diving the Submarine," in *Russian Cobra*.

98   *The first surveillance*: "Sound Surveillance System (SOSUS)," November 21, 2002, GlobalSecurity.org (accessed August 5, 2003):
http://www.globalsecurity.org/intell/systems/ sosus.htm

98   *K-129, like all the Soviet*: Minutes of the Tenth Plenary Session of the United States–Russia Joint Commission on Prisoners of War/Missing in Action (subsequently abbreviated USRJC), Moscow, August–September 1994.

99   *The U.S. Pacific coast system*: Jeffrey T. Richelson, *The U.S. Intelligence Community*, 4th ed. (Boulder, Colo.: Westview Press, 1999), p. 233.

99   *Even though K-129*: E. V. Miasnikov, "Characteristics of Noise Created by Submarines," Appendix I in "The Future of Russia's Strategic Nuclear Forces" (Moscow Institute of Physics and Technology, 1995), via Federation of American Scientists (FAS) (accessed March 21, 2002):
http://www.fas.org/spp/eprint/snf03221.htm

100   *He ordered the submarine*: Podvig, *Russian Strategic Nuclear Forces*, p. 278.

101   *Huge antenna frames*: James Bradford, *Body of Secrets: Anatomy of the Ultra-Secret National Security Agency* (New York: Random House, 2001), pp. 76–77.

CHAPTER 7

PAGE

106   *The ship's doctor*: Allbeury, "Life Support," in *Russian Cobra*.

107   *They were fed four meals*: Ibid., "Food Fit for a King."

117 *With no indication*: Retired high-ranking U.S. naval official, involved in the K-129 incident in the aftermath of the sinking of the Soviet submarine, in 1968–69. Interviews conducted by author at several sites around the Pacific during August 2001 and April 2003. Interviewee requested anonymity.

117 *It was March 8*: Vladimir Ryzhkov, "Russia's Festive Postmodernism," *Moscow Times*, April 30, 2002, via Center for Defense Information (CDI), Washington, D.C. (accessed December 16, 2003):
http://www.cdi.org/russia/204-2.cfm

118 *"I know exactly the day"*: Irina Zhuravina, interviews (see Chapter 5).

Chapter 8

PAGE

122 *The steps required*: Allbeury, "Surfacing the Submarine," in *Russian Cobra*.

124 *In the general area*: Peter H. Dana, "Geographic Information Systems Loran-C Coverage Modeling," *Proceedings of the Twenty-second Annual Technical Symposium, October 18–21, 1993, Santa Barbara* (Bedford, Mass.: Wild Goose Association, 1994).

124 *By 1968, Soviet submarines*: J. R. Wilson, "Loran-C Gets New Lease on Life," January 1999 (accessed February 21, 2004):
http://thefreelancer.com/archives/loran.htm

128 *A rigidly enforced*: Podvig, *Russian Strategic Nuclear Forces*, p. 281.

129 *The seabed drops: Pacific Map: World of Ocean Floors* (Washington, D.C.: National Geographic Society, 1992).

132 *The exploding warhead*: Golosov, open letter (see Chapter 1).

134 *Only a top-secret*: "Operation Jennifer," Discovery Channel documentary on the K-129 incident and Project Jennifer. Retired Soviet submarine officers from the Pacific

Fleet and American naval and intelligence officials served as consultants on the documentary.

CHAPTER 9

PAGE

137 *The explosion and sinking*: Thomas O'Toole, "Ocean Gear Heard Soviet Sub Blast," *Washington Post*, March 23, 1975, p. 1.

139 *The Pacific SOSUS*: High-ranking U.S. naval official (retired), interview by author (see Chapter 7).

139 *There certainly was no way*: Scott D. Sagan, *The Limits of Safety: Organizations, Accidents, and Nuclear Weapons* (Princeton, N.J.: Princeton University Press, 1995), p. 80.

140 *The base provided*: "Pearl Harbor," GlobalSecurity.org, March 27, 2004, (accessed November 19, 2002): http://www.globalsecurity.org/military/facility/pearl_harbor.htm

142 *A one-megaton explosion*: Retired defense nuclear weapons scientist, Battelle Memorial Institute, interviewed by author, Columbus, Ohio, April 2003.

143 *This deadly radiation*: Ibid.

143 *Experts say*: Ibid.

145 *"I think you should"*: Memorandum from Spurgeon Keeny, National Security Council staff, to Walt W. Rostow, National Security File (Secret), Nuclear Weapons, USSR, Vol. 1, Box 34, April 19, 1966, Lyndon B. Johnson Library, Austin, Texas.

146 *The PAL fail-safe*: Steven M. Bellovin, "Permissive Action Links," AT&T Labs, October 2003. Bellovin is an AT&T Fellow in the Network Services Research Lab. (Accessed January 17, 2004): http://www.research.att.com/~smb/nsam-160/pal.html

148 *The crude devices*: Ibid.

149 *After all, the fail-safe*: Sagan, *Limits of Safety*, p. 158.

CHAPTER 10

PAGE

153 *The submarine had reported*: Shtyrov correspondence with Neumann.

153 *When the duty officer*: Excerpt from "History of Russia's Pacific Fleet, After the War and Today," July 2003. *Russian Academy of Sciences*, (accessed July 4, 2003): http://www.fegi.ru/prim/flot/flot1_14.htm

154 *In the Soviet navy*: Rear Admiral Y. A. Krivoruchko (Retired), interviewed by Paul Neumann. Translation and notes provided to author.

155 *Communist bureaucrats*: Soviet submarine commander, retired in Russia, interviewed by author.

156 *On or about March 21*: Sontag et al., *Blind Man's Bluff*, pp. 107–9.

156 *The Soviet search boats*: John Piña Craven, *The Silent War: The Cold War Battle Beneath the Sea* (New York: Simon & Schuster, 2001), p. 204.

158 *The subject was*: Clyde Burleson, Kursk *Down! The Shocking True Story of the Sinking of a Russian Nuclear Submarine* (New York: Warner Books, 2002), p. 86.

160 *Admiral Anatoliy Shtyrov*: Paul Neumann, article "Operation Jennifer Behind the Scenes," from interview and correspondence with retired Soviet admiral Anatoliy Shtyrov; excerpts provided to author.

161 *The DIA had been founded*: "The Defense Intelligence Agency, Forty Years of History" (updated August 20, 2002), (accessed November 1, 2003): http://www.dia.mil/History/40years/intro.html

163 *Before the investigation*: Craven, *Silent War*, p. 216.

163 *The oceanographic research*: "The UNOLS Fleet, 50 Years of Discovery: National Science Foundation 1950–2000," Commission on Geosciences, Environment and Resources, Ocean Studies Board, *The National Academies Press*: http://www.nap.edu/openbook/0309063981/html/114.html

164 *At the time the* Teritu: Dr. Jim McVey, scientist aboard the R/V *Teritu* during the late 1960s, interviewed by author, April 2004.

164 *The diesel engines*: Kolosov, interview by author.

165 *Before anyone could*: Barry Raleigh, dean of University of Hawaii School of Ocean and Earth Science and Technology (formerly Oceanographic and Geological Department), in e-mail correspondence with author, April 2003.

166 *A remodeled Admiral-class*: Mine Warfare Vessel Archive, (accessed February 13, 2004):
http://www.navsource.org/archives/11/02297.htm

167 *Within three years*: "The University's new oceanographic vessel," *Hawaii Business and Industry*, March 1971, pp. 71–73.

167 *More than thirty years*: Raleigh, correspondence with author.

CHAPTER 11

PAGE

168 *The Navy had recently*: William Broad, *The Universe Below* (New York: Touchstone/Simon & Schuster, 1997), p. 63.

169 *The expertise of the DSSP*: Craven, *Silent War*, p. 205.

170 *Another incident*: Robert Burns, Associated Press correspondent, "Distrust of U.S. Harks Back to '68 Loss of Sub," *Moscow Times*, August 24, 2002, p. 1.

170 *The submarine was apparently*: Sontag et al., *Blind Man's Bluff*, p. 113n.

171 *Retired admiral Ivan Amelko*: Shtyrov, interviews and correspondence with Neumann.

172 *The widely held theory*: Robert Burns, "Russians Suspicious of U.S. in Sub," Associated Press, August 22, 2000.

173 *"While on patrol"*: Minutes of the Seventh Plenary Session, USRJC, Moscow, December 6, 1993.

173 *At the time there was ample reason*: Shtyrov, "*Kursk* Disaster: How, who, why?" *Red Star* (Russian army newspaper), August 8, 2000.

174 *"There have been numerous"*: Central Intelligence Agency, Top Secret Intelligence Memorandum #0000267786, "Communist Harassment of U.S. Ships and Aircraft Harassment," January 27, 1968, declassified November 18, 1999.

174 *Admiral Gorshkov was a strong*: Donald D. Chapman, "Transformation of Soviet Maritime Operations," *Air Power Journal* (Summer 1990).

175 *Gorshkov was in charge*: Podvig, *Russian Strategic Nuclear Forces*, p. 619.

CHAPTER 12

PAGE

179 *A comment leaked*: O'Toole, "Ocean Gear Heard Soviet Sub Blasts."

181 *A number of U.S. Air Force*: Chronology of Spy Satellites, (accessed August 5, 2003):
http://informanage.com/international/intelligence/spychron

181 *This system, code-named TIROS*: "The TIROS Program," NASA, April 22, 1999 (accessed August 5, 2003):
http://www.earth.nasa.gov/history/tiros

182 *The MIDAS program*: "MIDAS," GlobalSecurity.org, October 8, 2002 (accessed August 5, 2003):
http://www.globalsecurity.org/space/systems/midas.htm

183 *The Americans also operated*: "Mizar, Service Ship Archive," NavSource Online, (accessed February 29, 2004):
http://www.navsource.org/archives/09/130272.htm

184 *The boat was*: Hutchinson, *Jane's Submarines*, pp. 168–69.

186 *By early summer*: Sontag et al., *Blind Man's Bluff*, pp. 97–98.

189 *The USS* Halibut *found*: Broad, *Universe Below*, p. 73.

191 *The myth later circulated*: O'Toole, "Ocean Gear Heard Soviet Sub Blast."

192 *But everything the* Halibut *found*: Broad, *Universe Below*, pp. 78–79.

192 *The special project director*: Dr. John P. Craven, retired civilian director, U.S. Navy, Deep Submergence Systems Project, interview by author, Hawaii, July 2003.

192 *Dr. Craven told*: Broad, *Universe Below*, p. 74.

CHAPTER 13

PAGE

195 *The Presidential Citation*: Walt W. Rostow, National Security File, USS *Halibut* folder, September 18, 1968 (Top Secret—partially declassified, April 25, 1994); Lyndon B. Johnson Library, Austin, Texas.

197 *The final military*: CIA Director George Tenet, "Written statement to the *Washington Post*," August 8, 2003 (accessed August 10, 2003):
http://www.washingtonpost.com

200 *An eyewitness account*: Sontag et al., *Blind Man's Bluff*, pp. 114–15.

201 *Other photographs revealed*: Huchthausen, *K-19: The Widowmaker*, pp. 172–73.

202 *The extensive damage*: Former U.S. Navy submariner and later a crew member on the *Glomar Explorer* salvage operation of K-129, interviewed by author in Portland, Oregon, April 2003. Interviewee requested anonymity.

CHAPTER 14

PAGE

205 *Pieces of evidence*: "What Is Analysis?" March 31, 2003, National Security Archives, Wesleyan College, North Carolina, (accessed May 29, 2003):
http://faculty.ncwc.edu/toconnor/392/spy/WHATisANALYSIS .htm

205 *The methodology employed*: E. Bright Wilson, *An*

Introduction to Scientific Research (New York: McGraw-Hill, 1952). Bayes' Theorem is a controversial analysis system, but was widely used by military intelligence agencies at the time.

205 *The analysis was conducted*: Former U.S. government intelligence analyst, interviewed by author in New York City, November 2001, on condition of anonymity.

205 *Areas of inquiry*: Ibid.

206 *Since so little hard evidence*: "What Is Analysis?"

208 *The U.S. Navy had limited*: Craven, *Silent War*, p. 205.

209 *What has not been revealed*: Former U.S. intelligence analyst, interviewed by author.

210 *This document, with its additional finding*: Ibid.

212 *"The captain [of R/V Teritu]"*: Raleigh, correspondence with author.

213 *That cover story*: Author's engineering experience in the field of high-pressure, high-heat containment.

213 *That kind of buildup*: Allbeury, "Life Support," in *Russian Cobra*.

214 *"The widely touted"*: Golosov, open letter, 2000.

CHAPTER 15

PAGE

219 *The document justifying*: Spurgeon M. Keeny, Jr., "Seventeen-Year Locusts," *Arms Control Today*, Arms Control Association, Washington, D.C., March 1999: http://www.armscontrol.org/act/1999_03/focmr99.asp

219 *The suddenness of*: Dr. John M. Clearwater, *Johnson, McNamara, and the Birth of SALT and the ABM Treaty 1963–69* (Dissertation.com, 1996), p. 145.

220 *Strategic Arms Limitation Talks*: Conversation between Soviet Ambassador Dobrynin and Secretary of State Rusk, July 23, 1968 (declassified 2003), National Security File Box 3, Lyndon B. Johnson Library, Austin, Texas.

220 *"The Sentinel System"*: Letter to Senator Philip A. Hart from Department of Defense, June 11, 1968.

221 *Secretary of Defense*: Keeny, "Seventeen-Year Locusts."

222 *Initial arguments*: Report Prepared by the Strategic Military Panel of the President's Science Advisory Committee; Washington, D.C., October 29, 1965. National Archives and Records Administration, RG218, JCS Files, 3212 (29 Oct 65) IR 4878.

222 *President Johnson, early*: "China as a Nuclear Power," prepared by the Office of International Security Affairs at the Department of Defense, October 7, 1964.

223 *The Pentagon not only*: "Report on the Proposed Army-BTL [Bell Telephone Laboratories] Ballistic Missile Defense System," Strategic Military Panel, National Security File, Office of Science & Technology, October 29, 1965. Vol. 1, Box 42, Lyndon B. Johnson Library, Austin, Texas.

224 *Warrant officer John Walker*: Ed Offley, "Spy net may have doomed *Scorpion* before it set out," *Seattle-Post Intelligencer*, May 21, 1999.

224 *American submariners*: Ibid.

225 *Although the Navy*: Ibid.

225 *The KGB paid Walker*: Pete Earley, "The John Walker Family Spy Case," Court TV's Crime Library: http://www.crimelibrary.com/terrorists_spies/spies/walker/1 .html

225 *Kalugin, who became*: "Cold War Espionage, Inside the KGB," CNN Interactive, (accessed March 21, 2002): http://www.cnn.com/SPECIALS/cold.war/experience/spies/ interviews/kalugin

227 *Before assuming*: "Andropov, Yuri Vladimirovich," *Learning Network Encyclopedia*: http://www.infoplease.com/ce6/people/A0803987.html

227 *"After years of scorn"*: Oleg Kalugin and Fen Montaigne, *The First Directorate* (New York: St. Martin's Press, 1994), p. 67.

CHAPTER 16

PAGE

231 *"The notion that cadets"*: Soviet submarine commander, retired in Russia, interviewed by author.

233 *"A full list of the crew"*: Former Soviet submarine commanders and admirals interviewed by Paul Neumann.

233 *Author Clyde W. Burleson*: Clyde W. Burleson, *The Jennifer Project* (College Station: Texas A&M University Press, 2000), pp. 112–13.

234 *American intelligence*: Former U.S. government intelligence analyst with knowledge of the CIA's intense interest in the contents of the recovered diary, interviewed by author in New York City, November 2001, on condition of anonymity.

235 *Suspicions about the motives*: Craven, *Silent War*, p. 279.

236 *Dr. Craven confirmed*: Ibid., p. 216.

CHAPTER 17

PAGE

240 *An example is a study*: Ansii Kullberg, "Al Qaida is a threat also in Europe," November 10, 2003, *The Eurasian Politician*, (accessed March 13, 2004):
http://www.cc.jyu.fi/~aphamala/pe/2003/quaideure.htm

240 *Andropov, who earlier*: Viktor Suvorov, *The Story Behind the Soviet SAS* (Hamish Hamilton Ltd., 1987) (accessed March 13, 2004):
http://www.spetsnaz.com.br/gru.htm

241 *In addition to training*: Robert S. Boyd, *"Spetsnaz*: Soviet Innovation in Special Forces," *Air & Space Power Chronicles*, (accessed November 7, 2003):
http://www.airpower.au.af.mil/airchronicles/aureview/1986/nov-dec/boyd.html

241 *The KGB "had its own"*: Suvorov, *Story Behind the Soviet SAS*.

242 *The units were slotted*: Bjorn Hammerback, "KGB Organization of the Committee for State Security," May

1999, Ulfsbo Farms, Ulfsbo Gård, (accessed November 5, 2003):
http://www.ulfsbo.nu/kgb/kgb_7.html

242 *In addition to having political:* David Wise "Closing Down the KGB," *New York Times Magazine*, November 21, 1991, p. 68.

245 *The intruders would not:* Allbeury, "Life on Board," in *Russian Cobra*.

247 *It is also logical:* David S. Yost, *Soviet Ballistic Missile Defense and the Western Alliance* (Cambridge, Mass.: Harvard University Press, 1998), p. 138.

248 *The Central Intelligence Agency:* Former U.S. intelligence analyst, interviewed by author.

248 *One former U.S. intelligence analyst:* Ibid.

CHAPTER 18

PAGE

250 *Each of the three-bedroom:* Nick Patton Walsh, "Andropov's Apartment," *The Guardian*, January 28, 2003.

251 *In the mid-1960s:* History of Oil in Russia, Sibneft Company: http://www.sibneft.com/pages.jsp

251 *This double threat:* CIA, "Soviet Strategic Attack Forces" (Top Secret), National Intelligence Estimate No. 11-8-69, September 9, 1969, National Archives and Records Administration (NARA) #NN3-263-95-001, January 31, 1995, p. 7.

253 *And China had two:* Weapons of Mass Destruction Around the World, Project 629 Golf, Federation of American Scientists (updated June 10, 1998):
http://www.fas.irg/nuke/guide/china/slbm/golf.htm

253 *The Americans, therefore:* "Type 031 (Golf Class) Missile Submarine," *Chinese Defence Today* (accessed April 10, 2003):
http://www.sinodefence.com/navy/sub/golf.asp

254 *Years earlier, China had:* "Peoples Republic of China Nuclear Weapons Employment Policy," DIA, p. 4.

255 *The best solution:* Elizabeth Wishnick, *Mending*

Fences: The Evolution of Moscow's China Policy from Brezhnev to Yeltsin (Seattle: University of Washington Press, 2001), p. 6.

256   *Red China's rhetoric:* "Peoples Republic of China Nuclear Weapons Employment Policy," DIA.

256   *The Soviet leadership:* Andrei A. Kokoshin, *Soviet Strategic Thought, 1917–91* (Cambridge, Mass.: MIT Press, 1998), p. 5.

258   *Soviet intelligence agents:* "The KGB's 1967 Annual Report—Top Secret" as reported to the Central Committee of the CPSU and issued to Soviet leader Leonid Brezhnev, May 6, 1968; archived by CNN Interactive, http://www.cnn.com/SPECIALS/cold.war/episodes/21/documents/kgb.report/

259   *It seemed a perfect plan:* Steven P. Adragna, *On Guard for Victory: Military Doctrine and Ballistic Missile Defense in the USSR* (Washington, D.C.: Pergamon-Brassey's International Defense Publishers, 1987), p. 16.

CHAPTER 19

PAGE

264   *A retired Cold War–era:* Former U.S. government intelligence analyst spoke to the author about the likely leading plotters in the K-129 incident, in New York, November 2001, on condition of anonymity.

265   *Suslov was born:* Serge Petroff, *The Red Eminence: A Biography of Mikhail A. Suslov* (Clifton, N.J.: Kingston Press, 1988) p. 1.

266   *While his name did not appear:* Former U.S. intelligence analyst, interview.

266   *During the troubled:* Perry Anderson, review of *Khrushchev: The Man and His Era*, by William Taubman, *Atlantic Monthly* 291, No. 31 (April 2003).

266   *Suslov was a brilliant:* Ronald Hingley, *Joseph Stalin: Man & Legend* (New York: Konecky & Konecky, 1974), p. 388.

266   *He was the party liaison:* Christopher Andrew and

Oleg Gordievsky, *KGB: The Inside Story of Its Foreign Operations from Lenin to Gorbachev* (New York: HarperCollins, 1990), p. 651.

266 *Evidence has recently*: Michael Wines, "New Study Supports Idea Stalin Was Poisoned," *New York Times*, March 5, 2002.

267 *Suslov knew*: Adragna, *On Guard for Victory*, p. 18.

267 *Suslov had other well-honed*: Petroff, *Red Eminence*.

269 *But he took his schemes*: Former U.S. intelligence analyst who worked in Soviet section, interviewed by author, New York, November 2001.

269 *In 1956, Khrushchev*: Christopher Andrew and Vasili Mitrokhin, *The Sword and the Shield: The Mitrokhin Archive and the Secret History of the KGB* (New York: Basic Books, 1999), p. 201.

269 *Later he would use*: Dr. Stephen Kotkin, director of Russian Studies, Princeton University, in correspondence with author, May 20–22, 2003.

269 *Suslov was the ringleader*: Roy Medvedev, *All Stalin's Men: The Six Who Carried Out the Bloody Policies* (Garden City, N.Y.: Anchor Press/Doubleday, 1984), p. 65.

270 *It was Suslov who headed*: Andrew and Gordievsky, *KGB: Inside Story*, p. 491.

270 *American author Harrison*: Harrison E. Salisbury, *The New Emperors: China in the Era of Mao Zedong and Deng Xiaoping* (Boston: Little, Brown, 1991), pp. 153–54.

271 *The incident has been described*: Vladislav M. Zubok, "Deng-Xiaoping and the Sino-Soviet Split 1956–1963," Cold War International History Project, Woodrow Wilson Center, Washington, D.C.

271 *His insider experience*: "Mikhail Andreyevich Suslov," *Encyclopaedia Britannica*, from Encyclopædia Britannica Premium Service:
http://www.britannica.com/eb/article?eu=72323

271 *They had to have access*: Medvedev, *All Stalin's Men*, p. 163.

CHAPTER 20

PAGE

277 *While the Nixon transition:* Nixon and Ford: *Uneven Access, CIA Briefings of Presidential Candidates,* Center for the Study of Intelligence, Central Intelligence Agency, Washington, D.C., May 1996.

278 *It was the way:* Andrew and Gordievsky, *KGB: Inside Story,* p. 537.

279 *Haig insisted the photo:* Sontag et al., *Blind Man's Bluff,* pp. 116–17.

280 *"The discovery of a high probability":* Craven, *Silent War,* p. 221.

281 *Reports that an unmarked packet:* Former U.S. intelligence analyst, interviewed by author.

281 *The KGB had covertly:* John Kenneth White, Department of Politics, Catholic University of America, introduction to "Seeing Red: The Cold War and American Public Opinion," National Archives and Records Administration, Washington, D.C.

281 *A high-ranking Soviet:* Ibid.

282 *"The Soviet Union cannot look":* Henry A. Kissinger, *The Necessity for Choice: Prospects of American Foreign Policy* (Westport, Conn.: Greenwood Press, 1984 Reprint), p. 241.

283 *Long before Kissinger:* "Henry Kissinger—Biography," Nobelprize.org (modified April 29, 2004, accessed January 31, 2005):
http://nobelprize.org/peace/laureates/1973/kissinger-bio.html

284 *A growing body of information:* William Burr, ed., *The Kissinger Transcripts: The Top Secret Talks with Beijing and Moscow* (New York: The New Press, 1998), pp. 50–51.

285 *Declassified transcripts:* Ibid.

285 *Agence France Presse revealed:* Agence France Presse, "Kissinger Offered China U.S. Intelligence," Washington, D.C., January 11, 1999.

286 *"When one of three states":* Wishnick, *Mending Fences,* p. 5.

287 *Dobrynin told his superiors:* A. Dobrynin, Memorandum to members of the Politburo and A. Gromyko, July 12, 1969, regarding back-channel meetings with Henry Kissinger (accessed October 12, 2003):
http://www.turnerlearning.com/cnn/coldwar/detente/dete_rel.html

CHAPTER 21

PAGE

289 *The Soviet officers:* Retired Soviet submarine commander in the Kamchatka Flotilla at the time of the K-129 incident, interviewed by author's Russia-based researcher, Eugene Soukharnikov.

289 *In no case had a nuclear:* Sagan, *Limits of Safety*, p. 45.

290 *At the end of the Cold War:* John Greenwald, "Spy vs. Spy," *Time*, November 2, 1992.

291 *He frequently met: History of Russia's Pacific Fleet After the War and Today* (Russian publication), translated by author's Russia-based researcher, Eugene Soukharnikov. Kissinger provided Dobrynin the results of an American operation to raise the Soviet submarine K-129. The documents included the identification of the bodies of three of the sailors recovered in the salvaged wreckage.

291 *A likely purpose:* Kissinger, *Necessity for Choice*, p. 202.

293 *Something strange:* Petroff, *Red Eminence*, p. 169.

294 *General Grechko, along with:* "Mikhail Suslov," *Britannica Concise Encyclopedia*, from Encyclopædia Britannica:
http://concise.britannica.com/ebc/ article?eu=405253

295 *It ended with* Pravda's: Petroff, *Red Eminence*, p. 169.

296 *Central Committee members:* Serge A. Mikoyan, "Western Winds Behind Kremlin Walls, Eroding the Soviet 'Culture of Secrecy,'":
http://www.cia.gov/csi/studies/fall_winter_2001/article05.html (2001)

296 *A significant new procedure:* Podvig, *Russian Strategic Nuclear Forces*, p. 282.

297 *The KGB was stripped:* "Special Departments in the Armed Services," May 1989, Federation of American Scientists:
http://www.fas.org/irp/ world/russia/kgb/su0520.htm

298 *President Nixon did not rely:* Ron Kampeas, AP writer, "Nixon Used Madman Strategy," *Dallas Morning News*, December 26, 2002, p. 29A (citing declassified documents, December 2002, National Security Archive).

301 *Upon returning to the agency:* Craven, *Silent War*, p. 249.

301 *The clandestine Forty:* Brent Scowcroft (national security advisor) affidavit, as referenced in Case Summary of *Military Audit Project* v. *Casey et al.*, United States Court of Appeals, 211 U.S. App. D.C. 135, May 4, 1981 (decided), p. 9.

CHAPTER 22

PAGE

303 *The project to raise:* Mark Riebling, "Blowback," Chapter 16 of *Wedge: The Secret War Between the FBI and CIA*:
http://www.secretpolicy.com

304 *The first major Nixon:* Burr, *The Kissinger Transcripts*, p. 14.

304 *Kissinger used the border:* Ibid., pp. 5–6.

305 *At the very time:* L. Fletcher Prouty, "The Forty Committee," Committee on Foreign Relations, U.S. Senate, Congressional Research Service, Library of Congress, declassified 1977.

305 *The strategy of intrigue:* Kokoshin, *Soviet Strategic Thought*, p. 126.

306 *However, a large number:* Burr, *Kissinger Transcripts*, pp. 5–7, 12–15.

306 *Secret meetings between:* William Burr, ed., "Negotiating U.S.-Chinese Rapprochement," National Security Archive, May 22, 2002.

307 *Later, the U.S. Congress:* Colonel Daniel Smith, (Retired), Chief of Research, Center for Defense Information, "A Brief History of 'Missiles' and Ballistic Missile Defense," (accessed December 3, 2003):
http://www.cdi.org

307 *A flurry of other agreements:* SALT I, Interim Agreement between the U.S. and USSR on Certain Measures with Respect to the Limitation of Strategic Offensive Arms, May 26, 1972.

310 *Some items may have:* Broad, *Universe Below*, p. 74.

310 *There is a well-established:* Ibid., pp. 78–79.

311 *If the Soviets learned:* Burleson, *Jennifer Project*, p. 55.

313 *Détente did nothing:* "The Brezhnev Era," Learning Network:
http://www.infoplease.com

CHAPTER 23

PAGE

315 *But when the CIA was given:* "Project Jennifer, Hughes *Glomar Explorer*," Federation of American Scientists, March 8, 1999 (accessed July 1, 2003):
http://www.fas.org/irp/program/collect/jennifer.htm

316 *The recovery operations:* Roy Varner and Wayne Collier, *A Matter of Risk: The Incredible Inside Story of the CIA's Hughes* Glomar Explorer *Mission to Raise a Russian Submarine* (New York: Random House, 1978), p. 125.

317 *The Hughes Glomar:* Broad, *Universe Below*, pp. 79–80.

317 *Hughes Tool Company:* Varner and Collier, *Matter of Risk*, pp. 34–35.

318 *To some in the know:* Interview, John P. Craven, retired director, Navy's Deep Submergence Systems Project.

318 *Their arguments against:* Burleson, *Jennifer Project*, p. 43.

319 *Contracts were let:* Richard A. Sampson, "The

Hughes Glomar Explorer Project," *OPSEC Journal*, 2d edition 1995, OPSEC Professionals Society.

319 *Years later, even after:* Broad, *Universe Below*, p. 248.

320 *Secret subcontracts:* Varner and Collier, *Matter of Risk*, pp. 40–49.

323 *The Nixon assignment:* Broad, *Universe Below*, p. 78.

324 *The deep-sea mining:* David Helvarg, *Blue Frontier: Saving America's Living Seas* (New York: W. H. Freeman & Co, 2001), Chapter 1.

325 *While the cover story:* Seymour Hersh, "Participant Tells of CIA Ruses to Hide Glomar Project," *New York Times*, December 10, 1976, p. 1.

326 *The career CIA agents:* Sampson, "Glomar Explorer."

327 *One of the roughnecks:* "Behind the Great Submarine Snatch," *Time*, December 6, 1976, p. 23.

327 *The mineral-laden nuggets:* Sampson, "Glomar Explorer."

328 *In total, Project Jennifer:* Burleson, *Jennifer Project*, p. 77.

CHAPTER 24

PAGE

329 *The job could be done only:* Former submariner aboard USS *Seawolf*, which participated in later phases of the K-129 recovery operation, interviewed by author, July 2003.

329 *Relocating and marking:* "Submarine Development Squadron Five," Global Security.org (accessed April 16, 2004):
http://www.globalsecurity.org/military/agency/navy/subdevrons.htm

330 *Ironically, the USS* Halibut: USS *Halibut* (SSGN587):
http://www.home.earthlink.net/geflynn/halibut.htm

330 *Specialized vessels could then return:* "Exploring the Oceans: The Scientist at Sea," *Oceans Alive!* (Boston: Museum of Science, 1998):
http://www.mos.org/oceans/scientist

331 *The special CIA ship:* William Cole, "Recovery of Ehime Maru Tests Navy Skill," *Honolulu Advertiser,* October 22, 2001.

333 *One by one, each section:* Varner and Collier, *Matter of Risk,* pp. 143–48.

335 *Each trip to the bottom:* Ibid., pp. 149–50.

335 *Once the retrieval:* Broad, *Universe Below,* p. 78.

336 *The CIA circulated:* Burleson, *Jennifer Project,* p. 51.

338 *The radioactive wreckage:* The author has extensive training and experience in handling and characteristics of nuclear materials. He served as a Navy crewman aboard a nuclear-powered submarine and worked more than twenty years as a civilian contractor in many of the major nuclear labs and facilities involved in the development and manufacture of nuclear weapons and nuclear reactors.

338 *After the initial section:* Seymour Hersh, "Human Error is Cited in '74 Glomar Failure," *New York Times,* December 9, 1976, p. 1.

CHAPTER 25

PAGE

339 *On several occasions:* Burleson, *Jennifer Project,* p. 111.

340 *That location would have placed:* Sontag et al., *Blind Man's Bluff,* p. 112.

340 *A number of other reports:* "Selected Accidents Involving Nuclear Weapons 1950–1993," Greenpeace archives, March 1996.

341 *Another rumored site:* Podvig, *Russian Strategic Nuclear Forces,* p. 290.

341 *The Challenger was conducting:* Ships of the World: An Historical Encyclopedia, Houghton Mifflin:

http://www.college.hmco.com/history/readerscomp/ships/
html/sh_000106_shipsofthewo.htm

342 *An anonymous note:* Sontag et al., *Blind Man's
Bluff,* p. 275.

342 *Someone had made an effort:* Shtyrov correspondence with Neumann.

344 *When the first trawler:* Burleson, *Jennifer Project,*
p. 112.

345 *Years later, Shtyrov:* Admiral Shtyrov, excerpts of
transcripts from Neumann.

345 *During the first weeks:* Sampson, "Glomar Explorer."

346 *Within hours of taking office:* John L. Helgerson,
CIA Briefings of Presidential Candidates 1952–1992, Central
Intelligence Agency, May 22, 1996.

346 *Project Jennifer was so sensitive:* Ibid.

CHAPTER 26

PAGE

349 *The ship docked:* Burleson, *Jennifer Project,* p.
133.

350 *The trip from Hawaii:* Ibid., pp. 134–35.

350 *In the dark of night:* Former Lockheed engineer
who worked on Project Jennifer, interviewed by author,
Washington, D.C., February 2003, on condition of
anonymity.

353 *Recently there was confirmation:* Weir and Boyne,
Rising Tide, pp. 99–100.

356 *From Long Beach Harbor:* Former Lockheed engineer, interview.

356 *The site is today:* Lynn Graebner, Exclusive Reports, *San Francisco Business Times,* September 24, 1999.

357 *A Lockheed worker:* Former Lockheed engineer,
interview.

358 *The nine-hundred-acre Hunters:* Environmental
Protection Agency, Document CA1170090087, November
15, 2002.

CHAPTER 27

PAGE

360 *According to that story*: "Blind Man's Bluff," A&E Television Network, The History Channel, 2000.

362 *The CIA learned*: James B. Bruce, "Laws and Leaks of Classified Intelligence: Costs and Consequences of Permissive Neglect," The Centre for Counterintelligence and Security Studies (CI Centre):
http://www.cicentre.com/Documents/DOC_Classified_Leaks.htm

364 *A second layer*: Sontag et al., *Blind Man's Bluff*, p. 277.

365 *Coincidentally, there is*: Andrew Toppan, "Salvage of German U-Boats," *Haze Gray and Underway Naval Information Center*, Science Military Naval FAQ, Part G7, March 2000:
http://www.hazegray.org/faq/smn7.htm#G7

365 *The first major news leaks*: Burleson, *Jennifer Project*, pp. 140–41.

366 *The CIA then successfully*: William Colby and Peter Forbath, *Honorable Men* (New York: Simon & Schuster, 1978), p. 389.

366 *The first reporter*: Ibid., p. 415.

368 *Kissinger gave Dobrynin*: Borodin, ed., *History of Russia's Pacific Fleet*, Russian Academy of Sciences.

CHAPTER 28

PAGE

369 *Director Colby wrote*: Colby and Forbath, *Honorable Men*, pp. 417–18.

370 *Finally, the cover*: Jack Anderson with Daryl Gibson, *Peace, War, and Politics* (Forge reprint edition, 2000), p. 278.

371 *Anderson later criticized*: Ibid.

373 *The refloating itself*: Case summary, *Military Audit Project v. Casey et al.*, p. 28.

373 *The charade continued*: "Justice Plans Suit Over

Colby Book," *Washington Post*, September 21, 1981, p. 9.

375 *To this date, top-level officials:* Richard Helms with William Hood, *A Look Over My Shoulder: A Life in the CIA* (New York: Random House, 2003).

377 *The mystery surrounding:* American authors and journalists often become more determined to learn the truth when confronted by a government stamp of secrecy. This has certainly been the case with the K-129 incident. In addition to the works cited more extensively by the author, other notable aspects of the mystery have been covered in such books as *Spy Sub: Top Secret Missions to the Bottom of the Pacific*, by Roger C. Dunham (1997); *Wedge: The Secret War Between the FBI and CIA*, by Mark Riebling (1994); *K-19: The Widowmaker*, by Peter Huchthausen (2002); *Hostile Waters*, by Huchthausen, Igor Kurdin, and R. Alan White (1997); *Kursk Down*, by Clyde Burleson (2002); *A Matter of Risk*, by Roy Varner and Wayne Collier (1978); and *Rising Tide: The Untold Story of the Russian Submarines*, by Gary E. Weir and Walter J. Boyne (2003).

378 *There is a small, but revealing:* George H. W. Bush, Memorandum for the Record, "Meeting with the President, Oval Office, December 1, 1976," dated December 2, 1976, declassified January 2001.

378 Time *magazine in its:* "Submarine Snatch," *Time*.

378 *Project Jennifer was so wrapped:* A former U.S. government intelligence analyst who worked on Project Jennifer told the author: "You don't need to tell many lies to successfully hide an incident. The lies just have to be believable, and they need to be told over and over again. In this case, they only needed three. One, the submarine was on the bottom in one piece. Two, the claw cracked and all but the forward section fell back to the bottom of the ocean. Three, the submarine sank at 40° N latitude, 180° W longitude. No matter what information leaked out afterward, if these three lies were believed, nobody would ever discover the truth." Interviewed in New York City, November 2001, on condition of anonymity.

CHAPTER 29

PAGE

380 *The fact that this "mad" proliferation*: The *Federal'naya Sluzhba Bezopasnosti*, abbreviated FSB, is known as the Federal Security Service in the United States. See "Intelligence Resource Program," Federation of American Scientists:
http://fas.org/irp/world/russia/fsb/

381 *The government's defense*: Case Summary, *Military Audit Project* v. *Casey et al.* (see Chapter 21).

382 *The FOIA case was brought*: Case Summary, *Phillippi* v. *CIA* (Turner et al.), U.S. Court of Appeals, 211 U.S. App. D.C. 95, June 25, 1981 (decided).

384 *This Glomar exception*: Assistant Solicitor, Office of U.S. Solicitor General, Glomar Responses to FOIA Requests, memorandum of September 4, 1998.

385 *The world knew*: Robert M. Gates, *From the Shadows: The Ultimate Insider's Story of Five Presidents and How they Won the Cold War* (New York: Simon & Schuster, 1996), pp. 553–54.

386 *But even this goodwill*: Margaret Shapiro, "Gates Meets Yeltsin in Kremlin; Director Details Secret Savaging of Soviet Sub," *Washington Post*, October 17, 1992, p. 14.

CHAPTER 30

PAGE

387 *The two presidents announced*: "History of the U.S.-Russia Joint Commission on POWs and MIAs," Federal Research Division, Library of Congress, February 5, 2003 (accessed February 27, 2003):
http://lcweb2.loc.gov/frd/tfr/tfrhist.html

388 *Ambassador Toon addressed*: Minutes of the Sixth Plenary Session, USRJC, Moscow, August 31, 1993.

392 *The meeting ended angrily*: Minutes of the Eighth Plenary Session, USRJC, Washington, D.C., February 28, 1994.

392 *The photograph was reportedly:* Mormul, *Accidents Under Water*, p. 294.

393 *The Tenth Plenary:* Minutes of the Tenth Plenary Session, USRJC, Moscow, August 31, 1994.

394 *In the Eleventh Plenary:* Minutes of the Eleventh Plenary Session, USRJC, Washington, D.C., December 7, 1994.

394 *The ever more bitter:* Minutes of the Sixteenth Plenary Session, USRJC, Moscow, November 9, 1999.

395 *"Russia's initial suspicion":* Burns, "Russians Suspicious of U.S. in Sub."

396 *In 1968, the Pacific Fleet:* CIA, NIE, May 16, 1968 (see Chapter 5).

397 *The new official version:* Golosov, open letter.

398 *Another memorial:* Irina Zhuravina, interviews conducted in Moscow.

399 *The official silence:* Ed Offley, military reporter, *Seattle Post-Intelligencer*, May 21, 1998.

EPILOGUE

PAGE

402 *A year after the end:* Charles Smith, "Russian Navy Still Has Nuclear Punch," *World Net Daily*, September 6, 2000.

402 *Now, instead of two:* Lewis M. Simons, "Weapons of Mass Destruction: An Ominous New Chapter Opens on the Twentieth Century's Ugliest Legacy," *National Geographic Magazine*, November 2002, pp. 18–19. The author is a freelance writer who won the 1986 Pulitzer Prize for international reporting.

402 *Terrorist states are eagerly:* Sharon Jayson, "Virtual State of Terrorism," *Austin American Statesman*, December 2, 2002, sec. B, p. 1.

403 *Russian Federation:* Associated Press, "Report Warns of Nuclear Threat," *Dallas Morning News*, March 13, 2003, sec. A, p. 5.

403 *The stated aim of al-Qaeda:* Bill Gertz, "Terrorists

Aim at Pearl Harbor," *Washington Times*, March 3, 2003.

403 *There is more than ample proof*: Vernon Loeb, staff writer, "New Bases Reflect Shift in Military," *Washington Post*, June 9, 2003, p. 1.

404 *The three largest powers*: Hutchinson, *Jane's Submarines*, Appendix 1, pp. 204–14.

404 *Many of those are advanced*: Christopher Drew, author of *Blind Man's Bluff*, interviewed by Jeff Stein, in "Submariners: Heights of Risk, Depths of Courage," *New York Times on the Web*, December 31, 1998.

404 *The Defense Intelligence Agency*: Glenn Kessler, "N. Korea Nuclear Estimate to Rise," *Washington Post*, April 28, 2004, p. 1.

405 *In addition, the CIA*: Edith M. Lederer, AP writer, "U.S. Rates Chance of al-Qaeda WMD Attack," AP wire, June 10, 2003.

405 *As ludicrous as it sounds*: Andrew Selsky, Associated Press writer, "Drug Smugglers Obtain Submarine," AP wire, September 8, 2000.

405 *China's aggressive development*: George Gedda, AP writer, "Bush Looks to China for Aid," *Dallas Morning News*, October 18, 2002, p. 1A.

405 *In the event of another coup*: "The Ally of Evil," Foreign Affairs in *Atlantic Monthly*, June 2003, p. 34.

406 *Robert Baer, a twenty-two-year veteran*: Robert Baer, "The Fall of the House of Saud," *Atlantic Monthly*, May 2003, pp. 53–55.

407 *The threat that stateless*: The National Security Strategy of September (NSS 2002) of George Walker Bush, released by the White House on September 17, 2002.

407 *Only a fail-safe device*: Bill Keller, "The Thinkable," *New York Times Magazine*, May 4, 2003, p. 50.

INDEX